India Studies in Business and Economics

The Indian economy is considered to be one of the fastest growing economies of the world with India amongst the most important G-20 economies. Ever since the Indian economy made its presence felt on the global platform, the research community is now even more interested in studying and analyzing what India has to offer. This series aims to bring forth the latest studies and research about India from the areas of economics, business, and management science. The titles featured in this series will present rigorous empirical research, often accompanied by policy recommendations, evoke and evaluate various aspects of the economy and the business and management landscape in India, with a special focus on India's relationship with the world in terms of business and trade.

More information about this series at http://www.springer.com/series/11234

Naseer Ahmed Khan
Editor

Challenges and Issues in Indian Fiscal Federalism

Springer

Editor
Naseer Ahmed Khan
School of Economics
University of Hyderabad
Hyderabad, Telangana
India

ISSN 2198-0012 ISSN 2198-0020 (electronic)
India Studies in Business and Economics
ISBN 978-981-10-6216-2 ISBN 978-981-10-6217-9 (eBook)
https://doi.org/10.1007/978-981-10-6217-9

Library of Congress Control Number: 2017950261

Printed on acid-free paper

This Springer imprint is published by Springer Nature
The registered company is Springer Nature Singapore Pte Ltd.
The registered company address is: 152 Beach Road, #21-01/04 Gateway East, Singapore 189721, Singapore

Foreword I

I am happy to write the foreword to this book, which is a collection of selected papers presented at the national seminar on "Challenges and Issues in the Fiscal Federalism of India" organized by the School of Economics, University of Hyderabad towards the end of March 2016. The papers included in this volume cover varied aspects of federalism. Besides addressing the core issue of fiscal imbalances and ways to correct them, the articles touch on several issues confronting the Indian fiscal system at the centre, state and local levels. The articles are well researched and well argued. This book is a valuable addition to the literature on Fiscal Federalism.

Fiscal federalism is the economic counterpart to political federalism. Fiscal federalism is concerned with the assignment, on the one hand of functions to different levels of government, and on the other with appropriate fiscal instruments for carrying out these functions. It is generally believed that the Central Government must provide national public goods that render services to the entire population of the country. A typical example cited is Defence. Local governments are expected to provide goods and services whose consumption is limited to their own jurisdictions. The argument here is that output of such goods and services can be tailored to meet the preferences and circumstances of the people in that jurisdiction. Such a process of decentralization enhances the economic welfare above that which could result from the more uniform levels of such services that are likely under a centralized regime. Apart from the provision of national public goods, the Central Government is to be vested with the responsibilities for economic stabilization and for income redistribution. While income redistribution to some extent is possible even within sub-national government jurisdictions, a truly redistribution effort is possible only at the national level. An equally important question in fiscal federalism is the determination of the specific fiscal instruments that would enable the different levels of government to carry out their functions. This is the 'tax-assignment problem' which is discussed very much in the literature. In determining the taxes that are best suited for use at different levels of government, one basic assumption that is made is in relation to the mobility of economic agents, goods and resources. Very often it is assumed that while there is no mobility across national barriers, there is much greater mobility at decentralized levels. This proposition holds good only partly in an era of globalization. Once again, it is generally argued that the decentralized levels of government should avoid non-benefit taxes on mobile units. This has the implication that Central Government should have the responsibility to levy non-benefit taxes and taxes on mobile units or resources. Building these principles into an actual scheme of assignment of taxes to different levels of government in a Constitution is indeed very difficult. Different Constitutions interpret differently what is mobile and what is purely a benefit tax. For example, in the United States and Canada, both federal and state governments have concurrent powers to levy income tax. On the contrary, in India, income tax is levied only by the Central Government though shared with the States. It is interesting to note that the revenues collected by the Federal or Central government vary very sharply among different countries. For example, the federal government collects 69% of the total revenue in Australia, 65% in India and 48% in Canada. Thus, the traditional issues in fiscal federalism have been, how to determine the assignment of taxes and responsibilities to different levels of government. Recognizing, the possibility of imbalance between resources and responsibilities, many countries have a system of internal governmental transfers. In fact, intergovernmental transfers constitute a distinctive economic policy instrument in fiscal federalism. For example, intergovernmental transfers as a percentage of provincial or state revenues have been 41% in Australia, 40% in India and 20% in Canada in recent years. Correcting vertical and horizontal imbalances has been a major concern with which fiscal federalism has wrestled with. While actual designs and fiscal transfer systems differ across federations, these constitute experiments in search of satisfying the twin objectives of equity and efficiency in a multi-tiered system of government. Conceptually, the emphasis has been on providing enough resources at the sub-national level to ensure provision of a set of services at comparable or minimum acceptable levels in all jurisdictions.

The Indian Constitution lays down the functions as well as taxing powers of the Centre and States. It is against this background that the issues relating to the correction of vertical and horizontal imbalances have been addressed by every Finance Commission, taking into account the prevailing set of circumstances. Central transfers to States are not, however, confined to the recommendations of the Finance Commissions. There are other channels such as those through the Planning Commission as well the discretionary grants of the Central Government.

The Fourteenth Finance Commission has broken new path in terms of allocation of resources. One of the major recommendations of the Commission has been to increase the share of tax devolution to 42% of the divisible pool. This is a substantial increase by almost 10%. The Fourteenth Finance Commission has argued that this does not necessarily affect the overall transfers but only enhances the share of unconditional transfers. The Chairman writes "The balance in fiscal space thus remains broadly the same in quantitative terms but tilts in favour of states in qualitative terms through compositional shift in favour of devolution and hence fiscal autonomy". It is true that centrally sponsored schemes which have ballooned in recent years and may have "encroached" on the territory of states. But over years, the performance of central government is judged not only on the basis of actions taken which fall strictly in its jurisdiction but also on initiatives undertaken in the areas which fall in concurrent and even state lists. Centralized planning has something to do with it. "Image building" has also contributed to it. One of the reasons attributed for increasing the share of tax devolution is that the share of cess and surcharges (which are not shared with states) as a proportion of gross tax revenue has increased from 7.53 in 2000–2001 to 13.14% in 2013–2014. With the increased tax devolution to states, we should not be surprised if this ratio goes further. It is legitimate to argue as the Fourteenth Finance Commission has done in favour of increasing the share of unconditional transfers. However sooner or later, a point will be reached when such a transfer can only be at the cost of fiscal space available to the centre to discharge its obligations including correction of inequalities. Any further increase must be carefully calibrated. At some stage, even the Constitution may have to be amended to freeze the proportion. Otherwise, even the centre will lose the 'incentive' or 'will' to tax.

In deciding on the horizontal distribution among states, equity considerations have dominated. While this is legitimate, two factors need to be borne in mind. First, in the present scheme of tax assignment, some of the taxes have been listed in the centre purely from the angle of administrative convenience and prevention of leakage. Some part of tax revenue legitimately belongs to states. In the days when income tax was the primary tax shared with states, "collection" was also a criterion in determining the share that goes to the states. States which contribute more to the central pool should not be ignored. Second the above-mentioned consideration applies even more strongly "when the tax devolution share touches such a high level as 42%". Therefore some consideration must be given to assigning some weight to "contribution" even though one must accept that there are problems in conceptualizing a variable to measure it.

I recommend this book strongly to students, administrators and policy makers—all of whom will find the book instructive and interesting.

Dr. C. Rangarajan
Chairman, Madras School of Economics, Chennai, India;
Chancellor, University of Hyderabad, India;
Ex-Governor, Reserve Bank of India

Foreword II

In this volume, Dr. Khan has put together an interesting set of research papers. The volume is an outcome of the conference organized by University of Hyderabad and includes a set of very relevant papers on varied topics in Indian fiscal federalism. The papers are mostly empirical, dealing with the measurement of differences in fiscal capacity among the states, impact of intergovernmental fiscal arrangements on growth and social outcomes, as well as some specific sectors in Indian economy. There are papers covering the issues of governance and the effectiveness of fiscal rules as well.

The changing economic and political landscape has put Indian federalism in a predicament requiring significant policy and institutional changes. The end of single-party rule and emergence of coalition governments at Union and State levels, the rise of regional parties as pivotal members of ruling coalitions, declining time horizons in the political landscape has altered the fabric of Indian federalism in fundamental ways. There is lack of trust between the Union and States when the ruling parties in the latter are not a part of the central coalition. More importantly, in the prevailing environment, there is a dire need for institutions of intergovernmental coordination, bargaining and conflict resolution. The abolition of the Planning Commission, while desirable in many ways, has also added to the institutional vacuum in intergovernmental coordination. NITI Ayog can and should step into this arena, but it is still in its nascent stage. In the prevailing environment, ensuring objectivity and transparency promoting intergovernmental relationships is extremely important for ensuring stability and enabling environment for the development of India as a nation.

The market-based reforms has unleashed the forces of competition in the market. Concomitantly, the role of the State has changed from one of participant in the production—distribution system to that of an enabler and a regulator to ensure fair competition in the market. In a globalizing environment, provision of competitive levels of social and physical infrastructure has become extremely important. Given the predominant role of the subnational governments in India in the provision of social services and co-equal role with the Centre in the provision of physical infrastructure, the focus has shifted to promoting competitive federalism. However, it is important to prevent predatory competition and the preconditions for efficient intergovernmental competition are that there should be a measure of competitive equality among the jurisdictions and cost–benefit appropriability. In this context, the issues of governance, taxable capacity differences, ensuring intergovernmental transfers to offset revenue and cost disabilities and effect of transfers on growth and social development and the importance and effectiveness of fiscal rules—all become extremely important. While the papers included in the volume may not provide definitive answers to most of the question, they initiate useful research in these manifold aspects of federalism. The issues flagged in these papers should be taken forward and taken up for further research.

Dr. M. Govinda Rao
Emeritus Professor, NIPFP, New Delhi;
Chief Economic Adviser, Brickwork Ratings;
Member, Fourteenth Finance Commission (2013–14),
GoI

Acknowledgements

I express my sincere thanks to TIES (The Indian Econometric Society), for sponsoring the national seminar organized in the School of Economics, University of Hyderabad, on March 30–31, 2016. The chapters included in this volume were originally presented at this seminar.

We would specially like to express our sincere gratitude to Prof. B. Kamaiah, ex-Dean, School of Economics, for his support and guidance due to which we were able to conduct this seminar successfully. Finally, I must thank the Springer team for publishing this volume which would be useful for policy makers, faculty, research scholars and the entire student community.

Contents

Editor and Contributors

About the Editor

Dr. Naseer Ahmed Khan is a professor at the School of Economics, University of Hyderabad, India. Prior to this, he taught at the Institute of Chartered Financial Analysts of India (ICFAI) University, Hyderabad. His areas of interest include public finance, international trade, business economics and macroeconomics. He has published papers in journals of international repute and has also edited a volume titled "Transition to Market-oriented Economy", published by the ICFAI University Press.

Contributors

Sajad Ahmad Bhat School of Economics, University of Hyderabad, Hyderabad, Telangana, India

J.S. Darshini Post Graduate School of Economics, GFGC, Bangalore, India

Akshay Dhume Gokhale Institute of Politics and Economics, Pune, India; Centre for Development Studies, PES University, Bangalore, India

Nagesha G. Post Graduate School of Economics, GFGC, Bangalore, India

Aadil Ahmad Ganaie School of Economics, University of Hyderabad, Hyderabad, Telangana, India

K. Gayithri Faculty of Economics, Institute for Social and Economic Change, Bangalore, India

K.S. Hari Gokhale Institute of Politics and Economics, Pune, India

Bandi Kamaiah School of Economics, University of Hyderabad, Hyderabad, Telangana, India

Pradeep Kamble School of Economics, University of Hyderabad, Hyderabad, India

Arshi Khan Department of Political Science, Aligarh Muslim University, Aligarh, India

Naseer Ahmed Khan School of Economics, University of Hyderabad, Hyderabad, Telangana, India

Lalitagauri Kulkarni Gokhale Institute of Politics and Economics, Pune, India

Nityasundar Manik School of Economics, University of Hyderabad, Hyderabad, Telangana, India

Ashok Mittal Department of Economics, Aligarh Muslim University, Aligarh, India

Ranjan Kumar Mohanty National Institute of Public Finance and Policy (NIPFP), New Delhi, India

M.P. Muhammed Riyas School of Economics, University of Hyderabad, Hyderabad, India

Abbas Haider Naqvi Institute of Economic Growth, Delhi, New Delhi, India

M. Govinda Rao NIPFP, New Delhi, India; Takshashila Institution, Bangalore, India

Y.V. Reddy Hyderabad, India

J.V.M. Sarma School of Economics, University of Hyderabad, Hyderabad, India

Waseem Ahmad Sofi Department of Political Science, Aligarh Muslim University, Aligarh, India

Chapter 1
Fiscal Federalism in India: Emerging Issues

Y.V. Reddy

Abstract The finance commission was devised in our constitution as a mechanism for providing predictability in the fiscal federal relations for 5 years and flexibility to review and revise the relations generally every 5 years, and the Planning commission was an innovation of union government that gave flexibility to accommodate fiscal compulsions of socio-political developments from time to time. The finance commissions, 13 of them and the planning commission determined the federal fiscal relations for well over six decades since independence. NITI Aayog is established in January 2015, and the origins of NITI Aayog could be traced to the disenchantment with the Planning commission. Though the nomenclature of NITI Aayog is different, the process of setting up is similar to planning commission. The 14th finance commission has provided an operational frame work to dispense with the distinction between Plan and Non plan. The success of NITI Aayog will depend on the manner in which new realities of economic management are captured in the process of planning being involved in it. NITI Aayog now will also hope fully address New Realities, sooner than later to avoid a vacuum.

keywords NITI Aayog · Competitive federalism · Tax devolution · New realities

In our Constitution, the Finance Commission was devised as a mechanism for providing predictability in the fiscal federal relations for 5 years and flexibility to review and revise the relations generally every 5 years only. Planning Commission was an innovation of Union Government that gave flexibility to accommodate fiscal compulsions of sociopolitical developments from time to time. The Finance Commissions, 13 of them and the Planning Commission determined the federal fiscal relations for well over six decades since independence, till recently with the abolition of Planning Commission in August, 2014, the report of 14th Finance Commission in December, 2014 and establishment of NITI Aayog (National Institute for Transforming India) as part of 'cooperative federalism' in January 2015 constitute significant developments.

Y.V. Reddy (✉)
Hyderabad, India
e-mail: office.yvr@gmail.com

N.A. Khan (ed.), *Challenges and Issues in Indian Fiscal Federalism*,
India Studies in Business and Economics, https://doi.org/10.1007/978-981-10-6217-9_1

The origins of NITI Aayog could be traced to the disenchantment with the Planning Commission on two important fronts, viz. the perception that it was not able to capture what has been described as the new realities of macro-economic management at the national level, and that it has not been conducive to sound fiscal relations between the Union and the States.

Though the nomenclature of NITI Aayog is different, the process of setting up is similar to Planning Commission, viz. through a Cabinet Resolution based on the initiative of Prime Minister. The National Development Council has been replaced with a Governing Council but with a similar composition. However, NITI Aayog has an additional option of creating Regional Councils. NITI Aayog's composition and structure remain similar to Planning Commission in terms of its being co-terminus with political cycles of the Union Government.

It is different from the Planning Commission in terms of articulating what has been described as 'the new realities', and expressing intention to change the nature of working of the organisation to capture the 'new realities'. The articulation also emphasises that States have been co-opted as partners and will be consulted in the formulation of policies. Further, its role has been defined to go beyond the limited sphere of the public sector and the Government of India, and it is intended be a catalyst to the developmental process.

The 14th Finance Commission submitted its report in December 2014, a few days ahead of the announcement about establishment of NITI Aayog. The 14th Finance Commission took cognizance of concerns relating to Union-State fiscal relations gathered from its interactions with Ministries in the Union, States, Political parties and intellectuals. Accordingly, a comprehensive view of Union-State fiscal relations was taken, recognising that there are three channels of fiscal transfers. The first one relates to tax devolution as a share of divisible pool of taxes, which is in the nature of entitlement of the Union and States based on assessment of their resources and needs by the Finance Commission. The second relates to grants-in-aid in the recommendations of Finance Commission, which are in the nature of transfer of funds from Union to States, unlike devolution which is sharing of funds. The third channel is transfer of resources by Union to States outside the award of Finance Commission, essentially by the Union Government which in the past was, on the advice of Planning Commission. Consideration of the contours of the third channel of transfers was considered essential by the 14th Finance Commission for taking a comprehensive view of fiscal relations in making its recommendations mainly on core mandate.

There were suggestions that the Finance Commission could be made a permanent body and that the working of the Planning Commission should also be entrusted to the Finance Commission. The 14th Finance Commission expressed itself against such a suggestion. However, it suggested that the transfers from the Union to the States outside the recommendations of the Finance Commission should be through a new institutional arrangement that should involve Union, States and domain expertise, ideally under the aegis of inter-state Council. In a way, therefore, the importance of involvement of the States in designing the transfers from the Union to the States outside the Finance Commission was emphasised.

There is, thus, a convergence between this approach of the Finance Commission and the objectives of NITI Aayog.

It is very clear that the Finance Commission has recognised the importance of transfers from the Union to the States outside the mechanism of the Finance Commission. It made some recommendations for institutional arrangements for such transfers outside the Finance Commission that would strengthen the Union-State fiscal relations. In many ways, therefore, the rebalancing of Union-State fiscal relations contemplated by the 14th Finance Commission will depend on the manner in which transfers outside the Finance Commission are designed. As per the official notification, NITI Aayog appears to be the agency that would be central to this task, since its functions described in 15 heads under the title 'New Role' include 'Cooperative and Competitive Federalism; Shared National Agenda; States Best Friend at the Centre, Decentralised Planning and Vision and Scenario Planning'.

In the inevitable process of rebalancing Union-State relations consequent upon the recommendations of the 14th Finance Commission, several issues emerge and NITI Aayog has a responsibility to address those, as per its mandate. I propose to address these issues now.

First, the 14th Finance Commission has provided an operational framework to dispense with the distinction between Plan and non-Plan. This should enable NITI Aayog to take a comprehensive and in-depth view of the strategies and policies of each sector in general and public expenditures in each sector in particular. The removal of a distinction should also enable reversal of the neglect of non-Plan activities like maintenance and 'general services' often described as non-developmental expenditure and also maintenance of existing public assets created under the Plan.

In the budget speech for 2015–2016, the Finance Minister, Mr. Arun Jaitley, said: 'This is the last year of the 12th Plan. Successive committees have questioned the merit in having Plan and Non-Plan classification of Government expenditure. A broad understanding over the years has been that Plan expenditures are good and Non-Plan expenditures are bad. This results in skewed allocations in the Budget. We need to correct this and give greater focus to Revenue and Capital classification of Government expenditure. We have, therefore, decided that the Plan-Non-Plan classification will be done away with from fiscal 2017–18. The Finance Ministry will closely work with the State Finance Departments to align Central and State Budgets in this matter'. The removal of distinction is not merely an issue of classification; it is more than that, and NITI Aayog has a legitimate role in it.

Second, the indicative ceiling on transfers outside the Finance Commission has been removed. At the same time, the rationale for such transfers has been clearly indicated in terms of externalities, minimum standards of services across the country, and inter-state infrastructure in select States. In some ways, the legitimacy and the rationale for transfers through a body such as NITI Aayog has been established by the Finance Commission—a Constitutional body. In this regard, NITI Aayog may consider the experience of mechanisms of fiscal transfers in other federations since almost all of them deal with fiscal transfers as distinct from sharing of divisible pool of taxes which is the remit of Finance Commission.

Third, a new institutional mechanism has been proposed for transfers outside the recommendations of Finance Commission in the interest of sound fiscal federalism. NITI Aayog could take advantage of the underlying logic of such institutional mechanisms and devise its work methods consistent with the spirit of the recommendations. The sectors and activities for which Union transfers to States should take place, the design of such schemes and the distribution of resources among the States will have to be worked out in a forum that has representation of the Union, the States and the domain expertise.

Fourth, the 14th Finance Commission has eschewed prescribing conditionalities or policies that are considered desirable at a national level. Some of the overlap between the Finance Commission and the Planning Commission has been addressed by the Finance Commission by relinquishing most of the State specific or project specific grants-in-aid and associated conditionalities, in its recommendations. For example, incentives or disincentives or rewards to States for appropriate policies have been left out of the Finance Commission's considerations and, thus, legitimately fall under NITI Aayog. By relinquishing its marginal role as promoter of economic reforms periodically, the Finance Commission has put additional responsibility on NITI Aayog to promote appropriate policies and schemes both in the Union and among States on a continuous basis.

Fifth, successive Finance Commissions have recognised the fact that budgetary situation of the Union Government had direct bearing on state finances, but could not impose any conditions for reform of finances of the Union Government nor could evolve a system under which the Union Government adhered to its commitment to fiscal responsibility. In the current federal fiscal structure of India, revenue account transfers from the Union to the States constitute more than one-third of the total revenue resources of the States, and hence if Union's revenue performance declines, States also get affected. The creation of incentive fund suggested by the 11th Finance Commission, the conditional transfers and debt relief linked to fiscal responsibilities of States by the 12th Finance Commission and, incentive grants recommended by 13th Finance Commission were instrumental in bringing about prudent management of State finances. Currently, since challenges relate to Union finances, the 14th Finance Commission emphasised the importance of fiscal councils. A weak fiscal position of the Union not only has bearing on macro-economic management and stability, but also impacts State finances. NITI Aayog has an opportunity and, indeed, an obligation to contribute to fiscal responsibility in both Union and State Governments consistent with developmental priorities and sound fiscal federal relations. NITI Aayog is in a better position to contribute to these objectives since it is a continuing body and plays a critical, though advisory, role in regard to Union finances, State finances and transfers from Union to States on a continuous basis.

Sixth, the Finance Commission has eschewed categorisation of States, but this does not, in any way, restrict freedom of NITI Aayog for categorisation for specific purposes relating to development. In particular, the States of north-eastern region would require special attention in this regard as explained in the report of the 14th Finance Commission itself. In a way, therefore, the responsibility relating to special problems of select Stats would squarely be that of NITI Aayog.

Finally, areas under Schedule VI of the Constitution in north-eastern States remain outside the ambit of the measures recommended by the 14th Finance Commission for Panchayats and Municipalities. These have been excluded from the consideration of the Finance Commission in the Terms of Reference. This was necessitated by the fact that the Constitution mandates the Union Government to play a direct role in supporting the development of these areas. However, the quantum of assistance given over the years to these regions by Ministries in the Union Government has been very limited. NITI Aayog could consider a larger assistance and more effective intervention for the upgradation of administration as well as development of these areas to make-up for what the Finance Commission was not permitted to do.

It is quite conceivable that Way Forward, the Constitution of the Finance Commissions could also undergo some changes. Finance Commission is essentially an institution in the nature of an arbitrator giving award in matters relating to sharing of divisible pool of taxes between Union and States, and among the States. However, in this framework, having a serving Member of the Planning Commission, who is a functionary of Union Government associated with political parties, in the Finance Commission as a part time Member, clearly indicates that an interested party is also officiating as an arbitrator—a clear case of conflict of interest. Since the distinction between Plan and non-Plan has been dispensed with by the Finance Commission, and since the overlap between transfers through Finance Commission's recommendations and other transfers have been almost eliminated, this is an appropriate time to discontinue the practice.

The 14th Finance Commission emphasised the role of State Finance Commissions and recognised the critical role of States in regard to local bodies. In this, there is an element of empowering of States in the fiscal management. NITI Aayog could revisit the institutional arrangements for planning at State level to make State level planning institutions more effective. Approach to planning at level of local bodies could be reviewed, taking account of the recommendations of 14th Finance Commission, especially on resource mobilisation, including bond financing.

The Terms of Reference of Finance Commissions other than the core Terms of Reference have been expanding over a period and have also been varying. Many of them had overlap with work of the erstwhile Planning Commission, while a few others related to tax reforms, expenditure reforms, public enterprise reforms, pricing of public utilities, etc. Further, the recommendations in regard to other Terms of Reference have provisionally been treated as some suggestions and seldom acted upon vigorously. At the same time, the other Terms of Reference reduce the focus and the attention that the Finance Commission could give to its core Terms of Reference. The 14th Finance Commission recognised this and limited its recommendations relating to noncore Terms of Reference essentially to areas that have fiscal implications. NITI Aayog may legitimately address on a continuous basis the undeniably important policy issues often incorporated in other Terms of Reference of the Finance Commissions. NITI Aayog may also contribute to rationalisation of the other Terms of Reference of the 15th Finance Commission by attending to them on its own initiative.

The success of NITI Aayog will depend on the manner in which new realities of economic management are captured in the processes of planning being evolved by it. It will also depend on the processes that it institutes to rebalance the fiscal relations between the Union and States, mainly relating to transfers from Union and States outside the devolution recommended by Finance Commission. There are two institutional structures that determine the nature of fiscal federalism in India. One, namely, 14th Finance Commission has done its job of addressing new realities. The second, Planning Commission in the past and NITI Aayog now will also hopefully address new realities, sooner than later, to avoid a vacuum.

Part I
Fiscal Federalism and Resolving the Fiscal Imbalances

Chapter 2
Making Federalism Work for India's Development

M. Govinda Rao

Abstract Fiscal federalism in independent India evolved over the last 70 years has held the country together, provided identity and scope for various religious, ethnic, linguistic groups to function and has provided a reasonably flexible institutional framework for the functioning of the multilevel governance. There is clearly a strong idea of India gained during the independence struggle and cemented over the years after independence. At the same time, it would be erroneous to conclude that the system has worked to the satisfaction of all the groups and surely there is considerable scope for improvement in several areas. Indeed, development of the country and improving the well-being of 1.2 billion people depends on harnessing their energies which can be achieved only when we have an institutional framework to combining the advantages of a large market unfettered by impediments with sufficient scope to achieve regional specialization depending upon comparative advantage and with the regional governments cooperating and competing with one another to provide efficient level of social and physical infrastructure.

Keywords Fiscal federalism · India

2.1 Introduction

Alexis de Tocqueville, in his celebrated work *Democracy in America* written more than 150 years ago extolled, 'The federal system was created with the intention of combining the different advantage which result from the magnitude and the littleness of nations'. In economic terms, this implies reaping the economies of scale while providing public services according to the diversified preferences of people. This provides a large unified common market and enables efficiency gains through

M.G. Rao (✉)
NIPFP, New Delhi, India
e-mail: mgovinda.rao@nipfp.org.in

M.G. Rao
Takshashila Institution, Bangalore, India

N.A. Khan (ed.), *Challenges and Issues in Indian Fiscal Federalism*,
India Studies in Business and Economics, https://doi.org/10.1007/978-981-10-6217-9_2

intergovernmental competition to provide efficient levels of public services. In political terms, this implies a building a strong national policy by combining the subnational entities while providing adequate political space to them. In emotional terms, this provides a national bond while retaining multiple local identities. The realization of these advantages depends on the way in which the different units combine and extent of cooperation and harmony in the functioning of the federal system. Indeed, federalism is not an option but an imperative for a country like India inhabited by over 1.2 billion people with wide social, ethnic, religious, linguistic besides economic diversities.

Fiscal federalism in independent India evolved over the last 69 years, has held the country together, provided identity and scope for various religious, ethnic, linguistic groups to function and has provided a reasonably flexible institutional framework for the functioning of the multilevel governance. There is clearly a strong idea of India gained during the independence struggle and cemented over the years after independence. At the same time, it would be erroneous to conclude that the system has worked to the satisfaction of all the groups and surely there is considerable scope for improvement in several areas. Indeed, development of the country and improving the well-being of 1.25 billion people depends on harnessing their energies which can be achieved only when we have an institutional framework to combining the advantages of a large market unfettered by impediments with sufficient scope to achieve regional specialization depending upon comparative advantage and with the regional governments cooperating and competing with one another to provide efficient level of social and physical infrastructure.

The first 40 years after independence was marked by restricting the role of the market as well as subnational governments. The resource allocation in the country was dictated by plan priorities and centralized planning restricted the role of the subnational governments in resource allocation. The realization that planned development strategy undermined the role of the market as well as subnational governments in accelerating growth, reducing poverty and ensuring human development, economic reforms to liberalize and open up the economy were initiated in 1991. Although the growth rate of the economy has steadily accelerated, from an average of 3.5% during the first 40 years to 5.8% in the next 20 years and 7.5% during 2000–2001, there is growing awareness that the economic performance of the country has been far below the potential. A number of reasons for this have been speculated including the difficulties in building consensus on reforms in a democratic polity and the influence of special interest groups resulting in the crawling pace of reforms. Indeed as Morris and Johnson in their review of the Mirrlees report on Tax reform in England state, those who gain from the reforms are not grateful and those who lose are vengeful and therefore, we experience a tyranny of status quo in reforms.

One of the most important reasons for the gap between the potential and actual growth performance is the lack of coordination between the Union and the States in carrying out reforms. The Seventh Schedule to the Indian Constitution assigns functional responsibilities in terms Union, State and Concurrent Lists. The taxes are assigned according to the principle of separation where the powers are assigned either to the Union and States. However, the separation is only in the legal sense and there is considerable overlap in the tax bases of the Union and States. Thus, the taxes on agricultural incomes and wealth are assigned to the States whereas taxes on non-agricultural incomes and wealth can be levied only by the Union government. This makes the levy of comprehensive income tax difficult and as the States do not levy the taxes on agricultural incomes, it has opened up a major avenue for evasion of the tax. Similarly, the levy of comprehensive goods and services tax has become difficult as the states which have the power to levy sales taxes on goods cannot levy taxes on services. Furthermore, the Union government has the power to levy excise duty on all manufactured products which is actually the sales tax at the first point of sale, but cannot extend the tax to subsequent stages. There have been serious attempts to harmonize the tax system and levy the GST at both Union and State levels by amending the Constitution for about a decade, but the exercise in mired in political gamesmanship and lack of consensus required for Constitutional amendment. Hopefully, current session of the Parliament will approve the Constitutional amendment to pave the way for the reform which is considered to be an important reform in terms of raising revenue productivity, ensuring a common market in the federation promoting export competitiveness.

On the expenditure assignments too, considerable degree of cooperation is necessary to enable both the Union and states to provide public services according to the diversified preferences of the people while reaping the cost advantages arising from economies of scale. The Constitution assigns expenditure functions in terms of Union, State and Concurrent Lists. However well, it is designed to conform to comparative advantage, the assignment system results result in significant overlapping and there must be a mechanism to promote cooperation, ensure coordination and promote healthy and regulate predatory competition. High degree of overlapping exists in concurrent subjects like energy, environment and education. The spirit of cooperative federalism is particularly important in the case of anti-poverty interventions. Much of the funding for anti-poverty interventions will have to be defrayed by the Centre, but implementation of these programmes will have to be done at subnational levels. The Union government may also have to spend to ensure minimum standards of meritorious public services even if they fall in the State List and this has to be done through specific purpose transfers. Even in the case of Union subjects, it may be necessary to use the States as agencies to deliver the services to take advantage of varying local conditions. Another area where the Union and States have to work together is in ensuring healthy inter-governmental competition. Wallace Oates (1999) called it 'laboratory federalism'. Ensuring a measure of competitive equality among the jurisdictions and avoiding predatory competition through effective regulation is critical to reap the gains from intergovernmental competition. Therefore, there must be a clear mechanism to ensure coordination, promote cooperation and activate healthy competition among the states.

In general, the asymmetry between tax powers and expenditure functions is a feature seen in all federations. General purpose transfers by way of tax devolution or block grants are given to enable the States to provide comparable levels of public services at comparable tax rates. In addition, it is important to ensure minimum standards of meritorious public services with nation-wide externalities. Ensuring minimum standards of meritorious public services with nation-wide externalities is achieved through specific purpose transfers. In India, the Constitution provides for tax devolution and block grant from the Union to the States based on the recommendation of the Constitutional body, the Finance Commission appointed by the President every five years. So far, 14 Finance Commissions have made recommendations and these have been generally accepted and implemented. Questions have been raised on the design of the general purpose transfers as (i) it does not fully offset the fiscal disabilities of the states and (ii) it entails adverse incentives on tax effort and expenditure economy. The 14th Finance Commission has attempted to meet these challenges by increasing the tax devolution to the States from 32% of the divisible pool to 42%, consolidating all general purpose transfers including those given by the Planning Commission and including revenue and cost disability factors including the forest cover in the States in the devolution formula.

The major problem is in the disbursement of specific purpose transfers. These are given by various central ministries ostensibly to ensure minimum standards of meritorious public services with nation-wide externalities for all citizens irrespective of their place of residence. Serious questions have been raised on the existing centrally sponsored schemes in terms of number of services chosen for equalization, their one size fits all design and inability of many of the states which are in need of such assistance to avail them for want of fiscal space to make matching contributions. Transfers to a large number of schemes for equalization result in the thin spread of resources. The NDA government after assuming power appointed a Committee under the Chief Minister of Madhya Pradesh to rationalize the schemes, but even after consolidation, there are more than 30 schemes and with uniform matching contributions of 40% of the cost required from the states. With such large number of schemes chosen, it is not possible to link the transfers to outcomes. In fact, these schemes seem to serve more a political purpose of appeasing various sections rather than ensuring minimum standards of meritorious public services.

The most important requirement for the successful working of a federation is the institutional mechanism for intergovernmental coordination, bargaining and conflict resolution. Absence of such a mechanism is a major vacuum in Indian federation. It is necessary and important to foster the spirit of trust and cooperation between the Union and the states and among the States inter se, enable health intergovernmental bargaining and resolve conflicts and regulate inter-governmental competition. With the end of single party rule in both the Union and States and emergence of coalition governments at the Union level with regional parties being pivotal members, formal institutional mechanism for intergovernmental bargaining and conflict resolution has become necessary to minimize the coordination and other transaction costs of multilevel decision making. In other words, bargaining, coordination and conflict resolution in a multilevel system are important and at present, there is no institution undertaking this task in India. Indeed, this has resulted in either no coordination/conflict resolution, or ad hoc arrangements. Article 263 provides a basis for creating such an independent institution and the Government set up the Inter-State Council for the purpose. However, instead of setting it up as an independent neutral institution, the Government of India constituted the Inter-State

Council under the Union Home Ministry. Similarly, with the establishment of the Planning Commission under a Cabinet Resolution in 1950, the National Development Council was constituted to facilitate collaborative planning exercise. The Council comprised members of the Union Cabinet, Deputy Chairman and Members of the Planning Commission and the Chief Ministers of the States. However, rather than being a cementing institution and a neutral referee, the Council became a speech making body. The meetings became a forum for voicing the opinions and grievances. The meetings too became infrequent and since 2005 there were just two meetings of the Council. With the abolition of the Planning Commission, the NDC too has seen its last. However, one of the mandates of NITI Ayog established in the place of the Planning Commission is to promote cooperative federalism and enable healthy intergovernmental competition. While the jury on its functioning is still out, it is important to make this a Constitutional body rather than based on the Cabinet Resolution. Hopeully, with passage of time, Inter-State Council will be merged with the NITI Ayog and given a Constitutuional Status to make it an independent body to promote trust and cooperation between the Union and States.

One of the major shortcomings of Indian federalism is the failure to decentralize below the State level. Some of the States are larger than many countries and therefore, decentralization is necessary to ensure effective delivery of public services in response to the diversified requirements of people and effective participation in the political processes. Indeed, everyone wants decentralization, but only up to his level. This is amply demonstrated by the States with few exceptions, which in spite of the amendments to the Constitution to devolve powers to urban and rural local governments have failed to do so. Inability to achieve sub-state decentralization is one of the most important shortcomings of Indian federation.

The above discussion makes it clear that making federalism to work effectively for India requires reforms in decentralization policies and federal institutions. Sustained development requires the participation of diverse groups in a harmonious manner. It is important to nation-wide product and factor markets which requires creation of nation-side markets for goods and services as well as capital and labour unhindered by impediments. Similarly, for reasons of both efficiency in service delivery and accountability, it is important to foster the spirit of cooperation and achieve efficiency gains through intergovernmental competition.

Chapter 3
Cooperative Federalism: Implications for Social Sector Expenditure in India

K.S. Hari

Abstract The centre-state relations in India have endured drastic changes during the last two decades of economic reforms. The economy moved away from a centralized federalism to that of cooperative and competitive federalism. The decision of the Union government to accept the recommendations of the 14th Finance Commission (FFC) (2015) to increase tax devolution to 42% of the sharable pool of taxes has increased the flow of untied resources to states is a major boost to the federal autonomy in the country. During the period 2015–2020, the untied statutory transfers would be more than 70% of the aggregate resource transfers from the Union to States and will add the autonomy of states in the allocation of resources. As per the Constitution of India, major taxes are collected by the Union government from the point of efficiency and equity and the proceeds of the same are shared with the state governments. On the other hand, even though major social services like education and health care are on the concurrent list of the Constitution, major expenditure responsibilities are with the state governments.

Keywords Fiscal federalism · Social sector expenditure
Centre state relations in India · 14th Finance Commission

3.1 Introduction

The centre-state relations in India have endured drastic changes during the last two decades of economic reforms. The economy moved away from a centralized federalism to that of cooperative and competitive federalism. The decision of the Union government to accept the recommendations of the 14th Finance Commission (FFC) (2015) to increase tax devolution to 42% of the sharable pool of taxes has increased the flow of untied resources to states is a major boost to the federal autonomy in the country. During the period 2015–2020, the untied statutory

K.S. Hari (✉)
Gokhale Institute of Politics and Economics, Pune, India
e-mail: harineelamana@gmail.com

N.A. Khan (ed.), *Challenges and Issues in Indian Fiscal Federalism*,
India Studies in Business and Economics, https://doi.org/10.1007/978-981-10-6217-9_3

transfers would be more than 70% of the aggregate resource transfers from the Union to States and will add to the autonomy of states in the allocation of resources. As per the Constitution of India, major taxes are collected by the Union government from the point of efficiency and equity and the proceeds of the same are shared with the state governments. On the other hand, even though major social services like education and health care are on the concurrent list of the Constitution, major expenditure responsibilities are with the state governments.

The process of cooperative federalism started in the early 1990s in India, but there was a reversal of the process during the period 2006–2015. This was especially true during the period of UPA government, when a major chunk of the transfer from that of Union government to state governments were either routed through the Centrally Sponsored Schemes or through the Planning Commission. These conditional transfers have created a scenario of 'one size fit for all' approach where states were forced to spend on their non-priority areas as well. The FFC have taken the bold initiative of reversal of this centralization of power and recommended more decentralization of power and resources in the country. Last three Union Budgets (2015–2016, 2016–2017 and 2017–2018) have clearly indicated the movement of the economy towards providing more fiscal space for the states. A key recommendation of the FFC was to reduce the number of Centrally Sponsored Schemes to minimum sectors where there are interstate externalities like polio vaccination, etc. NitiAyog (the agency that replaced Planning Commission of India) recommended scrapping of many Centrally Sponsored Schemes (Niti Ayog 2015). The reduction of the number of schemes under the Centrally Sponsored Schemes has drastically reduced the allocation of funds from Central government to the concerned departments in the Union Budget 2015–2016. Hence, a major issue, post-Budget 2015–2016 is the sharp decline in allocations to the social sector in the form of various conditional grants to the states. This decline has happened to accommodate a large increase in tax devolution. As per Budget 2015–16, enhanced tax devolution should result in an increase in the flow of untied funds to the tune of Rs. 186,150 crores and a reduced flow of grants to the tune of Rs. 87,730 crores. Chakraborty (2015) reiterates the need for getting expenditure priorities right at each levels of government in this context.

Indian states historically spend a very meagre amount of their GDP on social sectors, especially on education and health care and this acts as a major reason for the human development backlog across Indian states.[1] The combined expenditure of the States and Centre in education, key component of social sector, has always been under the United Nations mandate of 6% of GDP in India. In the present context, whether the increased allocation of unconditional grants to the states and reduction of Centrally Sponsored schemes will motive the states to incur more expenditure on the social sectors is the major question this chapter tries to address. The main objective of the present chapter is to understand the changing pattern of

---

[1]See Joshi (2006) for a detailed discussion on the performance of Indian states in social sector expenditure in the 1990s compared to pre reform period.

the transfer from the Union government to State governments and the likely impact it can have on the priority sector expenditure of the state governments in India.

Recent literature on receipts of Central transfers in states and the net effect to states expenditure had given a mixed result. Chakraborty (2016) estimated that the net gain to the state of Bihar through devolution of more tax share compensates more than loss of direct grants. In the case of Maharashtra, Shetty (2016) showed the unutilized fiscal space post FFC. World Bank (2016) also had shown a net gain to states post FFC recommendations. A critique of these studies was done by Choudhury et al. (2016) by comparing the revised budget figures of 2014–2015 with that of 2015–2016. This study argues that the existing studies have an upward bias in the net gain and the corresponding increase in the social sector expenditure. This study finds methodological problems in comparison of 2014–2015 actuals with that of revised and budget figures for 2015–2016 and 2016–2017, respectively. The comparison based on revised budget figures gives a decline in the central transfers and the expenditure on social sectors as a percentage of Gross State Domestic Product (GSDP) in a number of states.

In the light of this mixed results, the existing chapter looks into this issue using the actual budget figures for 2014–2015 and 2015–2016, and revised estimates for 2016–2017 and budget estimates for 2017–2018 for the major states of India. The chapter is divided into four sections. The long-term movement of the Indian economy from that of a centralized planned regime to that of cooperative federalism is discussed in Sect. 1. The long-run experience of the states on Social Sectors is discussed in Sect. 2. The third section gives a detailed account of the question whether increased autonomy will boost the social sector expenditure. The final section of the chapter gives conclusion and some policy implications.

3.2 Centralized Federalism to Cooperative and Competitive Federalism the Long Road Travelled

The Constitution of India proclaims India as a Union of States and defines the functions and duties of the different layers of the government. In the initial years after Independence, there was a growing centralization of power in the country. This was made possible mainly through the functioning of the erstwhile Planning Commission. Even though the Constitution demarcates the functioning of various levels of government, the Centre used to be more powerful in allocation and distribution function. The state plan needs the final approval of the National Development Council and that made the Centre more powerful. The establishment of the big public sector units was another mechanism through which the central government had shown enormous dominance over the states. The Industrial licensing was another tool that was used for centralization of power in India. During the first three decades after independence, it was the Central government that dominated the economic decision-making in India.[2] States were having predominantly limited role in the economic policy making. But an interesting feature during the phase of high centralisation was that the major expenditure responsibilities were still with the state governments. As is clear from Table 3.1, state's revenue expenditure as a percentage of the combined expenditure of centre and states is more than 50%. But the states own tax revenue as a proportion of the total tax revenue of the government was marginally above 30% during the high centralization phase. This made the states to depend more on the Central government for resources to meet the expenditure requirement and that give limelight to the Planning Commission as a policy making body in India. Hence, the first four decades since Independence India had experienced a growing centralization of power and functioning.

The second phase of cooperative federalism in India started in the early 1990s at the time of dominance of regional parties in Indian politics. The distinguishing feature of cooperative federalism is the primacy it accords to the state and the local government in providing public services and in exercising a decisive voice in setting central government policies.[3] The term 'cooperative federalism' is not well defined in any of the Indian policy documents. To the states, the idea was to get the Centre to consult them in all matters that concerned them. An environment was created whereby the states came to have a larger say in the Centre's policies than before, with both positive and negative results (Bagchi 2003; Rao and Singh 2006). The 73/74th Indian Constitutional Amendments gave further boost to the idea of cooperative federalism in the Country. Presently, India has three-tier system of government and governance consisting of the Union government, State governments and Local governments. The Indian constitution provides the framework for administrative, developmental and financial responsibilities (mainly taxation powers and borrowing capacities) and relationships between these different levels of governance. The reform era had shown faster growth in most of the Indian states and the states own tax revenue has improved tremendously (Table 3.1) but there was manifold increase in the expenditure responsibilities of the states. Almost all Indian states failed to allocate sufficient resources for the Social Sector as per the United Nations norms. Hence, the social indicators had shown a very slow growth pace in India compared to the income growth. This has created a scenario where the central government started directly spending resources in many areas that were earlier the responsibility of the state governments. The growing centralization of the social sector can be seen in the changing share of the Centre and states in the total social sector expenditure. The period 2004–2005 to 2014–2015 saw a rapid increase in the number of Centrally Sponsored Schemes and the amount of resources transferred directly for such schemes, bypassing the formulae based

[2]Bagchi (2003) gives a detailed account of the movement of the Indian economy from Centralized Federalism to that of cooperative and competitive federalism.

[3]For theoretical explanation on the detailed characteristic features of cooperative federalism see Inman and Rubinfeld (1997).

Table 3.1 States share in receipts and expenditure of the government: selected parameters in percentages

Heads	1950–1951	1960–91	1970–1971	1980–1981	1990–1991	2000–2001	2005–2006	2014–2015
State's revenue expenditure as a proportion of revenue expenditure of Centre and States	51.16	59.8	60.2	59.62	55	59.3	55.5	61.38
State's total expenditure as a proportion of total expenditure of government (Centre and States)	51.75	56.8	53.9	54.8	52	62.2	60	64.03
State's own revenue receipts as proportion of states total revenue expenditure	80.75	64.2	60.6	60.07	54	50.2	59.4	53.6
State's own tax revenue as proportion of total tax revenue of government	35.41	33.7	32.5	33.59	34	69.1	69.3	69.04
State's total revenue as proportion of total revenue of government (Centre and states)	47.84	58.7	58.4	63.08	63	62.5	65.6	62.63

Source Indian Public Finance Statistics and RBI Study on State Finances (Various Issues)

transfer of the Finance Commission. Planning Commission and the Central government departments increased the amount of tied grants to the state governments. A part of the state plan budget has been devoted as the matching grant for the centrally sponsored schemes and that reduced the available fiscal space of the state government. The growing Centralization of the social sector policies has often been criticized by the policy makers and the state governments as 'One Size does not fit for all'. Many states found the schemes as repetitive and not up to the priority of the respective states and found as a mechanism by the central government to intrude into the autonomy of the state. Many sectors that were not having interstate externalities also come into the purview of Centrally Sponsored Schemes.

The 14th Finance Commission (2015) had reiterated the idea of cooperative and competitive federalism in the country and the provisions were made for higher allocation of untied grants to the states to meet their expenditure responsibilities. As per the 14th Finance Commission Report (2015), the aggregate transfer from the Union to States (including direct transfers) as a percentage of gross revenue receipts of the Union has ranged between 44.7 and 53.7%. Expressed as a percentage of the divisible pool, these transfers have been in the range of 58.3–71.4%. The Finance Commission transfers comprised 58.5% of the aggregate transfers from the Union to the States, with the 'other' transfers comprising 41.5%. Only 10.1% of 'other' transfers were through normal central assistance. The remaining portion largely comprised of what are generally described as 'non-formula based' or 'discretionary transfers'. The FFC recommended increase in the amount of 'formula' based 'non-discretionary' or untied transfers during the period 2015–2016 to 2019–2020. Further as per the FFC recommendation and the Niti Ayog (2015) recommendations, the Central government has reduced the number of Centrally Sponsored Schemes and amount of direct transfer through departmental channels. Whether the adequate fiscal space provided by the increased devolution of taxes and grants by the FFC are sufficient for meeting the increased expenditure responsibilities in the absence of CSS and whether it will automatically lead to more spending by the states on priority areas like education and health care are discussed in the following section.

3.3 Social Sector Expenditure: The Story Across Indian States

Social Sector mainly consists of social services and the rural development in the Indian context. As per the Constitution of India, major expenditure responsibilities on this sector lies with the respective state governments. The poor outcome indicators of majority of the Indian states are often related with poor expenditure allocation for these sectors by the state governments. States historically spend a very meagre amount of their GDP on social sectors and this has often been cited as a major reason for the human development backlog across Indian states (Dev and Mooij 2002; Shariff et al. 2002). The role of state and public policy for the development of social sectors is well documented in the literature.

Even though primarily a state priority, Central government also do spend on social sector in India since majority of them comes under the Concurrent list of the Constitution. But the combined expenditure of the States and Centre has always been under the United Nations mandate of 6% of GDP in India. The long-term average expenditure of the Central government in this sector is below 1% of GDP. The long-term movement of the same is given in the Fig. 3.1. It is interesting to note that during the period 2004–2005 to 2014–2015, the Central government expenditure on social sector had almost doubled. This is the second phase of centralization as discussed in the previous section. The Centrally Sponsored Schemes and the direct transfer of resources through implementing agencies have boosted the Central government expenditure on this sector. Programmes like National Health Mission, SarvasikshaAbiyan, etc., have contributed higher expenditure directly by the Central government (Rath 2013).

The increased allocation of the Central government funds through CSS has contributed to an increase in the social sector expenditure as a proportion of the total expenditure as well during the period 2004–2005 to 2014–2015 (Fig. 3.2). Education is a major area where there was more than proportionate increase in the

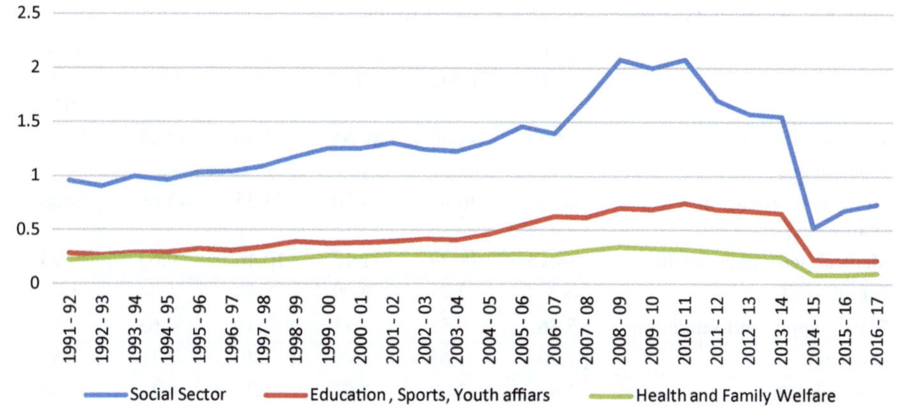

Fig. 3.1 Union government expenditure on social sector as % of GDP

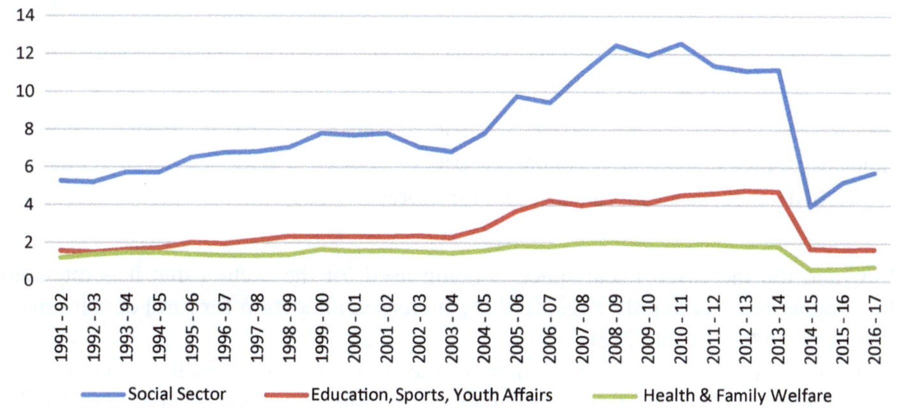

Fig. 3.2 Union government expenditure on social sector as % of total expenditure

Central government expenditure during this phase. This growing centralization of the social sector expenditure has invited criticisms from the state governments as elaborated in the FFC and in the Report of the Sub group of Chief Ministers on Rationalization of Centrally Sponsored Schemes (Niti Ayog 2015). This enrichment in the functioning of the state governments had an adverse impact on many state budgets since majority of these schemes are having matching contribution from the state governments as well.

As discussed in the previous sections, state governments are the major stakeholders on social sector in India and their share in the expenditure has remained stagnant for almost two decades. The year post FFC (2015–2016), there was an increase of more than 4% in the states allocation towards the social sectors, a clear indication that states are responding positively towards the recommendations of the

Table 3.2 Sectorial expenditure of states in social sector

Sector	1990–1991	1995–1996	2000–2001	2005–2006	2010–2011	2015–2016 (RE)
Total social sector expenditure	37.34	35.40	35.03	32.80	37.88	41.91
Education, sports, art and culture	46.49	46.63	49.70	43.35	43.89	39.06
Medical and public health	14.18	11.24	11.12	10.46	9.65	9.95
Family welfare	NA	2.71	2.00	1.50	1.54	1.85
Water supply and sanitation	5.86	6.51	7.11	7.41	4.63	5.15
Housing	1.60	1.67	1.49	1.49	2.16	2.51
Urban development	1.95	2.07	2.52	3.79	6.12	5.41
Welfare of Scheduled Caste, Scheduled Tribes and OBC	5.61	5.83	5.46	6.35	6.42	6.80
Labour and labour welfare	1.33	1.18	1.01	0.90	0.92	0.97
Social security and welfare	4.08	3.89	4.13	5.14	9.09	8.98
Nutrition	1.58	3.45	2.08	2.18	3.06	2.37
Relief on account of natural calamities	2.58	3.12	3.26	4.65	2.00	1.29
Others	0.65	0.83	0.63	1.08	0.99	0.69
Rural development	14.08	10.87	9.49	11.69	9.53	14.97

Source Budget documents of Various States for respective Years

FFC and the increased fiscal space is being used for the sectors that it is intended for. The increase is mainly a result of the increased allocation for rural development across the states (Table 3.2).

In order to understand the changes in the social sector expenditure in the high growth phase of the states, we have made an attempt to analyse the percapita social sector expenditure in India for the major states. The percapita expenditure shows an interesting picture that the better off states in terms of human development are the one that leads in the percapita expenditure on social sectors. The states like Bihar and Odisha spend half the amount of expenditure in Kerala and Maharashtra. The long-term trend shows a very slow growth in the social sector allocation by the states (Table 3.3).

Having analysed the state level scenario in the social sector, an analysis of the combined expenditure of centre and states will give a holistic view about the overall expenditure going to this crucial sector. The combined expenditure on social sector is more than 25% of the aggregate expenditure of both levels of government. If one looks at the post-reform period (Fig. 3.3), the expenditure remained stagnant around 20% till 2004–2005 and then gradually increased. The healthcare sector has virtually remained stagnant below 5% of the overall expenditure. It is the education that contributed more to the social sector expenditure in India.

Table 3.3 Per capita expenditure on social sectors (2004–05 prices)

State	1993–1994	1995–1996	2000–2001	2005–2006	2010–2011	2014–2015
Andhra Pradesh	1012	1130	1462	1714	2820	2184
Bihar	811	761	1015	890	1273	2813
Gujarat	1112	1176	2206	1902	3415	4851
Haryana	1114	1484	1539	1958	3258	4861
Karnataka	1128	1139	1548	1811	2943	4272
Kerala	1325	1300	1830	2132	2806	4944
Madhya Pradesh	1159	1206	1323	1277	2116	3591
Maharashtra	1286	1362	1828	2196	3317	4694
Orissa	1037	925	1198	1324	2157	3612
Punjab	1057	1164	1420	1440	1876	3020
Rajasthan	999	1143	1436	1691	2112	3939
Tamil Nadu	1277	1277	1738	2034	3635	5145
Uttar Pradesh	684	678	803	1026	1692	2382
West bengal	837	822	1354	1288	2274	3169

Source Own calculation based on budget figures of various states

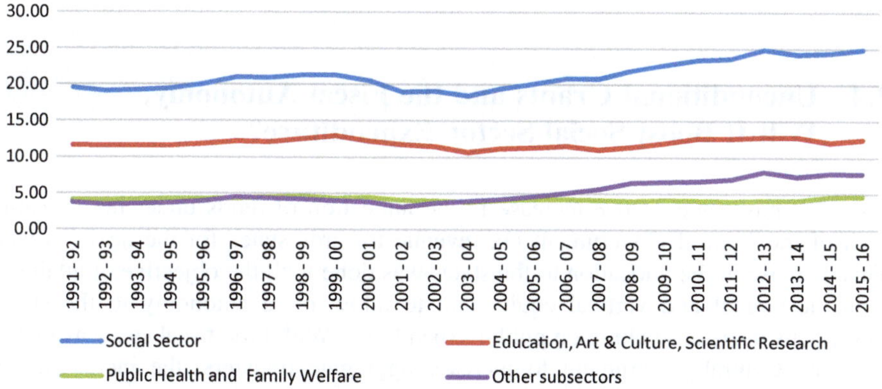

Fig. 3.3 Combined (Centre + States) social sector expenditure as a percentage of total expenditure

The GDP of the country had recorded an average growth rate of 5–6% since the early 1990s and had touched 8% during the high growth phase of 2004–2005 to 2007–2008 (Nagaraj 2013), whether this has accompanied by a corresponding increase in the revenue mobilization and expenditure expansion is a serious issue,

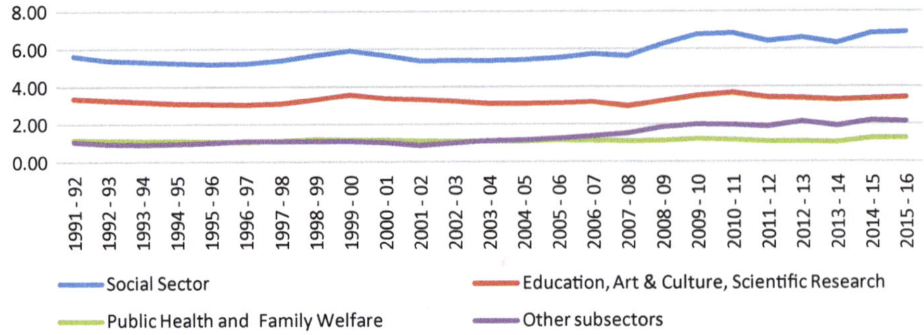

Fig. 3.4 Combined (Centre + States) social sector expenditure as percentage of GDP

since it is through such an effort that inclusive growth was likely to be planned in India during the 10th Plan period. A comparison of the social sector expenditure with GDP is done in Fig. 3.4 to understand the long-term trend post-1991. The long term trend gives a clear stagnation of the social sector expenditure in India around 6% for the last 25 years. The combined expenditure on education was below 4% of GDP and that of health care failed to reach even 1% of GDP. It is in this context that the FFC had recommended more untied grants to the state governments with the objective of more autonomy. Whether such an autonomy worked in increasing the allocation of resources for the social sectors is examined in the subsequent section.

3.4 Unconditional Grants and the Fiscal Autonomy, Will It Boost Social Sector Expenditure?

The FFC has made a 10% increase in the allocation of funds under the divisible pool of the Central Government tax revenue towards states for the next 5 years. This increase in the allocation to the states was done with the objective of attaining more horizontal and vertical equity and to allow more autonomy to the states towards its decision-making on public expenditure. With little fiscal space available with the Central government to increase aggregate transfers, the increased tax devolution was primarily intended to change the composition of Central transfers to states.

The changing structure of the transfers to the state and increased allocation of the funds through the FFC route is clear from Table 3.5. During the 13th Finance Commission period (2010–2011 to 2014–2015), the proportion of the transfer through scheme related and other central transfer, through Planning Commission and Central Ministries have increased from 28.92 to 37.90%. Correspondingly, there was a decline in the formulae based untied grants. Since 2015–2016 onwards, the share of tax devolution has increased leading to a decline in the other forms of transfers. The formulae based transfer during 2017–2018 (BE) constitutes around 72%. It is thus evident that Finance Commission transfer is the route through which most funds are being transferred to states and there is minimum discretion left with the Centre government. The discontinuation of the plan, non-plan classification and reduction in the number of centrally sponsored schemes have increased the importance of Finance Commissions in determining the transfer.

The increase in the total transfer is visible from the improved figures for transfer as a percentage of GDP. It has increased by more than 1% of GDP during the FFC compared to 13th Finance Commission period. Here, again the higher devolution of states share in taxes showed an improvement during the FFC (Table 3.4).

The increase in the net transfer of resource is clearer from Fig. 3.5. The proportion was below 50% of the Gross Tax Revenue of the Central government during the grant phase of 13th Finance Commission. The proportion had increased more than 10% points from around 45 to 55%. As we saw earlier, a major proportion of this transfer is through Finance Commission route and hence untied.

As state level comparison of Social Sector expenditure during 2014–2015 and 2015–2016, the pre- and post-FFC implementation years indicates a favourable change that happened across Indian states in allotment of higher amount towards social sectors. Table 3.5 gives another interesting story that it is the backward states that are leading in allocating more resources towards social sectors post FFC implementation. This will have a long-term positive impact on the social sector development of the respective states. Bihar, Odisha, Madhya Pradesh and Uttar Pradesh allocate a sizeable amount on social sectors. Other states also recorded a decent improvement in the social sector expenditure post FFC. The relative change in the social sector expenditure as a percentage of GSDP from 2014–2015 to 2015–2016 indicates that except Bihar and Maharashtra all other states have a positive improvement (Fig. 3.6). Relatively high improvement was visible in Uttar Pradesh, Madhya Pradesh and Odisha in 2015–2016 compared to 2014–2015.

The importance of education cannot be overemphasized in the present knowledge-based economy. The knowledge economy driven by information technologies (IT) requires highly educated people. Primary education is critical. Coming now to relative expenditure incurred on two components of social sectors, viz. education and health, the increasing trend in their expenditures can be noticed during the post FFC periods. The degree of improvement varies from state to state and some states have recorded a slight decline in 2015–2016 followed by a compensating increase in the following years (Table 3.6).

Health and Family Welfare is an area often neglected in India. The expenditure across majority of the states indicates that even though there is a trend improvement, sufficient level of public investment is yet to reach in this crucial sector.

Table 3.4 Central transfers to states

Category	2010–2011	2011–2012	2012–2013	2013–2014	2014–2015	2015–2016	2016–2017 (RE)	2017–2018 (BE)
Devolution of States' share in taxes	219,303	250,522	291,547	318,230	337,808	506,193	608,000	674,565
Finance commission grants	49,875	51,595	51,402	60,631	77,198	84,579	99,115	103,101
Scheme related and other central transfer to states	109,510	123,532	127,737	136,440	253,231	238,572	277,649	303,412
Total transfer to states	378,688	425,649	470,686	515,301	668,237	829,344	984,764	1,081,078
Composition of transfers								
Share of tax devolution (%)	57.91	58.86	61.94	61.76	50.55	61.04	61.74	62.40
Share of finance commission Grants (%)	13.17	12.12	10.92	11.77	11.55	10.20	10.06	9.54
Share of scheme related and other transfers (%)	28.92	29.02	27.14	26.48	37.90	28.77	28.19	28.07
Transfers as % of GDP								
Share of tax devolution (%)	3.03	2.87	2.93	2.83	2.71	3.70	4.03	4.00
Share of finance commission grants	0.69	0.59	0.52	0.54	0.62	0.62	0.66	0.61
Share of scheme related and other transfers	1.51	1.41	1.28	1.21	2.03	1.74	1.84	1.80
Total transfers as % of GDP	5.22	4.87	4.73	4.59	5.37	6.06	6.53	6.42

All Figures in Rs. Crores
Source Union Budget Various Years

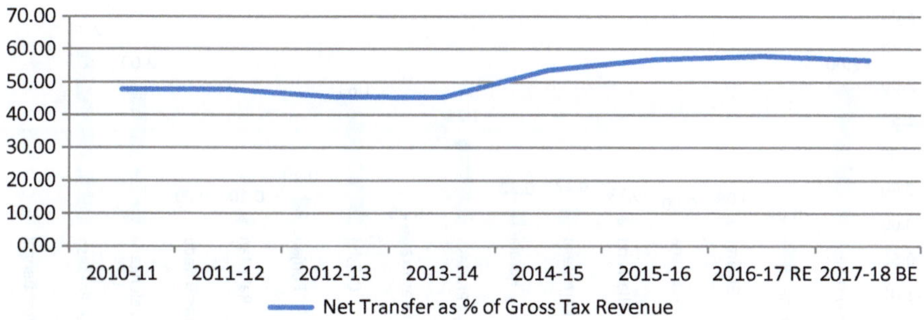

Fig. 3.5 Net transfer of resources to states as a percentage of gross tax revenue of central government

Table 3.5 State government expenditure on social sectors as a percentage of GSDP

S. No.	State	2014–2015	2015–2016	2016–2017 (RE)	2017–2018 (BE)
1	Andhra Pradesh	7.36	9.36	9.54	9.72
2	Bihar	11.26	10.59	12.31	14.71
3	Gujarat	5.26	5.34	5.31	5.21
4	Haryana	6.24	6.24	7.61	8.34
5	Jharkhand	8.15	8.28	12.27	11.84
6	Karnataka	5.27	5.53	5.85	5.54
7	Kerala	5.16	5.37	5.64	5.94
8	Madhya Pradesh	8.71	9.96	9.98	10.04
9	Maharashtra	4.85	4.60	5.29	5.16
10	Odisha	8.60	10.23	11.02	11.49
11	Punjab	4.20	4.60	4.59	NA
12	Rajasthan	6.59	6.69	7.98	7.61
13	Tamil Nadu	5.62	5.71	5.50	5.24
14	Telangana	4.55	6.55	7.41	8.27
15	Uttar Pradesh	8.09	10.57	10.92	NA
16	West Bengal	6.51	6.49	6.54	6.04

Note Detailed Budget of Punjab and Uttar Pradesh for 2017–18 are not available
Source Respective State Government Budgets, 2017–18

In the absence of proper insurance coverage, the out of pocket expenditure on health care in India is very high and unless a substantial improvement happens in public investment, the deficiencies of the sector will affect the long term health of an average Indian (Table 3.7).

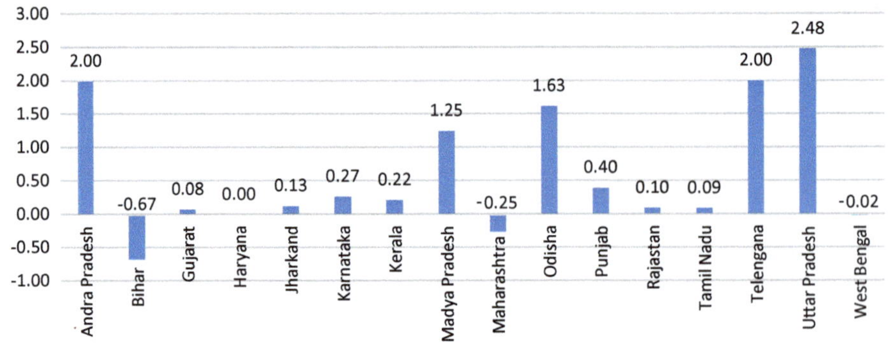

Fig. 3.6 Change in social sector expenditure as a percentage of GSDP in 2015–2016 over 2014–2015

Table 3.6 State government expenditure on education as a percentage of GSDP

S. No.	State	2014–2015	2015–2016	2016–2017 (RE)	2017–2018 (BE)
1	Andhra Pradesh	2.19	2.78	2.87	2.87
2	Bihar	4.42	3.93	4.31	4.88
3	Gujarat	1.98	1.94	1.82	1.79
4	Haryana	2.59	2.53	2.91	3.17
5	Jharkhand	2.68	2.75	3.55	3.84
6	Karnataka	2.05	1.89	1.91	1.61
7	Kerala	2.44	2.47	2.50	2.54
8	Madhya Pradesh	3.43	3.27	3.73	3.69
9	Maharashtra	2.24	2.15	2.16	2.19
10	Odisha	3.06	3.38	3.53	4.02
11	Punjab	2.07	2.28	2.22	NA
12	Rajasthan	2.89	2.83	3.43	3.31
13	Tamil Nadu	2.27	2.15	2.13	2.15
14	Telangana	1.37	1.84	1.55	1.66
15	Uttar Pradesh	3.39	4.14	4.39	NA
16	West Bengal	2.42	2.07	2.10	2.12

Note Detailed Budget of Punjab and Uttar Pradesh for 2017–18 are not available
Source Respective State Government Budgets, 2017–18

Table 3.7 State government expenditure on health and family welfare as a percentage of GSDP

S. No.	State	2014–2015	2015–2016	2016–2017 (RE)	2017–2018 (BE)
1	Andhra Pradesh	0.65	0.85	0.84	0.94
2	Bihar	0.96	0.94	1.39	1.21
3	Gujarat	0.71	0.72	0.73	0.71
4	Haryana	0.59	0.63	0.81	0.86
5	Jharkhand	0.71	1.08	0.93	0.93
6	Karnataka	0.63	0.57	0.60	0.55
7	Kerala	0.73	0.74	0.81	0.84
8	Madhya Pradesh	0.99	1.00	0.98	1.09
9	Maharashtra	0.51	0.50	0.56	0.48
10	Odisha	0.99	1.08	1.27	1.38
11	Punjab	0.64	0.77	0.73	NA
12	Rajasthan	0.96	1.03	1.14	1.17
13	Tamil Nadu	0.52	0.51	0.51	0.52
14	Telangana	0.37	0.65	0.71	0.57
15	Uttar Pradesh	1.15	1.36	1.48	NA
16	West bengal	0.80	0.76	0.67	0.55

Note Detailed Budget of Punjab and Uttar Pradesh for 2017–2018 are not available
Source Respective State Government Budgets, 2017–2018

3.5 Conclusion

Fourteenth Finance Commission has made revolutionary changes in the Centre State fiscal relations by increasing the sates share in the divisible pool of central taxes to 42% during the period 2016–2020. The experience during the first 2 years of implementation of FFC gives a positive trend. The share of the formulae based transfer of resources has increased drastically and that had contributed towards availability of more untied funds to the states. Almost all States have responded positively with the suggestion of FFC and improved their allocation for social sectors. Still, more concrete efforts are required to improve the quantum of social sector expenditure at the state level and extra caution should be there so that increased fiscal space is used more judiciously for human welfare.

References

Bagchi A (2003) Rethinking federalism: changing power relations between the center and the states. Publius J Federalism 33(4)

Chakraborty P (2015) Finance commission's recommendations and restructured fiscal space. Econ Polit Weekly 50(12)

Chakraborty P (2016) Restructuring of central grants: balancing fiscal autonomy and fiscal space, Econ Polit Weekly 51(6)

Choudhury M, Mohanty RK, Dubey JD (2016) Impact of the recommendations of the 14th FC: central transfers and social sector expenditures in the 1st year. NIPFP, New Delhi. Working paper no. 183
Dev M, Mooij J (2002) Social sector expenditures in the 1990s: an analysis of central and state budgets. Econ Polit Weekly 37(9)
Government of India (2015) Report of the fourteenth finance commission, New Delhi
Inman RP, Rubinfeld DL (1997) Rethniking federalism. J Econ Perspect 11(4)
Joshi S (2006) Impact of economic reforms on social sector expenditure in India. Econ Polit Weekly 41(04)
Nagaraj (2013) India's dream run 2003–08: understanding the boom and its aftermath. Econ Polit Weekly 48(20)
NitiAyog (2015) Report of the Sub group of Chief Ministers on Rationalization of Centrally Sponsored Schemes, NitiAyog, New Delhi
Rao MG, Singh N (2006) The political economy of India's fiscal federal system and its reform. Publius J Federalism 37(1)
Rath A (2013) Growing centralization of social sector policies in India. Econ Polit Weekly 48(4)
Shariff A, Gosh P, Mondal SK (2002) State—adjusted public expenditures on social sector and poverty alleviation programmers. Econ Polit Weekly 37(8)
Shetty SL (2016) Underutilized fiscal space: Maharashtra's budget post fourteenth finance commission. Econ Polit Weekly 51(21)
World Bank (2016) India development update: financing double digit growth. World Bank Group

Chapter 4
A Comparison of Fiscal Capacity of States in India: A Regression Approach

Ashok Mittal and Abbas Haider Naqvi

Abstract The States with low taxable capacity need special help in terms of more funds for providing the social and economic services. In addition to 'equalization', another important consideration in a sound federal fiscal transfer scheme is for 'relative tax effort'. It is also one of the important objectives of a federation to induce federating units to make high resource mobilization efforts as is warranted by their capacity. Both fiscal capacity and tax efforts are very important criteria in the scheme of federal fiscal transfers aiming at achieving objectives of equity and efficiency. However, the usefulness of these criteria depends entirely upon their accurate measurement. A wrongly construed or arbitrarily measured taxable capacity or effort can defeat the very purpose of inclusion of these criteria in the scheme of devolution. Here, in this paper the focus is only on fiscal capacity and it is also treated as a measure of horizontal imbalances.

Keywords Fiscal capacity · Horizontal imbalance · Federal transfers
Own tax revenue

Any federal formation is motivated by several factors. In addition to facilitate accessibility to unified common national market, getting best use of the scarce resources of the country and providing common defence facilities, a federation also aims at achieving 'equality of all citizens'. In the presence of regional disparities, inherent or otherwise, the very objective of forming a federation necessitates reducing horizontal fiscal imbalances. In the literature on federal finance, more than vertical fiscal imbalances (VFI), it is the horizontal fiscal imbalances (HFI) that has received lot of attention (Rao 1981). Horizontal fiscal imbalances arise due to the

A. Mittal (✉)
Department of Economics, Aligarh Muslim University, Aligarh, India
e-mail: askmittal@yahoo.com

A.H. Naqvi
Institute of Economic Growth, Delhi, New Delhi 110007, India
e-mail: naqviabbashaider@gmail.com

N.A. Khan (ed.), *Challenges and Issues in Indian Fiscal Federalism*,
India Studies in Business and Economics, https://doi.org/10.1007/978-981-10-6217-9_4

differences in the fiscal capacities and due to varied expenditure needs. Any scheme of federal fiscal transfers pursuing the objective of equalization should recognize the underlying differences in the capacity of the States to raise funds from their tax resources for financing their expenditure and investment programs.

The States with low taxable capacity need special help in terms of more funds for providing the social and economic services. In addition to 'equalization', another important consideration in a sound federal fiscal transfer scheme is for 'relative tax effort'. It is also one of the important objectives of a federation to induce federating units to make high resource mobilization efforts as is warranted by their capacity. Both fiscal capacity and tax efforts are very important criteria in the scheme of federal fiscal transfers aiming at achieving objectives of equity and efficiency. However, the usefulness of these criteria depends entirely upon their accurate measurement. A wrongly construed or arbitrarily measured taxable capacity or effort can defeat the very purpose of inclusion of these criteria in the scheme of devolution (Rangarajan and Srivastava 2011; Pratibha 2012). Here, in this paper the focus is only on fiscal capacity and it is also treated as a measure of horizontal imbalances.

4.1 Review of Some Important Studies

G. Balasubramanian, J.Govindadass and Prasant Kumar Panda (2012) in their paper "*Finance Commission Transfers and Fiscal Equalization in India: Evidence from Panel Data*" examined the fiscal equalization aspect of Finance Commission (FC) transfers in India using the fixed effect panel regression models and it was found that FC transfers are regressive in nature and fails to equalize fiscal capacity of the States.

Swati Raju (2012) in her paper "*State Fiscal Capacity and Tax Effort: Evidence for Indian States*" tried to measure the internal fiscal capacity or the potential to create 'space' in the seventeen non-special category States of India through a tax effort analysis for Own Tax Revenues over the period 2005–06 to 2009–10. Estimates indicate a high tax effort index for the middle and lower income States while the high-income States exhibit a low tax effort. Consequently, the scope to augment revenues for the middle and lower income States is limited, whereas the high-income States enjoy greater latitude for revenue augmentation particularly in Sales Tax.

ICRA Rating Feature (2010) in their report for "*Thirteenth Finance Commission*" mentioned that according to Thirteenth FC's recommendation that the share of States in the divisible pool of Union taxes be increased and that the level of Central grants to the States be raised significantly would boost the States' revenue receipts over the period 2010–11 to 2014–15. However, in ICRA's view, renewed buoyancy of Central and State tax revenues, and structural improvements accruing from greater expenditure control would be essential to improve the States' revenue balances in the medium-to-long term.

Mahesh C Purohit (2006) in his paper "*Tax Efforts and Taxable Capacity of Central and State Governments*" relates taxable capacity to the average efforts of 16 major states in India and takes into account independent variables that influence the capacity factors of States. The final results of the regressions estimated for each of the taxes indicate that Gujarat ranks first in tax effort. West Bengal and Andhra Pradesh stand second and third, respectively. Basically, for those who have a lower rank, actual revenue is lesser than total taxable capacity.

Nirvikar Singh and GarimaVasishtha (2004) in their paper "*Some Patterns in Center-State Fiscal Transfers in India: An Illustrative Analysis*" employed panel data on Center-State transfers to examine how the economic and political importance of the States influences the level and the composition of per capita transfers to the States, as well as differences in temporal patterns of Planning Commission and Finance Commission transfers. They find evidence that States with indications of greater bargaining power seem to receive larger per capita transfers, and that there is greater temporal variation in Planning Commission transfers.

4.2 Meaning and Measuring Fiscal Capacity

According to Mathews and Sweeney (1977) "A fiscal unit's taxable capacity in particular to a revenue source may be defined as the amount of tax the unit can raise by applying a standard rate schedule to its own revenue base". Advisory Commission on Intergovernmental Relations (ACIR 1971) says "fiscal capacity is a quantitative measure intended to reflect the resources which a taxing jurisdiction can tax to raise revenue for public purpose". It is important to make clear that tax capacity is usually related to 'activity variables' such as income or the tax base, so that an increase in the level of activity variable would enhance tax capacity. On the other hand, tax effort refers to the various administrative and legislative efforts to expand the base, rationalization of the tax structure and reduction in the incidence of tax avoidance and evasion. Thus, it is possible for a high-income economy to have a high tax capacity but low tax effort if it does not take initiatives to maximize its tax revenue "potential".

When the federal government transfers resources to the federating units with an objective of equalization, it becomes essential to assess the interstate differentials in fiscal potential.

In this context, the problem of measurement of fiscal potential arises and this problem can be broadly addressed to in two different ways:

1. Macroeconomic approach: Income measure of fiscal capacity.
2. Tax yield/revenue approach to measuring fiscal capacity.

4.3 Macroeconomic Approach: Income Measure of Fiscal Capacity

Income approach measures fiscal capacity in terms of income of the country/state. Based on "Income approach" there are number measures which have been used for the purpose of the comparative study of tax effort. These measures could be put into the following categories.

i. Per capita tax ratio as a measure of tax effort (PCTR)
ii. Tax income ratio (T/Y)
iii. Incremental tax income ratio ($\Delta T/\Delta Y$)
iv. Income elasticity of tax revenue ($\Delta T/\Delta Y * T/Y$)
v. Modified T'/Y' ratio to reflect relative taxable capacity and tax efforts.

However, the macro approach has some theoretical and practical problems. Conceptually, even in a "best-case", the gross local product may not reflect the actual differential abilities of local governments to mobilize resources since income may not be received where it originates. Moreover, the fiscal capacity of a State depends not only on the income but also on inter state shifting of State and local taxes. Taxable capacity depends not only on income produced but also on income accrued.

Besides, no doubt regional income is one of the major and important determinants of fiscal potential, fiscal capacity is influenced by a number of other factors like structural composition of the economy, level of consumption, price variation, distribution of personal income, wealth of the State and so on, which do not get captured by income measure.

4.4 Tax Yield/Revenue Approach to Measuring Fiscal Capacity

The second approach which is a 'micro–oriented' approach to the fiscal capacity issue is often the tax yield approach. The tax yield approach particularly evaluates the taxable resources, i.e. it estimates the amount of tax revenue any State would produce when subjected to various levels of taxation, and make inter-state comparisons.

The yield approach can further be classified into:

a. Regression Analysis Approach (Oommen 1987; Sen 1997; Rao 2006).
b. Representation Tax System Approach (Chelliah and Sinha 1982; Thimmaiah 1979).

4.5 Methodology

The present paper adopts the regression approach for assessing the fiscal Capacity of the Indian states. This study confines itself to the estimation of 16 Major States. Paper is based on the data pertaining to years 2008–2009 to 2013–2014. Here in this paper an attempt has been made to compare the fiscal capacity of two periods, i.e. (2008–2009 to 2010–2011) and (2011–2012 to 2013–2014). The data are collected from the RBI, Central Statistics office (CSO), Ministry of Transport & Highways, Ministry of Power and from other sources. To avoid the impact of fluctuations in a particular year, the study uses three yearly averages for tax revenue, GSDP and all other variables.

For the estimation of the fiscal capacity of different major own-tax revenue of States, the study uses the regression approach. Major tax revenues are: Land Revenue & Agriculture Income Tax, Stamp Duty and Registration Fee, Sales Tax, Motor Vehicle Tax & Passengers and Goods Tax, State Excise Duty and Electricity Duty.

SALES TAX

Sales tax is levied on all sales and/or purchases in the states. This study uses the independent variable of GSDP as the potential base for sales tax. The equation used is as follows:

$$\log(\mathrm{STAX}) = \mathrm{a} + \mathrm{b}\log(\mathrm{GSDP})$$

where,

STAX revenue from total sales tax minus central sales tax; and
GDSP gross state domestic product Table (4.1).

For estimating the fiscal capacity of Sales Tax, the revenue from central taxes is not included in the total sales tax yield. For estimating the fiscal capacity of sales tax GSDP from different states is taken as a potential base. The result of regression is presented in Table 4.2 which indicates that Maharashtra UP and Tamil Nadu ranks first, second and third, respectively in their fiscal capacity in both the periods. Goa got lowest sixteenth rank in both the reference period.

Table 4.1 Sales tax regression results

Year	(2008–2009) to (2010–2011)	(2011–2012) to (2013–2014)
Constant	−1.717	−2.004
Log(GSDP)	1.045 *p*-value (0.000)	1.089 *p*-value (0.000)
R-square	0.878	0.899

Table 4.2 Estimated fiscal capacity of sale tax

(2008–2009) to (2010–2011)				(2011–2012) to (2013–2014)		
States	Tax revenue actual (Rs. Lakh)	Fiscal capacity (Rs Lakh)	Rank	Tax revenue actual (Rs Lakh)	Fiscal capacity (Rs Lakh)	Rank
Andhra Pradesh	2,487,891	1,148,573	8	4,270,823	1,944,524	8
Assam	365,481	382,122	15	625,071	605,833	15
Bihar	380,431	688,195	14	949,040	1343,541	12
Goa	121,794	110,189	16	166,546	173,700	16
Gujarat	1,996,797	1,864,860	4	3,865,566	3,323,809	4
Haryana	942,304	912,946	11	1,538,676	1,591,897	11
Karnataka	1,689,670	1,479,933	6	2,876,142	2,499,425	6
Kerala	1,332,704	958,513	9	2,270,453	1,638,865	10
MP	827,452	943,711	10	1,462,434	1,713,915	9
Maharashtra	3,527,976	3,874,510	1	5,819,953	6,936,543	1
Orissa	567,297	688,492	13	965,884	1,119,590	14
Punjab	801,001	814,453	12	1,371,307	1,307,102	13
Rajasthan	1,056,587	1,155,146	7	1,869,703	2,229,534	7
Tamil Nadu	2,398,348	2,079,732	3	4,633,998	3,761,451	3
UP	2,104,792	2,231,776	2	3,662,556	3,874,268	2
West Bengal	1,091,350	1,689,763	5	1,929,527	2,994,578	5

4.6 Land Revenue and Agriculture Income Tax

Land revenue includes land tax or the basic land revenue, cesses based on the land revenue, special crop cesses, and surcharge and betterment levy. The amount of tax payable depends on the size of landholdings as well as on the productivity of the land. Both these factors also determine the income generated from agriculture. Thus, GSDP originating in the agricultural sector can be regarded as the potential base for land revenue.

Agriculture income tax is not levied in many states. However, land revenue is levied in all the states. But in this analysis, both land revenue and agriculture income tax added together and GSDP from agriculture sector is taken as the potential base for the estimation of tax potential. The equation used is

$$\log(\text{L\_Rev.\&\,AIT}) = a + b\log(\text{GSDPa})$$

where

L_Rev. & AIT Land revenue & Agriculture income tax
$GSDP_a$ Gross State Domestic Product from Agriculture Table (4.3).

Table 4.3 Land revenue and agriculture income tax regression results

Year	(2008–2009) to (2010–2011)	(2011–2012) to (2013–2014)
Constant	−1.223	2.118
Log(GSDPa)	0.822 *p*-value (0.018)	0.334 *p*-value (0.303)
R-square	0.341	0.075

The results of Land and Agriculture income tax are given in Table 4.4. The results of the regression are estimated for the two periods 2008–2009 to 2010–2011 and 2011–2012 to 2013–2014 by using 3- year averages for all the variables. Uttar Pradesh ranks first in both the period and Maharashtra ranks second in the same periods. West Bengal got the third rank in first reference year, i.e. in 2008–2009 to 2010–2011 and achieved fifth rank in the period 2011–2012 to 2013–2014. Goa and Assam got sixteenth and fifteenth rank, respectively, in terms of revenue generating capacity.

Table 4.4 Estimated fiscal capacity of land revenue and agricultural income tax

(2008–2009) to (2010–2011)				(2011–2012) to (2013–2014)		
States	Tax revenue actual (Rs lakh)	Fiscal capacity (Rs lakh)	Rank	Tax revenue actual (Rs lakh)	Fiscal capacity (Rs lakh)	Rank
Andhra Pradesh	17,422	23,741	5	8407	27,992	7
Assam	18,995	9459	15	22,555	18,646	15
Bihar	12,157	15,942	12	19,265	25,036	10
Goa	944	748	16	13,598	6870	16
Gujarat	116,450	24,717	4	190,874	30,217	3
Haryana	934	17,750	11	1231	24,846	11
Karnataka	19,612	19,195	10	22,458	24,680	12
Kerala	8138	12,008	14	13,667	21,260	13
MP	29,323	19,862	9	43,155	28,632	6
Maharashtra	78,508	27,787	2	108,853	30,328	2
Orissa	34,387	12,303	13	44,723	20,845	14
Punjab	1666	21,614	7	3726	26,032	9
Rajasthan	17,745	22,240	6	29,311	30,196	4
Tamil Nadu	14,590	20,562	8	12,633	26,511	8
UP	78,219	43,474	1	68,543	36,270	1
West Bengal	106,486	26,600	3	220,881	29,736	5

4.7 Motor Vehicles Tax and Passengers and Goods Tax

Motor vehicles tax is levied under the Indian Motor Vehicles Act, 1939. Tax rates for motor vehicles tax vary from one state to another depending on the type of vehicle. Passengers and goods tax is a levy on the movement of goods and persons from one place to another.

In view of this, in this study, the fiscal capacity is estimated for the two taxes together. Accordingly, the following regression equation is estimated:

$$\log(\text{MVT\_P\&GT}) = a + b\log(\text{No.\_REG.V})$$

where,

MVT_P&GT Motor vehicles tax and passengers and goods tax
No._REG.V Number of registered Vehicles Table (4.5).

In case of motor vehicles tax and passengers and goods tax number of registered motor vehicle is taken as a potential base for estimating the fiscal capacity of different states. The results of this tax is given in Table 4.6 for both the periods. Maharashtra, Tamil Nadu and Gujarat are the states who got first, second and third rank, respectively, in terms of their fiscal potentials in both the period except Gujarat which achieved rank fourth in the period (2011–2012–2013–2014). Goa ranks sixteenth in both the periods which is lowest in the ranking of fiscal capacity of all the states.

4.8 State Excise Duty

It is levied on all kinds of alcoholic liquor, opium, hemp and other narcotics. For this duty, either the total value of consumption of liquor and narcotics or the total quantities of consumption of various goods subject to state excise duty could be taken as the potential base. Due to non-availability of complete data we have chosen a proxy base, i.e. GSDP for this duty.

$$\text{Log}(\text{SE}) = a + b\log(\text{GSDP})$$

where

SE State Excise Duty and
GSDP State Domestic Product Table (4.7).

Table 4.5 Motor vehicle tax & passengers and goods tax regression results

Year	(2008–2009) to (2010–2011)	(2011–2012) to (2013–2014)
Constant	0.611	0.222
Log(No. of Reg.V)	0.676 *p*-value (0.001)	0.752 *p*-value (0.000)
R-square	0.579	0.743

Table 4.6 Estimated motor vehicles tax and passengers and goods tax

(2008–2009) to (2010–2011)				(2011–2012) to (2013–2014)		
States	Tax revenue actual (Rs lakh)	Fiscal capacity (Rs lakh)	Rank	Tax revenue actual (Rs lakh)	Fiscal capacity (Rs lakh)	Rank
Andhra Pradesh	215,277	190,460	5	357,733	346,051	5
Assam	62,088	53,868	15	79,207	82,760	15
Bihar	199,906	74,683	14	199,856	127,968	14
Goa	27,194	35,613	16	39,662	48,586	16
Gujarat	170,354	235,728	3	241,812	402,652	4
Haryana	70,754	126,401	11	138,418	208,138	10
Karnataka	336,483	179,798	6	621,031	328,228	6
Kerala	113,331	135,936	9	192,760	232,675	9
MP	243,387	156,698	8	387,362	261,001	8
Maharashtra	363,462	283,432	1	551,828	504,998	1
Orissa	147,606	89,453	13	219,636	147,060	13
Punjab	57,758	135,879	10	105,493	206,786	11
Rajasthan	159,844	164,969	7	250,963	283,211	7
Tamil Nadu	336,357	262,509	2	626,125	464,949	2
UP	170,809	232,990	4	297,178	420,759	3
West Bengal	77,279	94,314	12	211,279	165,460	12

Table 4.7 State excise duty regression results

Year	(2008–2009) to (2010–2011)	(2011–2012) to (2013–2014)
Constant	−2.871	−2.245
Log(GSDP)	1.090 *p*-value (0.018)	1.012 *p*-value (0.027)
R-square	0.340	0.303

In the Table 4.8, fiscal capacity of State excise duty is estimated and it is clearly visible from the table that Maharashtra, UP, Tamil Nadu and Gujarat are the top most states in terms of revenue potential. Goa, Assam and Bihar again accorded lowest rank in fiscal capacity in both the periods.

4.9 Electricity Duty

This duty refers to the tax imposed by the state governments on the consumption of electricity. This study takes total consumption of electricity by all types of consumers (leaving aside the consumption on street lighting, traction, etc., which is for public consumption) as the potential tax base.

Table 4.8 Estimated state excise duty

(2008–2009) to (2010–2011)				(2011–2012) to (2013–2014)		
States	Tax revenue actual (Rs lakh)	Fiscal capacity (Rs lakh)	Rank	Tax revenue actual (Rs lakh)	Fiscal capacity (Rs Lakh)	Rank
Andhra Pradesh	662,196	174,205	8	874,726	289,369	8
Assam	25,366	55,274	15	57,114	97,905	15
Bihar	109,472	102,102	14	257,027	205,231	12
Goa	11,077	15,108	16	21,374	30,663	16
Gujarat	5921	288,810	4	8114	476,226	4
Haryana	194,779	137,105	11	330,612	240,270	11
Karnataka	699,354	226,926	6	1,114,839	365,402	6
Kerala	153,733	144,250	9	230,543	246,851	10
MP	295,244	141,928	10	504,818	257,339	9
Maharashtra	515,075	619,238	1	947,919	943,472	1
Orissa	86,779	102,148	13	153,421	173,241	14
Punjab	209,465	121,713	12	336,219	200,053	13
Rajasthan	244,393	175,245	7	396,663	328,589	7
Tamil Nadu	687,071	323,603	3	1,219,025	534,237	3
UP	570,319	348,317	2	981,500	549,112	2
West Bengal	143,670	260,584	5	264,683	432,231	5

Table 4.9 Electricity duty regression results

Year	(2008–2009) to (2010–2011)	(2011–2012) to (2013–2014)
Constant	−2.658	−2.411
Log(Elec_CONSUME)	4.786 *p*-value (0.000)	4.503 *p*-value (0.000)
R-square	0.638	0.609

$$\log(\text{E\_Duty}) = \text{a} + \text{b} \log(\text{Elec\_CONSUME})$$

where,

E_Duty Electricity Duty and
Elec_Consume Electricity Consumption Table (4.9).

The results of electricity duty for both the reference year is given in Table 4.10 which indicates that Maharashtra, Gujarat, Andhra Pradesh and Tamil Nadu got top most rank in both the periods. Except Tamil Nadu which got fifth rank in the second reference year (2011–2012 to 2013–2014). Goa have excluded due to non-availability of data relating to revenue received from the electricity duty. Bihar, Assam and Kerala got bad ranks in revenue generating capacity.

Table 4.10 Estimated Electricity Duty

(2008–2009) to (2010–2011)				(2011–2012) to (2013–2014)		
States	Tax revenue actual(Rs Lakh)	Fiscal capacity (Rs Lakh)	Rank	Tax revenue actual (Rs lakh)	Fiscal capacity (Rs lakh)	Rank
Andhra Pradesh	22,123	98,227	3	31,644	157,819	3
Assam	3034	3472	14	4168	3767	14
Bihar	6649	3121	15	7447	3467	15
Gujarat	275,873	103,133	2	418,705	170,373	2
Haryana	11,872	31,886	12	18,983	47,732	12
Karnataka	57,092	52,618	7	80,268	89,278	6
Kerala	3383	12,964	13	2494	17,061	13
MP	132,196	42,672	10	165,034	62,804	9
Maharashtra	347,148	147,031	1	561,151	263,468	1
Orissa	42,768	32,968	11	59,404	56,441	11
Punjab	76,145	43,821	8	155,253	58,732	10
Rajasthan	75,328	54,131	6	135,706	87,815	7
Tamil Nadu	71,273	92,159	4	113,907	128,400	5
UP	28,196	86,600	5	59,770	142,929	4
West Bengal	67,373	42,746	9	119,407	63,146	8

4.10 Stamp Duty and Registration Fee

A stamp duty and registration fee is paid to the government while transferring or registering various financial instruments or deeds relating to financial transactions.

The base of the tax is generally the value of property bought and/or sold in the state. However, due to non-availability of data relating to various categories of property transacted, GSDP is taken as the factor influencing the potential revenue that can be obtained from this tax.

$$\log(\mathrm{STAMP\_DT}) = a + b\log(\mathrm{GSDP})$$

where

STAMP_DT Stamp duty and registration fee and
GSDP Gross state domestic product Table (4.11).

In this case of stamp duty and registration fee the results are obtained with the help of regression equation, the results are given in Table 4.12 which shows that Maharashtra, UP, Tamil Nadu and Gujarat are the top 4 states in the country which

Table 4.11 Stamp duty and registration fee regression results

Year	(2008–2009) to (2010–2011)	(2011–2012) to (2013–2014)
Constant	−5.435	−4.268
Log(GSDP)	1.437 *p*-value (0.000)	7.094 *p*-value (0.000)
R-square	0.827	0.782

Table 4.12 Estimated stamp duty and registration fee

(2008–2009) to (2010–2011)				(2011–2012) to (2013–2014)		
States	Tax revenue actual (Rs Lakh)	Fiscal capacity (Rs Lakh)	Rank	Tax revenue actual (Rs Lakh)	Fiscal Capacity (Rs Lakh)	Rank
Andhra Pradesh	313,440	181,771	8	530,496	317,788	8
Assam	11,415	40,020	15	23,751	80,437	15
Bihar	93,759	89,874	14	228,436	205,576	12
Goa	12,614	7238	16	41,852	18,461	16
Gujarat	265,049	353,972	4	469,907	597,635	4
Haryana	164,641	132,558	11	318,142	251,049	11
Karnataka	302,846	257,573	6	544,941	427,156	6
Kerala	215,063	141,740	9	303,273	259,798	10
MP	192,557	138,739	10	374,288	273,871	9
Maharashtra	1,085,909	967,535	1	1,693,525	1,421,876	1
Orissa	42,381	89,927	13	55,434	165,833	14
Punjab	186,656	113,300	12	283,654	199,023	13
Rajasthan	155,354	183,203	7	311,208	373,353	7
Tamil Nadu	403,548	411,241	3	781,606	691,394	3
UP	489,172	453,142	2	883,394	715,889	2
West Bengal	186,297	309,091	5	386,266	528,525	5

are having high fiscal capacity in stamp duty and registration fee. Goa, Assam, Bihar and Orissa are the four states who got lowest ranks.

The given below Table 4.13 shows the tax wise comparative status of all states in both the periods. Maharashtra, UP and Gujarat are the states which are having best revenue potential. Goa, Assam and Orissa are the states which are the lowest revenue generating capacity states in the country in both the periods.

For getting a clear picture of fiscal capacity and horizontal imbalances of all the states Table 4.14 has been constructed and ranks have been accorded according to their fiscal capacity in both the reference year.

Coefficient of variation is also computed which shows negligible change in revenue potential of all the states in both the periods. Maharashtra tops the list of the states and Goa got lowest rank in both the reference periods.

Table 4.13 Comparative status of states-tax wise

States/Taxes	LR & AIT		ST		MVT & PG		SE		ED		SD & RF	
	RY1	RY2	RY1	RY2	RY1	RY2	RY1	RY2	RY1	RY2	RY1	RY2
Andhra Pradesh	5	7	8	8	5	5	8	8	3	3	8	8
Assam	15	15	15	15	15	15	15	15	14	14	15	15
Bihar	12	10	14	12	14	14	14	12	15	15	14	12
Goa	16	16	16	16	16	16	16	16	NA	NA	16	16
Gujarat	4	3	4	4	3	4	4	4	2	2	4	4
Haryana	11	11	11	11	11	10	11	11	12	12	11	11
Karnataka	10	12	6	6	6	6	6	6	7	6	6	6
Kerala	14	13	9	10	9	9	9	10	13	13	9	10
MP	9	6	10	9	8	8	10	9	10	9	10	9
Maharashtra	2	2	1	1	1	1	1	1	1	1	1	1
Orissa	13	14	13	14	13	13	13	14	11	11	13	14
Punjab	7	9	12	13	10	11	12	13	8	10	12	13
Rajasthan	6	4	7	7	7	7	7	7	6	7	7	7
Tamil Nadu	8	8	3	3	2	2	3	3	4	5	3	3
UP	1	1	2	2	4	3	2	2	5	4	2	2
West Bengal	3	5	5	5	12	12	5	5	9	8	5	5

RY1 = Reference year (2008–2009) to (2010–2011)
RY2 = Reference year (2011–2012) to (2013–2014)

Table 4.14 Fiscal capacities, all states

State	Fiscal capacity (Rs Lakh) (08–09 to 10–11)	Rank	Fiscal capacity (Rs Lakh) (11–12 to 13–14)	Rank
Andhra Pradesh	18.17	7	30.84	8
Assam	5.44	15	8.89	15
Bihar	9.74	14	19.11	13
Goa	1.69	16	2.78	16
Gujarat	28.71	4	50.01	4
Haryana	13.59	11	23.64	11
Karnataka	22.16	6	37.34	6
Kerala	14.05	10	24.17	10
MP	14.44	9	25.98	9
Maharashtra	59.20	1	101.01	1
Orissa	10.15	13	16.83	14
Punjab	12.51	12	19.98	12
Rajasthan	17.55	8	33.33	7
Tamil Nadu	31.90	3	56.07	3
UP	33.96	2	57.39	2
West Bengal	24.23	5	42.14	5
Coeff. V	69.99		69.12	

4.11 Summary and Conclusion

In estimating the fiscal capacity of all the major 16 states the paper adopts the regression approach. Numbers of determinants of taxes have been used for estimating the revenue potential of the state. The final result of the regression of all the states and for each tax is given in Table 4.14.

The paper presented a tax wise comparative status of states in terms of fiscal capacity for the year (2008–2009 to 2010–2011) and (2011–2012 to 2013–2014). It is found that relative performance of fiscal capacity in terms of all major taxes are same in all the states in both the periods. Fiscal potential of Maharashtra is highest in all taxes for both the reference periods, except land revenue and agriculture income tax in which it ranks second. Goa is the least fiscal potential state and its rank is 16 in all the major taxes in both the reference year. Assam is the second least fiscal potential state and the rank is 15 in all the taxes. Except electricity duty in which it ranks 14th in both the study periods.

The present paper also computed the total fiscal capacity and their respective ranks of all the states as a final result. Again it is clear that Maharashtra tops in revenue potential in both the periods. And Goa is the least revenue potential state. The total fiscal capacity of the states is also an indicator of horizontal imbalances. The horizontal imbalance is almost same in the two study periods. The coefficient of variation for the period (2008–2009) to (2010–2011) and (2011–2012) to (2013–2014) is 69.99 and 69.12%, respectively, which is almost same. From the above analysis it may be concluded that federal transfers are ineffective in reducing horizontal imbalance. The weightage given by Finance Commission to the states for the devolution of taxes should be reconsidered.

References

Balasubramanian G, Govindadass J, Panda PK (2012) Finance commission transfers and fiscal equalization in India: evidence from panel data. Int J Finance Policy Anal 4(1)

Chelliah RJ, Sinha N (1982) Measurement of tax effort of state governments (1973–76). Somaiya Publications, Bombay

ICRA Rating Feature (2010) Thirteenth finance commission: implications of key recommendations for state governments, ICRA Rating Services. http://www.icra.in/Files/Articles/FinanceCommission-13th-2001008.pdf

Mathews RL, Sweeney TA (1977) Concepts and measures of taxable capacity and tax efforts. In Mathews RL (ed) State and local taxation, Canberra

Oommen MA (1987) Relative tax efforts of states. Econ and Polit Weekly, 2(11): 466–470

Pratibha A (2012) Fiscal federalism in India: impact of union transfers on state finances. New Century Publications, Delhi

Purohit MC (2006) Tax efforts and taxable capacity of central and state governments. Econ Polit weekly

Raju S (2012) State fiscal capacity and tax effort: evidence for Indian states. Department of Economics, University of Mumbai, Mumbai

Rangarajan C, Srivastava DK (2011) Federalism and fiscal transfers in India. Oxford University Press, India
Rao H (1981) Centre-state financial relations: criteria of federal fiscal transfers and their application in India. Allied Publishers, New Delhi
Rao H (2006) Fiscal federalism: issues and policies. New Century Publication, Delhi
Sen TK (1997) Relative tax effort by Indian states. Working paper, New Delhi: National Institute of Public Finance and Policy
Singh N, Vasishtha G (2004) Some patterns in center-state fiscal transfers in India: an illustrative analysis, SCCIE Working Paper 04–18, Santa Cruz Center for International Economics
Thimmaiah G (1979) Revenue potential and revenue efforts of the southern states. Oxford and IBH, New Delhi

Chapter 5
Impact of Fiscal Transfers on Gross Domestic Product of Indian Federal States: A Panel Data Analysis

Lalitagauri Kulkarni and Akshay Dhume

Abstract The paper attempts to understand the impact of tax transfers and grants from the Central Governments to the States on the latter economic growth. The study is conducted for the period 2004–05 to 2012–13 and includes 11 'Special' Category states and 17 'Non-Special' Category states. The paper finds that while tax transfers have a positive impact on economic growth of the states; grants have a mixed impact on growth. Fixed Effect model was selected to analyze the data.

Keywords Fiscal transfers · Economic growth · Federal transfers
Panel data · Fixed effect model

5.1 Introduction

Recently the interest in cooperative federalism in India has been revived after the establishment of NITI Aayog and the official statement by the Government. Fiscal federalism is, 'understanding which functions and instruments are best centralized and which are best placed in the sphere of decentralized levels of government' (Oates 1999). In simple terms, fiscal federalism is the distribution of economic power in a government between a central authority and the constituent units. In theory, fiscal federalism becomes an issue of debate because it involves complex measurement of sub central governments' autonomy, their budget constraint, limited access to credit, and a common market sans barriers (Careaga and Weingast 2003); (Rodden 2002). This system is institutionalized, so that the central government may not alter it at will (Sorens 2008). The theoretical literature on economic growth as well as fiscal federalism recognizes the role of federal decentralization in balanced growth (Oates 1993) while economic growth theories

L. Kulkarni (✉) · A. Dhume
Gokhale Institute of Politics and Economics, Pune, India
e-mail: lalitagkulkarni@gmail.com

A. Dhume
Centre for Development Studies, PES University, Bangalore, India

N.A. Khan (ed.), *Challenges and Issues in Indian Fiscal Federalism*,
India Studies in Business and Economics, https://doi.org/10.1007/978-981-10-6217-9_5

include fiscal autonomy as an endogenous factor to achieve higher output per labour and higher level of steady state growth rate (Buckner 2006).

Empirically, fiscal federalism involves a variety of economic, political, geographical and regional issues and the debates on effects of federalism either of a political or an economic nature. In the present study, we aim at examining the effect of fiscal transfers on economic growth of Indian federal states in terms of the state GDPs. Economic growth is influenced by a number of factors. Many of these factors are external non-economic factors like technology, socio-political institutions, etc., which are beyond the control of macroeconomic policy. It is necessary to examine the policy controllable factors without being overwhelmed by the multiplicity of influences on economic growth. The present paper moots that an economic study should essentially focus on the endogenous economic variables which can be controlled fully or partially by economic policy. In absence of policy controllability, mere incorporation and understanding of exogenous factors is impotent.

To quote Rao and Singh (1998, p. 2), 'It is presumed that economic objectives are the sole consideration for determining the quantum of transfers and the design of transfer systems. Of course, even economic objectives have political undertones and in actual practice, the volume and the distribution of transfers to a large extent reflect political compromises, and they are designed to sub serve a host of political objectives. However, an emphasis on economic objectives helps to focus the analysis on the ideal design of the transfer schemes and the departures from this can then be analysed in terms of various noneconomic (political) objectives'.

India's newly constituted planning body, NITI Aayog, has made the term cooperative federalism popular in the recent times. The pre-requisite of the cooperative federalism is the assurance to the subnational governments that the dependence on union finances in form of fiscal transfers is beneficial for their economic growth. On this backdrop the present study aims at examining the effect of tax transfers and grants on the state's output. Although a plethora of literature is available on fiscal federalism in India, the empirical literature focusing on the impact of fiscal transfers on economic growth of Indian Federal States is scarcely found in the public domain (Rao and Singh 1998; Zhang and Zou 2001).

The present study tries to bridge this gap by examining the relation between fiscal transfers from the Union Government to the State Governments and the economic growth of states. The study classifies the fiscal transfers to examine the effect of tax devolution and grants separately on the economic growth. The study is based on panel data analysis of 28 states including 17 states listed under 'non-special' category and 11 states listed under 'special' category for the period 2004–05 to 2012–13.

The remainder of the study is divided into 5 sections. Section 2 discusses the theoretical background and extant empirical literature on this subject, sect. 3 provides an overview of the trends and nature of fiscal transfers in India. In sect. 4 we present the data and methodology followed by a discussion of results. Section 5 concludes the study.

5.2 Literature Survey

5.2.1 Fiscal Federalism and Economic Growth –Theoretical Underpinnings

The association between economic growth and fiscal transfers is elusive. The theory on fiscal decentralization argues for a positive association between both variables (Tiebout 1956; Musgrave 1959; Oates 1972). The theoretical literature on federalism focuses on division of functions and finances among the multiple layers of the Governments. The theory of fiscal federalism is about decentralization, and its eco-political effects. According to Bird, 'the main analytical task of fiscal federalism is to define the appropriate functions and finances of local governments as efficiently as possible—that is, in such a way as to maximize community welfare often represented, for analytical convenience, by the Median Voter Theorem' (Bird et al. 2003). With the decentralization of functions and taxes comes the issue of revenue gap and grants. The issues related to decentralization and fiscal transfers become more complex with greater heterogeneity of the local subnational units (Bird et al. 2003).

Buckner (1999) has derived upon the Diamond Overlapping Generations Model to explain the effects of fiscal federalism in relative preference framework. He states that whether the fiscal autonomy will be beneficial will be essentially determined by the relative preference of the younger population as against that of the older population. If the young desire higher consumption level then the savings will be lower under the fiscal autonomy.

A production function approach toward the supply of central and sub central public goods is taken by Davoodi and Zou (1998). The study concludes that maximization of output in a federal state can be achieved by allowing for regionally differentiated supply of sub-central public good (Buckner 2006).

Mankiw et al. (1992) discuss the importance of physical and human capital in the growth process of an economy. In a developing country like India where the states face disparities of various types, the central government is a required step in and provide funding for capital development. Thus, theoretically, fiscal channels play an important role in promoting economic growth. Feld et al. (2004) however suggest that the importance of fiscal channel is not reflected in the statistical significance of variables in empirical analyses of the association between GDP and fiscal variables.

5.2.2 Fiscal Federalism and Economic Growth—Empirical Studies

A larger body of public economics literature is devoted to relation between government expenditure and economic growth (Martinez-Vazquez and Mcnab 1997). The empirical studies on impact of decentralization and fiscal transfers on economic growth are conducted for China as well as India and other developing countries by World Bank. The study on India has reported a positive significant relation between decentralization and economic growth (Zhang and Zou 2001).

The empirical literature is divided on the benefits of fiscal federalism. Some studies report a positive impact of federalism on economic development. (Feld et al. 2004) empirically study the impact of different instruments of fiscal federalism on economic performance measured by GDP per capita using panel data for the 26 Swiss cantons from 1980 to 1998 and concludes that the intensity of tax competition, which is measured by the difference between a cantons tax rate and the average of its neighbours' tax rates, is at least not harmful for economic performance. Many studies using cross country comparisons show negative impact (Oates 1993, 1999; Reynolds and Smolensky 1974; Rodden 2002). The results of the empirical studies differ based on type of countries, country characteristics, degree of decentralization, etc. Studies on single countries (Akai and Sakata 2002) provide evidence that fiscal decentralization contributes to economic growth, in contrast to previous studies that have denied such a contribution. The state-level data for the United States enable us to estimate the effect of fiscal decentralization more objectively than previously, because the data set exhibits little cultural, historical, and institutional variation. The present study examines whether the same logic can be applicable in case of India.

Most of the empirical literature is pertaining to China. This literature indicates no significant negative effect of decentralization on economic growth. Given the peculiar eco-political institutional framework in China, the comparability of the results is questionable. The remaining empirical studies are mainly pertaining to the federal systems in developed countries, viz. Germany, Switzerland or USA. This shows a void in the literature as regards the effects of fiscal federalism on economic performance of the developing countries (Feld and Schnellenbach 2010).

The dissent in the literature on effects of fiscal transfers and decentralization is due to the fact that both the factors, measure of economic growth as well that of decentralization are highly imperfect. The empirical testing effect of transfers and decentralization on gross domestic product per capita is less than perfect because decentralization and growth both are broad concepts which themselves are correlated with many other variables (Martinez-Vazquez and Mcnab 1997). The growth of per capita income is a long-run variable influenced by numerous factors. On the other hand an acceptable measure of decentralization is always controversial as it involves a combination of all kinds of transfers from the central government to the states. In addition, it involves the redistribution aspect reflecting the local governments own capacity to raise revenues from its own resources.

The literature uses various indices of fiscal decentralization (Zhang and Zou 2001). These measures of decentralization are also criticized (Martinez-Vazquez and Mcnab 1997). Using any measure of decentralization for India needs to incorporate many socio economic political factors. Often the linkages are complex and difficult to capture in econometric modelling.

Empirical studies on fiscal decentralization and economic growth face the challenges of uniformity of data and conceptual definition of fiscal decentralization.

The data available for international cross-country studies from IMF (GFS) is not uniform due to differences in the reporting by the countries and gaps in the data. Conceptually, it is challenging to capture the decentralization and empowerment of local units through the taxation and spending estimates. These estimates do not correctly reflect the decision making power of the local and sub national Governments. A more sophisticated dataset is available for nineteen countries by Thornton (2007). The data gaps and quality is a major issue in case of most of the countries in Asia including India. This is an impediment to develop more sophisticated measures of fiscal decentralization.

On this tormented background, the present study tries to examine the effect of fiscal transfers on economic growth. The empirical studies concerning Indian fiscal transfers and economic growth are scarcely found in public domain. The present study attempts to analyze the effects of fiscal transfer on state per capita gross domestic products focusing on economic factors.

5.3 Fiscal Federalism in India: Cooperative, Combative, or Competitive?

The pre-requisite for cooperative federalism is transparency in fiscal transfers which is ensured by the constitutional provisions. One component of fiscal transfers are tax devolution based on constitutionally established finance commission formulae while the other component is the grants over and above the tax sharing. The grants are classified into the grants under finance commission and the grants for implementation of centrally sponsored schemes. In India, vertical fiscal imbalances as well as the horizontal fiscal imbalances are issues of constant debate among policy makers and academicians. Each of the components of fiscal transfers has specific eco-political significance. The motive behind transfer of taxes is to establish balance between states' revenue capacity and expenditure responsibilities. In addition to this, the redistribution of revenue through the finance commission formulae is designed to remove the horizontal imbalances among the states.

While this framework of fiscal transfers is expected to eventually lead to cooperative federalism, on the contrary it has led to combative federalism! One reason of the states' discontent is the classic equality-efficiency trade off. Economically advanced states feel that they are being punished for their efficiency as the finance commission formulae always devises inverse relation between share of states in central taxes and states GDP. Second reason for the states' grudge is to be found in political argument of centre being dominant paternalistic provider to the states. This is claimed to be creating the vertical imbalance. The vertical imbalance embedded in the constitution to retain national unity is acceptable. However, the vertical imbalance generated by grants and centrally sponsored schemes (CSS) circumventing the finance commission formulae is debatable.

Chart 5.1 States own tax revenue versus States share in central taxes (% of total GSDP). *Source* Derived from Database on Indian Economy, RBI

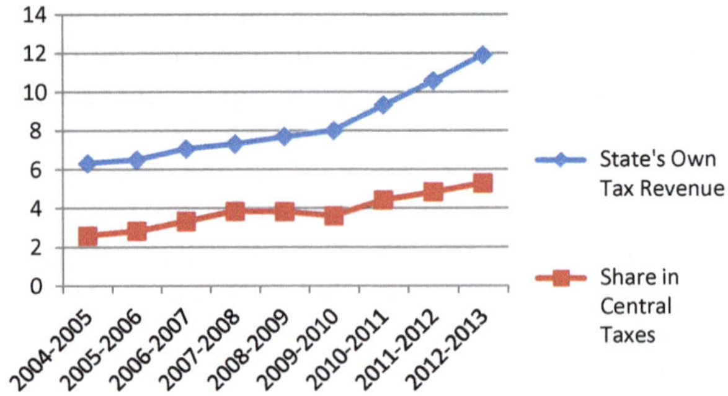

The grants for implementation of the centrally sponsored schemes (CSS) are out of the gamut of constitutional fiscal transfers. Although these grants are helping the states to implement various developmental schemes, these have been controversial in India. The CSS grants are disbursed at the discretion of the Central Government. So it is important to observe the trends in tax sharing vis-à-vis the CSS grants. The following charts throw light on these trends during the past decade.

As shown by Chart 5.1, the States' own tax revenue as percentage of aggregate state GDP is rising at a greater rate from 2009–10 as compared to the states share in central taxes taken together.

Chart 5.2 shows interesting trends in central tax devolution to states as compared to the grants received by states. The share of states in the central taxes is growing at a higher rate than the growth of share of grants to states as percentage of total state GDP. Only the year 2008–09 is exception to this trend when the central tax revenue dwindled due to corporate recession.

Chart 5.3 shows that the grants for centrally sponsored schemes are very small part of the total grants. However, their share in total grants is increasing. The grants for centrally sponsored schemes are totally discretionary component of fiscal transfers.

Each of the components of fiscal transfers, are based on separate driving factors. Taxes are determined by constitutionally established finance commission, while a

Chart 5.2 States share in central taxes versus Grants from the centre (% of total GSDP). *Source* Derived from Database on Indian Economy, RBI

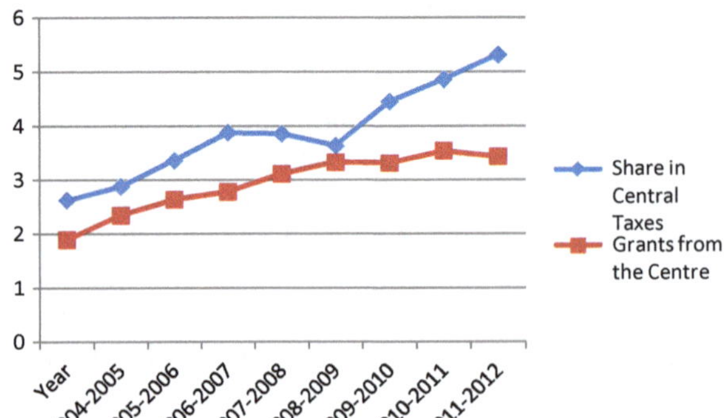

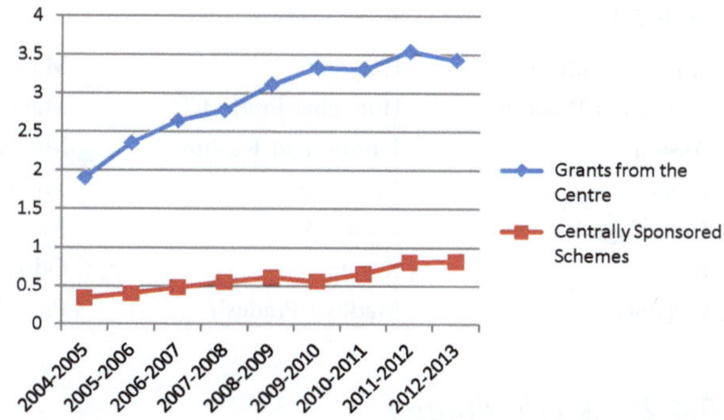

Chart 5.3 Grants from the centre versus Grants for centrally sponsored schemes (% of total GDP). *Source* Derived from Database on Indian Economy, RBI

portion of grants (Sect. 282 and CSS) is discretionary. Hence the source of fiscal transfers has a bearing on political aspects of states autonomy and centre's dominance especially when the ruling parties at these two layers of Government are different. For the Sect. 282 grants and CSS grants the states have to compete for the attention of the central Government. Thus, the components of fiscal transfers have major effect on whether the federalism in India turns out to be cooperative competitive or combative. On this background one should verify the economic effects of each of these components on economic growth of the states.

An attempt at a formal analysis of economic impact of fiscal transfers in India is important because the issue of fiscal transfers becomes controversial when the transfers are regarded by the states as unnecessary paternalistic overtures by the central government with a tacit motive to have political domination. An economic analysis will examine if this view is supported by economic logic and a promise of future economic growth.

5.4 Empirical Investigation

5.4.1 Data

The data used for the empirical analysis is sourced from the Reserve Bank of India Database on Indian Economy. The state-level data on tax revenue, state-level expenditure on economic and social services, tax receipts from central government and state GDP is sourced from State Finances: A Study of Budgets. The study focuses on the impact of fiscal transfers on the economic growth of the states for the period 2004–05 to 2012–13. The study covers 28 states. The list of states that have been included is provided in Table 5.1.

Table 5.1 States included in the study

Andhra Pradesh	Haryana	Maharashtra	Rajasthan
Arunachal Pradesh	Himachal Pradesh	Manipur	Sikkim
Assam	Jammu and Kashmir	Meghalaya	Tamil Nadu
Bihar	Jharkhand	Mizoram	Tripura
Chhattisgarh	Karnataka	Nagaland	Uttarakhand
Goa	Kerala	Odisha	Uttar Pradesh
Gujarat	Madhya Pradesh	Punjab	West Bengal

5.4.2 Methodology

Feld and Baskaran (1998) use panel data model with GDP as dependent variable and decentralization measures and a vector of control variables as independent variables. The study of OECD countries over 1975–2001 shows that the effects of decentralization on economic growth are different for different countries. Generally, the effects are insignificant.

As seen from the survey of literature, the extant empirical studies on effect of fiscal decentralization on economic growth in India are not found. The present study tries to bridge this gap. As mentioned in the literature survey, the methodology for empirical analysis of decentralization effects on economic growth has been challenging. The empirical studies are yet to settle the issue of the impact of decentralization on efficiency, growth, poverty and governance (Rao et al. 2011). The per capita state GDP as an indicator of economic growth is never a flawless indicator. In India, GDP is fraught with all kinds of empirical and conceptual problems like under reporting, different base years, etc. However, it is the most suitable measurable and empirically available indicator of economic growth.

The extant empirical studies on India present the models which incorporate all kinds of socio political factors examine the reasoning behind the distribution of revenue from centre to states and not its effects on the economic growth.

In the present study we have used the following set of independent variables. The Ratio of State's Own Tax Revenue Per Capita to Sum of All State's Own Revenue Per Capita to reflect the state's economic status and tax effort as compared to other states. We use the Ratio State's Share in Central Taxes Per Capita to Total of Share across States Per Capita as an indicator of tax transfer from Centre to states. This reflects the vertical transfers as well as horizontal transfers. Development Expenditure of State Per Capita is used as a proxy for human capital and overall productivity of the states.

The paper presents six models based on inclusion/exclusion of certain states. The details of these models are provided in Table 5.2.

The dependent variable is Gross State Domestic Product. The variables Ratio of State's Own Tax Revenue Per Capita to Sum of All State's Own Revenue Per Capita and Ratio of Grants from Centre to State Per Capita to Grants from Centre to All States Per Capita attempt to account for the transfers from the Centre to the

Table 5.2 States included/excluded in the models

Model	Description of model
Model 1	All states
Model 2	All states excluding Goa, Jharkhand, J&K, Nagaland
Model 3	All non-special category states
Model 4	Non-special category states excluding Goa and Jharkhand
Model 5	All special category states
Model 6	All special category states excluding J&K and Nagaland

Table 5.3 List of variables

Variables	Description of variables
Year	Year
GSDPPC	GSDP per capita
PSOTRPC	Ratio of state's own tax revenue per capita to sum of all state's own revenue per capita
PSSCTPC	Ratio state's share in central taxes per capita to total of share across states per capita
DESPC	Development expenditure of state per capita
PGCSPC	Ratio of grants from centre to state per capita to grants from centre to all states per capita

Note All variables included in the model are in log form. 'ln' represents log of the variable

States. All variables in the model enter in log form. The variables included in each of the models are presented in Table 5.3.

5.4.3 Model and Model Selection

Development of human and physical capital is essential for growth of an economy (Mankiw et al. 1992). Funds for this purpose are made available through grants from centre, share of state in central taxes, as well as through state's own tax receipts. Development expenditure accounts for available infrastructural facilities, which provide a base for further development and the amount that is spent towards development of human and physical capital.

Thus,

$$\text{GSDPPC} = f(\text{PSOTRPC}, \text{PSSCTPC}, \text{DESPC}, \text{PGCSPC}) \quad (1)$$

We argue that higher state's share in central taxes and grants from the centre would assist the state in its growth process. Development expenditure shall also bear a positive relationship with output in the economy as this expenditure is made on human and physical capital. Finally, the relationship between state's own tax

Table 5.4 Model selection

Model	Fixed effect versus OLS (*F*-test)	Decision	Random effect versus OLS (Breusch–Pagan LM test for random effect)	Decision	Fixed versus random effect (Hausman test)	Decision	Selected model
Model 1	39.58***	Fixed effect	491.68***	Random effect	57.95***	Fixed effect	Fixed effect
Model 2	26.39***	Fixed effect	260.16***	Random effect	58.68***	Fixed effect	Fixed effect
Model 3	58.35***	Fixed effect	388.99***	Random effect	30.28***	Fixed effect	Fixed effect
Model 4	77.11***	Fixed effect	390.32***	Random effect	19.03***	Fixed effect	Fixed effect
Model 5	27.30***	Fixed effect	135.25***	Random effect	19.79***	Fixed effect	Fixed effect
Model 6	12.65***	Fixed effect	11.96***	Random effect	29.43***	Fixed effect	Fixed effect

Note Test statistic ***$p < 0.01$, **$p < 0.05$, *$p < 0.1$

receipts and output is ambiguous. While, we may expect a positive relationship between the two variables, it can also be argued that a higher tax collection from the state's population and enterprises may have an adverse impact on the growth of the state's economy.

We will assume a log-linear functional form for the model. The model may then be represented as follows.

$$\ln \mathrm{GSDPPC}_{it} = \beta_1 + \beta_2 \ln \mathrm{PSOTRPC}_{it} + \beta_3 \ln \mathrm{PSSCTPC}_{it} + \beta_4 \ln \mathrm{DESPC}_{it} + \beta_5 \ln \mathrm{PGCSPC}_{it} + \varepsilon_{it} \quad (2)$$

The study checks for appropriateness of model/estimation procedure by testing for Fixed Effect versus OLS with F statistic, Random Effect versus OLS with Breusch–Pagan Lagrange Multiplier test and Fixed Effect versus Random Effect estimation with Hausman test. The results obtained from each of these test are presented in Table 5.4. It can be observed from the table that for all groups of states, the Fixed Effects Model is selected over OLS and Random Effects Model.

The fixed effects model captures the unobserved heterogeneity among the Indian states by emphasizing on the State-specific effects arising from various factors like geographical factors, rainfall, draught-prone areas, hilly regions, etc.

5.4.4 Results

Table 5.5 provides the summary of results for the panel data analysis for the 6 models. From the table we observe that,

- For all states (Model 1), the impact of increase in States' own per capita tax revenue, on the state GDP per capita is negative and statistically significant. All other models show similar impact except for Model 4 which includes Non-Special Category States Excluding Goa and Jharkhand. This result is expected, as the tax revenue is a withdrawal from gross domestic product.
- The impact of increase in Ratio State's Share in Central Taxes Per Capita to Total of Share Across States Per Capita, (PSSCTPC) is positive and statistically significant for all models except for Model 3. Model 3 includes all non-special category states. The state per capita GDP in these states shows negative impact of tax transfers.
- The impact of increase in Development Expenditure of the states per capita is positive and significant on the State per capita GDP for all Models. This is a good indication showing the welfare effect of development expenditure on economic growth.
- The impact of share of per capita Grants from centre to the state is negative for all models except Model 6 which is for all special category states excluding J&K and Nagaland. However, for Model 2 and Model 4 the coefficients on per capita grants are significant while for the remaining models the coefficients are insignificant.
- The impact of share in grants is statistically insignificant except for Model 2 (All States Excluding Goa, Jharkhand, J&K, and Nagaland) and Model 4 (Non-Special Category States Excluding Goa and Jharkhand).

Table 5.5 Summary of results

Variables	Model 1	Model 2	Model 3	Model 4	Model 5	Model 6
lnPSOTRPC	−0.213*** (0.0676)	−0.167** (0.0739)	−0.0482 (0.0721)	0.117 (0.0724)	−0.402*** (0.123)	−0.438*** (0.134)
lnPSSCTPC	0.273*** (0.0621)	0.350*** (0.0693)	−0.0309 (0.0774)	0.0347 (0.0824)	0.325*** (0.114)	0.371*** (0.131)
lnDESPC	0.466*** (0.0151)	0.461*** (0.0163)	0.436*** (0.0122)	0.423*** (0.0111)	0.532*** (0.0466)	0.562*** (0.0532)
lnPGCSPC	−0.0348 (0.0303)	−0.0593* (0.0347)	−0.0148 (0.0240)	−0.0483** (0.0239)	−0.0125 (0.0877)	0.000661 (0.102)
Constant	6.294*** (0.137)	6.356*** (0.147)	6.780*** (0.104)	6.852*** (0.0936)	5.120*** (0.512)	4.764*** (0.572)
Observations	252	216	153	135	99	81
Number of states	28	24	17	15	11	9
R-squared	0.837	0.840	0.913	0.934	0.777	0.778

Note Standard errors in parentheses ***$p < 0.01$, **$p < 0.05$, *$p < 0.1$

5.5 Conclusion

The study tries to observe the impact of fiscal transfers from the centre to the states on state level incomes with the help of panel data approach. The results of the empirical analysis indicate that:

- The tax revenue of the states leads to leakages in the per capita GDP of the states while per capita development expenditure by the states causes increase in the per capita state GDP this is consistent with the classroom macroeconomic theory.
- The results for the fiscal transfer variables are interesting. The Ratio of State's Share in Central Taxes Per Capita to Total of Share Across States Per Capita shows a positive and statistically significant impact on state per capita GDP this implies that the tax devolution by the centre has welfare effect on economic growth of the states. However, this effect is negative and statistically insignificant in case of all non-special category states. This may imply that the economic growth of these states is not dependent on the share of taxes from central Government.
- Another notable conclusion from the panel data analysis is that grants from the centre are mostly statistically insignificant in economic growth of states and show a negative impact on State GDP.
- The directions of the signs of coefficients both for tax share as well as for share in grants show that overall the fiscal transfers are of redistributive nature in India. In this sense, the Finance Commissions have mostly achieved their goals of re-distributional fiscal federalism Irrespective of the hue and cry about the central dominance in Indian fiscal federalism; the overall effect of tax transfers is economically beneficial. However, the economic welfare effect of grants seems to be ambivalent.

It would be prudent to emphasize on the transfers in form of sharable tax revenue rather than grants. The literature on political effects of fiscal transfers on states' independence commonly supports this argument in favour of the fiscal autonomy of the states.

The empirical results of the present study support this argument as the effect of tax transfers is proved to be more beneficial while the effect of grants is insignificant in improving economic efficiency and equity in terms of state GDP in India.

References

Akai N, Sakata M (2002) Fiscal decentralization contribute to economic growth: evidence from state-level cross-section data for United States. J Urban Econ 52:93–108

Bird R, Dafflon B, Jeanrenaud C, Kirchgässner G (2003) Assignment of responsibilities and fiscal federalism. Politorbis 32:58–78

Buckner JK (1999) Fiscal federalism and capital accumulation. J Public Econ Theory 1:205–224

Buckner JK (2006) Fiscal federalism and economic growth. J Public Econ 90:2101–2120

Careaga M, Weingast BR (2003) Fiscal federalism, good governance, and economic growth in Mexico. In: Rodrick d (ed) Search of prosperity: analytic narratives on economic growth. Princeton University Press, Princeton, pp 399–435

Davoodi H, Zou H (1998) Fiscal decentralization and economic growth: a cross country study. J Urban Econ 43:244–257

Feld LP, Baskaran T (1998) Fiscal decentralization and economic growth in OECD countries: is there a relationship? Memiograph. University of Heidelberg, Heidelberg

Feld LP, Schnellenbach J (2010) Fiscal federalism and long-run macroeconomic performance: a survey of recent research. International Center for Public Policy Working paper series, at AYSPS, GSU paper1009, International Center for Public Policy, Andrew Young School of Policy Studies, Georgia State University

Feld LP, Kirchgässner G, Schaltegger C (2004) Fiscal federalism and economic performance : evidence from Swiss Cantons. Jahrbuch fur Regionalwissenschaft/Rev Reg Res 25:3–25 (Public Finance)

Mankiw NG, Romer D, Weil DN (1992) A contribution to the empirics of economic growth. Quart J Econ 107(2):407–438

Martinez-Vazquez J, Mcnab R (1997) Fiscal decentralization, economic growth, and democratic governance. Georgia State University, International studies program working paper-43, 97-7

Musgrave RM (1959) The theory of public finance. McGrawHill, NY

Oates WE (1972) Fiscal federalism. Harcourt Brace Jovanovich, NY

Oates WE (1993) Fiscal decentralisation and economic development. Natl Tax J 46(2):237–243

Oates WE (1999) An essay on fiscal federalism. J Econ Lit 37(3):1120–1149. doi:10.1257/jel.37.3.1120

Rao MGR, Singh N (1998) Intergovernmental transfers: rationale, design and Indian experience, pp 1–22. Accessed http://people.ucsc.edu/~boxjenk/cre3.pdf

Rao MG, Raghunandan TR, Datta P, Amarnath HK (2011) Fiscal decentralization to rural local governments in India : selected issues and reform options. http://www.nipfp.org.in/media/medialibrary/2013/08/Fiscal_Decentralization_to_Rural_Local_Governments_in_India.pdf

Reynolds M, Smolensky E (1974) National tax association. Natl Tax J 27(4):515–530

Rodden J (2002) The dilemma of fiscal federalism : grants and fiscal performance around the world. Am J Polit Sci 46(3):670–687 (Published by : Midwest Political Science A)

Sorens J (2008) Fiscal federalism: a return to theory and measurement. SSRN working paper series. http://doi.org/10.2139/ssrn.1301096

Tiebout C (1956) A pure theory of local expenditures. J Polit Econ 64:24–416

Thornton J (2007) Fiscal decentralization and economic growth reconsidered. J Urban Econ 61 (1):64–70

Zhang T, Zou H (2001) The growth impact of intersectoral and intergovernmental allocation of public expenditure: with applications to China and India. China Econ Rev 12:58–81

Chapter 6
Analysis of Trends and Patterns of Southern States' Fiscal Indicators

K. Gayithri, Nagesha G. and J.S. Darshini

Abstract The paper makes an attempt to analyze the trends and patterns of revenue and expenditure structure of the Southern States of India and analyze the fiscal gap and dependence of the southern states. The paper is organized in the following order: section one briefly describes the fiscal situation of southern states namely Karnataka, Kerala, Andhra Pradesh and Kerala. Section two explains the trends and patterns of various fiscal gap of the respective southern states. Section three analyses the trends and patterns of central transfers to southern states following which some conclusions are presented.

6.1 Introduction

Finance Commissions in India have addressed the issues of vertical and horizontal imbalances from time to time that tend to influence the state finances in a significant manner. It would be of academic and policy importance to analyze the impact of these transfers on state finances. India is one of the world's largest fiscal federal systems. Since its inception India's federal structure was a two tier, namely Union (center) and States, FY1993 onwards this has expanded to three tiers structure with the addition of the rural and urban local government bodies. The prevailing transfer mechanisms and the transfers effected from time to time tend to have significant

K. Gayithri (✉)
Faculty of Economics, Institute for Social and Economic Change, Bangalore, India
e-mail: gayithri@isec.ac.in

N. G.
Post Graduate School of Economics, GFGC, Yelahanka, Bangalore, India

J.S. Darshini
Post Graduate School of Economics, GFGC, K.R Puram, Bangalore, India

N.A. Khan (ed.), *Challenges and Issues in Indian Fiscal Federalism*,
India Studies in Business and Economics, https://doi.org/10.1007/978-981-10-6217-9_6

implications on the state finances and the resultant state level fiscal management can be quite challenging for the states concerned. While some states have had greater dependence on the Center some have had reduced dependence.

The paper makes an attempt to analyze the trends and patterns of revenue and expenditure structure of the Southern States of India and analyze the fiscal gap and dependence of the southern states.

The paper is organized in the following order: section one briefly describes the fiscal situation of southern states namely Karnataka, Kerala, Andhra Pradesh and Kerala. Section two explains the trends and patterns of various fiscal gap of the respective southern states. Section three analyses the trends and patterns of central transfers to southern states following which some conclusions are presented.

6.2 Southern States Contribution to GDP of India

Analysis of the Southern States GSDP to total GDP of India (Table 6.1) reveals that the southern states share in the GDP has gradually increased and also constitutes a significant share. On an average all the four southern states of India accounts for 22.39% of GDP of India during the FY02 to FY15. Further individually Tamil

Table 6.1 Southern states share in GDP of India

Year	All SS	Karnataka	Kerala	Andhra Pradesh	Tamil Nadu
	Values are percent to GDP of India				
2002–03	19.18	4.70	3.14	5.80	5.53
2003–04	19.12	4.72	3.09	5.88	5.43
2004–05	20.94	5.14	3.68	6.93	5.18
2005–06	21.48	5.53	3.70	6.95	5.31
2006–07	22.00	5.87	3.66	7.07	5.40
2007–08	22.33	6.36	3.62	7.21	5.14
2008–09	22.93	6.95	3.64	7.22	5.12
2009–10	24.90	6.93	3.65	7.00	7.32
2010–11	25.95	7.75	3.58	7.00	7.61
2011–12	22.32	5.21	4.17	4.34	8.60
2012–13	22.52	5.66	4.20	4.11	8.54
2013–14	23.09	6.25	4.09	4.19	8.56
2014–15	23.34	6.49	4.10	4.21	8.54
2015–16 RE	23.34	6.48	3.88	4.35	8.63
Mean	22.39	6.00	3.73	5.88	6.78

Source Computed from the various documents of MOSPI

Nadu, Karnataka, Andhra Pradesh and Kerala GSDP account for 6.78, 6.00, 5.88 and 3.73 of GDP of India, respectively, during the same reference period.

6.3 Fiscal Situation of Southern States

6.3.1 Fiscal Indicators of Karnataka

Growth rates of the Karnataka's key fiscal indicators for the period FY02 to FY16 reveals that average annual growth rate (AAGR) of own tax revenues (OTR) in Karnataka accounts for 16.67%; this is higher than the AAGR of revenue expenditure (RE) and total expenditure (TE) which are 15.11 and 15.41, respectively, during FY02 to FY16. Further, the Gross State Domestic Product (GSDP) increased at 15.04 and capital expenditure (CE) grew at 18.36 percent during the same reference period. Whereas Karnataka's share in central taxes and central grants respectively accounts for 18.89 and 19.51 of AAGR respectively; it is important to note that the growth rates of these two indicators are higher than the AAGRs of any other fiscal indicators (refer Table 6.2).

Analysis found that the AAGR of revenue expenditure is more consistent; which is observed through relatively small variance (8.6%) as compared to all other fiscal indicators during the above reference period. Whereas the fiscal indicators like Non-tax revenue, capital expenditure, share in central grants and share in central taxes are more inconsistent. Indicators like GSDP, interest payments, own tax revenues and total tax revenue are relatively less consistent (with 2 digit variances).

It is also observed that the fiscal indicators like RE, TE, GSDP, IPs and OTRs AAGRs are more concentrated from its mean values in the order of ascending. Whereas NTR, CGs, CE, CTs, are more dispersed in the order of descending.

The descriptive statistical analysis (refer Table 6.2) explains that Government of Karnataka has to sustain its consistency of non-tax revenue, capital expenditure, and total expenditure in line with the revenue expenditure or more to sustain its fiscal health in the long run.

6.3.2 Fiscal Indicators of Kerala

Kerala's fiscal indicators as it is observed in Table 6.3 reveals that average annual growth rate of capital expenditure, non-tax revenue, share in central grants and central taxes accounts for 32, 24.9, 23.9, 17.1% respectively, during FY02 to FY15. This is followed by the TRRs with 16.7%, TE with 16.4%, OTR with 15.8, IPs with 11.2% during the same reference period.

It is important to notice that the growth rate of capital expenditure is higher than any other fiscal indicators analyzed (refer Table 6.3). However, the respective CE AAGR is more volatile compared to other indicators. In all other indicators

Table 6.2 Growth rates of key fiscal indicators of Karnataka

Year	OTR	NTR	Share in CTs	CGs	TRR	RE	CE	Total expenditure	Interest payments	GSDP
2003–04	20.40	131.46	16.48	19.34	28.39	13.13	3.19	11.79	12.70	8.36
2004–05	27.86	51.18	19.51	8.05	27.99	17.13	54.29	21.76	2.27	27.30
2005–06	15.93	−13.35	8.64	69.17	14.23	12.47	24.57	14.38	−0.77	17.49
2006–07	25.06	5.75	27.56	32.52	23.84	19.24	46.74	23.96	12.53	15.99
2007–08	11.53	−18.06	26.14	4.45	0.18	11.78	1.24	9.64	6.36	19.10
2008–09	6.38	−5.93	5.53	6.07	14.97	11.46	14.13	11.96	0.58	14.66
2009–10	10.61	5.53	2.88	47.84	13.55	14.11	22.96	15.80	15.03	8.78
2010–11	25.82	0.73	29.16	−12.88	18.41	13.67	44.42	19.92	8.21	21.67
2011–12	20.80	21.70	16.51	18.93	19.93	20.51	15.23	19.22	7.46	10.84
2012–13	15.66	−2.95	14.20	−4.39	11.99	17.17	−14.04	9.78	12.72	14.82
2013–14	16.46	1.66	9.18	16.51	14.54	16.90	−0.35	13.71	14.69	17.59
2014–15	12.10	16.27	6.12	60.67	16.30	16.17	16.47	16.22	19.99	11.49
2015–16 RE	7.68	15.42	63.66	−12.66	13.05	12.66	9.84	12.20	16.47	7.41
2016–17 BE	10.98	14.95	12.49	7.25	11.07	11.57	18.55	12.68	15.69	
Mean	16.64	16.11	18.89	19.51	16.72	15.11	18.36	15.41	9.86	15.04
SD	6.97	38.85	15.99	26.36	7.42	2.93	20.13	4.60	6.44	5.75
Variance	48.55	1509.59	255.73	694.59	55.06	8.60	405.16	21.12	41.44	33.05

Notes: *OTR* Own tax revenue; *NTR* Non-tax revenue; *CTs* Central taxes; *CGS* Central grants; *TRR* Total revenue receipts; *RE* Revenue expenditure; *TCE* Total capital expenditure; *TE* Total expenditure; *IPs* Interest payments; *GSDP* Gross state domestic product

Source Computed from various budget documents of GOK, RBI State Finances and MOSPI documents

Table 6.3 Average annual growth rates of various fiscal indicators

States	Descriptive statistics	OTR	NTR	CTS	CGs	TRR	RE	CE	TE	IPS	GSDP
Kerala	Mean	15.8	24.9	17.1	23.9	16.7	15.5	32.0	16.4	11.2	15.2
Karnataka	Mean	16.6	16.1	18.9	19.5	16.7	15.1	18.4	15.4	9.9	15.0
Tamil Nadu	Mean	15.6	15.3	15.6	25.2	15.8	11.9	53.7	19.7	11.0	16.7
Andhra Pradesh	Mean	11.0	7.8	16.6	20.7	11.6	10.9	15.1	11.2	7.5	9.4
Kerala	SD	7.75	22.72	8.53	43.85	6.85	10.58	95.19	20.79	8.63	24.05
Karnataka	SD	7.0	38.9	16.0	26.4	7.4	2.9	20.1	4.6	6.4	5.7
Tamil Nadu	SD	5.5	30.4	16.6	42.2	6.0	7.7	51.1	7.7	4.2	23.7
Andhra Pradesh	SD	17.1	25.5	16.5	46.5	14.4	11.9	25.5	13.3	13.9	8.9
Kerala	Variance	60.07	516.07	72.79	1922.62	46.97	111.88	9060.36	432.09	74.42	578.24
Karnataka	Variance	48.5	1509.6	255.7	694.6	55.1	8.6	405.2	21.1	41.4	33.0
Tamil Nadu	Variance	30.4	925.9	274.7	1783.6	36.0	58.8	2611.2	59.4	17.7	563.6
Andhra Pradesh	Variance	292.3	649.2	272.7	2166.7	207.4	140.8	648.3	176.1	193.0	79.7

Notes: *OTR* Own tax revenue; *NTR* Non-tax revenue; *CTs* Central taxes; *CGS* Central grants; *TRR* Total revenue receipts; *RE* Revenue expenditure; *TCE* Total capital expenditure; *TE* Total expenditure; *IPs* Interest payments; *GSDP* Gross state domestic product

Source Computed from various budget documents of Southern States, RBI State Finances and MOSPI

specifically CGs, NTR, TE, RE and CT are also more inconsistent as compared to all other Southern States.

6.3.3 *Fiscal Indicators of Tamil Nadu*

Tamil Nadu's fiscal indicators AAGRs of CE, SCGs, TE, GSDP are positioned at first four berths with 53.7, 25.2, 19.7, 16.7 during FY02 to FY15 (Table 6.3). Whereas the OTRs and CTs have same AAGRs of 15.6%, followed by NTR with 15.3 and IPs with 11% during the same reference period. In Tamil Nadu also the highest growth rate of CE, which is more inconsistent (similar to Kerala). CGs, NTRs, GSDP indicators also appears to be less consistent as compared to the IPs, OTRs.

6.3.4 *Fiscal Indicators of Andhra Pradesh*

In AP fiscal indicators like share in CGs and CTs, capital expenditure accounts for more than 15% of AAGR during the reference period FY02 to FY15 (refer Table 6.3). It is very important to notice that interest payments have the least AAGR as compared to all other Southern States. Secondly, NTRs growth rate is the second least both within AP's other fiscal indicators and between the southern States NTR growth rates.

In AP Growth rate of GSDP, RE TE, IPs are relatively more consistent than other fiscal indicators like OTR, TRR and share in CTs; whereas central grants are very inconsistent followed by NTR and CE.

6.4 Analysis of Vertical Fiscal Gaps of Southern States

The paper attempts to analyze the extent of vertical fiscal gap that exists in the southern Indian states during the period 2002–2015. Vertical fiscal gap indicates the extent of expenditure that has to be financed through other sources of revenue rather than states' own revenue source. The extent of vertical fiscal gap is measured in two different ways (based on the Kumudini et al. 2009) namely:

1. Vertical Fiscal gap (VFG_1): Gap between own non-debt revenue and total expenditure.
2. Vertical Fiscal gap (VFG_2): Gap between own non-debt revenue and primary expenditure.

The Vertical Fiscal gap (VFG_1) refers to the difference between the total revenue expenditure and capital expenditure and own non-debt receipts comprising of total

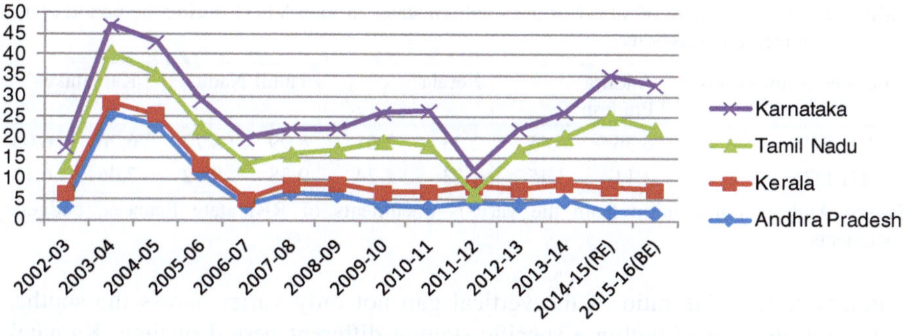

Chart 6.1 Trends and patterns of fiscal gap among southern states. *Source* Compilation from the various documents of RBI state finances, budget documents

Table 6.4 Relative share of VFG1 and VFG2 of the southern states in total VFG1 and VFG2

Year	Andhra Pradesh		Kerala		Tamil Nadu		Karnataka		All four states
	VFG1	VFG2	VFG1	VFG2	VFG1	VFG2	VFG1	VFG2	
2002–03	8.00	6.92	3.11	2.21	6.39	6.61	4.75	4.64	17.70
2003–04	21.25	14.51	2.75	3.93	12.24	8.38	6.44	5.74	47.05
2004–05	20.70	16.39	2.70	3.89	9.75	8.47	7.77	6.58	43.06
2005–06	10.59	10.41	2.01	2.66	8.84	8.49	6.70	6.37	29.03
2006–07	3.05	3.39	1.55	2.00	8.27	8.18	6.27	6.12	19.70
2007–08	5.74	5.92	1.88	2.38	7.40	7.28	6.16	5.94	22.20
2008–09	5.51	5.65	2.46	2.70	8.23	7.95	5.16	5.03	22.22
2009–10	2.25	2.58	3.26	3.29	12.21	11.71	6.99	6.77	26.03
2010–11	1.75	2.16	3.69	3.69	11.16	10.78	8.37	8.09	26.57
2011–12	2.59	2.92	3.82	3.82	−1.74	−1.24	5.73	5.60	12.26
2012–13	2.18	2.51	3.83	3.82	9.08	8.86	5.24	5.16	22.11
2013–14	2.95	3.25	3.98	3.97	11.35	10.93	5.93	5.78	26.21
2014–15(RE)	1.16	0.04	5.82	5.91	17.07	15.28	10.03	9.04	31.77
2015–16(BE)	1.06	0.46	5.56	5.68	14.56	13.15	10.69	9.60	29.73
Mean	5.91	5.50	3.32	3.57	9.63	8.92	6.88	6.46	26.83
Standard deviation	7.21	5.01	1.27	1.17	4.37	3.79	1.77	6.59	27.48

Source Authors compilation from the various documents of RBI state finances, budget documents

own tax and non-tax revenue, recovery of loans and advances and other non-debt capital receipts. The Vertical Fiscal gap (VFG_2) further excludes interest payment from the revenue expenditure to know the borrowing unrelated Fiscal gap that exists in the states (Chart 6.1; Table 6.4).

Vertical fiscal gap reveals the extent to which states' expenditure need to be to be financed through other sources of revenue other than their own revenue source. As it observed from Table 6.5, there is no uniformity in the fiscal health in the

Table 6.5 Average share of VFG1 of the southern states in total VFG1 during the period of 12th and 13th finance commissions

Finance commissions	Andhra Pradesh		Kerala		Tamil Nadu		Karnataka	
12 TH FC	6.36	6.45	2.23	2.61	8.99	8.72	6.26	6.05
13 TH FC	3.11	3.45	4.23	4.24	9.38	8.92	7.06	6.73

Source Authors compilation from the various documents of RBI state finances, budgetary documents

southern states. The ratio of the vertical gap not only varies across the southern states but also varies within a specific state at different period of time. Karnataka and Tamil Nadu have higher fiscal gap as compared to Kerala and Andhra Pradesh. The possible reasons for such large fiscal gap could be many. It needs careful examination of the trends in the revenue account and also the structure of expenditure among the states. As the central funds also play an important role in the fiscal position of the states it is also essential to look into the structural change in the flow of funds to these states. These necessitate the states to manage the state finances either by way of mobilizing more own revenue or compress or restructure the expenditure which tend to impact on the state finances in a significant manner.

With enhanced expenditure obligations and less elastic nature of tax and non-tax revenue the fiscal gap has widened at the state level. Some states such as Tamil Nadu and Karnataka have enhanced their revenue generation power which largely relates to tax revenue, gradual decline in the Non-Tax Revenue can be noticed in the southern states except in Andhra Pradesh. The revenue buoyancy is higher in Karnataka, Tamil Nadu, Kerala and Andhra Pradesh but in the recent years gradual fall their revenue can be noticed. Along with the improvement in revenue account states enactment of rule based fiscal correction through the enactment of Fiscal Responsibility and Budget Management Act (FRBM), Structural adjustment lending, etc., have forced the states to compress their expenditure by resorting to measures such as not filling vacancies, not fully implementing central pay scales, etc., (Karnataka). The reason of relative fall in the fiscal gap in Andhra Pradesh may be due to the improvement in the revenue receipts and relatively larger availability of central funds. Andhra Pradesh also has experienced a smaller increase in deficit as compared to other southern states.

The ratio of borrowing related expenditure is higher in Kerala when compared to Karnataka and Andhra Pradesh and remained more or less same in Tamil Nadu (Table 6.6). Due to lower own revenue efficiency, states need to finance their expenditure obligations through borrowing.

6.5 Share of Central Resources to Southern States

Analysis of four southern States (SS) reveals that average central taxes to southern States as a percent of total transfers to all States accounts to 19.23%; whereas the central grants to SS accounts to 16.63% of the total grants over the period of FY02

Table 6.6 Share of barrowing related VFG of the southern states in total VFG

Year	Andhra Pradesh	Kerala	Tamil Nadu	Karnataka
2002–03	9.21	4.12	6.14	4.88
2003–04	7.17	5.22	4.18	4.98
2004–05	6.73	6.55	5.61	3.92
2005–06	8.78	8.62	5.33	3.35
2006–07	8.02	8.05	7.00	4.11
2007–08	7.84	7.81	5.90	3.58
2008–09	7.38	5.71	4.57	3.52
2009–10	7.34	3.72	4.43	3.63
2010–11	8.16	3.56	5.23	3.93
2011–12	7.16	3.80	5.25	3.88
2012–13	7.18	3.71	5.65	3.92
2013–14	6.80	3.88	5.85	3.93
2014–15(RE)	4.15	6.38	5.72	3.78
2015–16(BE)	3.95	6.29	5.99	3.99
Mean	7.13	5.53	5.49	3.96
Standard deviation	1.49	1.79	0.74	0.46

Source Authors compilation from the various documents of RBI state finances, budgetary documents

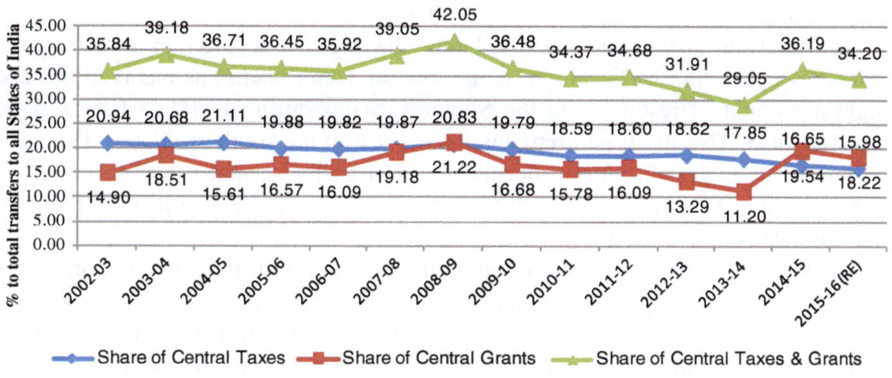

Chart 6.2 Share of Central Taxes, Grants to Southern States to total transfers. *Source* Computed from the various documents of RBI State Finances, Ministry of Finance, GOI, and State Budget documents

to FY15. Both the central taxes and grants to SS account to 35.86% during the same reference period. As it can be viewed from the Chart 6.2 that central tax transfers to SS are smoother (more statistical consistency) than the central grants.

It is important to know that Andhra Pradesh has received the highest central (tax and grants) transfers i.e. on an average 7.27% of GSDP during the FY02 to FY15. Tamil Nadu, Karnataka, and Kerala followed the second, third and fourth position,

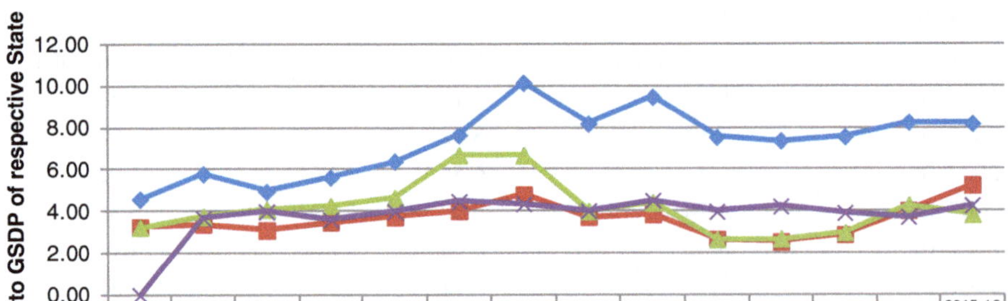

	2002-03	2003-04	2004-05	2005-06	2006-07	2007-08	2008-09	2009-10	2010-11	2011-12	2012-13	2013-14	2014-15	2015-16 RE
AP	4.60	5.80	4.96	5.63	6.40	7.64	10.16	8.18	9.48	7.54	7.36	7.56	8.24	8.18
Kerala	3.28	3.40	3.12	3.49	3.75	4.04	4.82	3.73	3.87	2.66	2.54	2.88	4.03	5.24
Tamilnadu	3.26	3.76	4.10	4.27	4.64	6.68	6.67	4.00	4.40	2.66	2.67	2.97	4.28	3.83
Karnataka	0	3.69	4	3.61	4	4.48	4.36	4.03	4.52	3.99	4.23	3.92	3.73	4.27

Chart 6.3 Share of Central transfers (tax and grants) to Southern States to respective GSDP. *Source* Computed from the various documents of RBI State Finances, Ministry of Finance, GOI and State Budget documents

respectively, by receiving on an average 4.16, 4.13 and 3.63% to their GSDPs during the same reference period (refer Chart 6.3).

The present study finds that the central tax and grant transfers are statistically more consistent to Karnataka as compared to other Southern States namely Kerala, Tamil Nadu and Andhra Pradesh (refer Chart 6.3).

The analysis also finds that AP being the highest position in receiving the resources in the SSs its fiscal gap is the lowest. Tamil Nadu has received the 2nd highest amount of resources in the Southern States during FY02 to FY15. After transfers also, TNs fiscal gap remains the highest in the southern States. This may be due to its largest fiscal gap during the pre-transfer scenario. Kerala's average fiscal gap prior to transfers was 5.14%, which accounts to 1.5% of its GSDP during the same reference period.

Karnataka's fiscal gap position both in the pre- and post-transfer situations is the second highest among the Southern States during the FY02 to FY15. Further Chart 6.4 reveals that central tax transfers to Karnataka from the various finance commissions is almost consistent of 5% of total transfers till eleventh finance commission. However, there is a declining trend during 12th and 13th FC and marginal climb of 0.39 in the present 14th FC transfers. As one can observe (from Chart 6.4) that, from 2nd FC onwards in Central tax transfers Karnataka's trend is more consistent than the other southern States.

As it is depicted in the chart 6.4 one can observe that consistently finance commission transfers as a percent to total transfers the respective southern states declined from Ninth Finance Commission onwards. The total share of these Southern States has declined to 17.96% in 14th Finance Commission from 23.4% in 9th Finance Commission. Roughly, Southern States GDP to India's GDP is 22.39% (Table 6.7) where as their share in finance commission is less than 18% during post FY02 to FY15. Paradoxically, the GDP share of these southern States is increasing

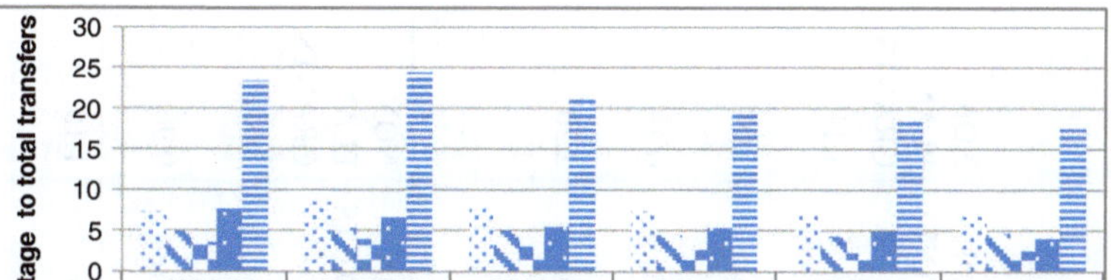

	1990-95 Ninth	1995-2000 Tenth	2000-05 Eleventh	2005-10 Twelth	2010-15 Thirteenth	2015-20 Fourteenth
ANDHRA PRADESH	7.34	8.46	7.7	7.35	6.93	6.73
KARNATAKA	4.93	5.34	4.93000056	4.46	4.32	4.71
KERALA	3.55	3.87	3.05	2.66	2.34	2.5
TAMILNADU	7.61	6.63	5.38	5.3	4.96	4.02
TotalSouthernStates	2343	243	2106000056	1977	1855	1796

Chart 6.4 Recent Finance Commission Transfers to Southern States. *Note* Andhra Pradesh (AP) (14th FC AP + Telangana), Source: Compiled from various finance commission reports

on the one side but the share in central tax transfers is consistently falling. One needs to explore the vital reasons for the deceleration of such transfers. Further, if the same trend continues the southern states will seriously suffer from the fund crunch.

In addition to examining the level of Vertical Fiscal gap among selected four states, this paper looks into the degree of dependence of those 4-major south Indian states on different components of central transfers from 11th finance commission to 13th finance commission following the methodology of C. Bhujanga Rao, K. Srivastava, 2014 with some modifications.

The above Table 6.7 depicts the extent of dependency of southern states across the states and time. As an in-depth analysis, this study also looks in to the relative share of different types of transfers in states Own Revenue and Borrowing. As the southern states come under the middle-income category the relative share of total transfers decreased over the period of time. Mainly from the twelfth finance commission the ratio of transfers in total states own revenue and borrowing showing the decreasing trend among all the four states. Comparatively out of four selected states Tamil Nadu is the lowest dependent compared to all other states. Andhra Pradesh is comparatively more dependent on transfers followed by Karnataka and Kerala, which also have had a marginal increase in their dependency. Over the period of Successive finance commission relative fall during twelfth and thirteenth commission is noticeable except in Andhra Pradesh due to larger flow of transfers to Telangana region (AP Andhra Pradesh + Telangana). In the first year of fourteenth commission again transfers showing a positive trend in all the four states. In the total transfers, Central Shared Tax is the major component and its share further raised in the recent commission period due to rise in the share of tax devolution. Among four states very less variations in the allocation of transfers can be noticed in Karnataka and it is higher in Andhra Pradesh.

Table 6.7 Decomposition and Pattern of Dependence of four southern states

STATES	Karnataka					Kerala				
Finance Commissions	TOTAL TRANSFERS	CENTRAL SHARED TAX	TOTAL GRANTS	PLAN GRANTS	NON-PLAN GRANTS	TOTAL TRANSFERS	CENTRAL SHARED TAX	TOTAL GRANTS	PLAN GRANTS	NON-PLAN GRANTS
11 TH FC (200004)	19.41	12.01	7.40	6.07	1.33	15.79	10.68	5.11	4.00	1.11
12 TH FC (200509)	6.50	3.52	2.97	1.79	1.18	6.80	4.17	2.63	1.55	1.08
13TH FC (201014)	6.42	3.69	2.73	1.94	0.79	5.16	3.22	1.94	1.45	0.49
14TH FC (201519) First year	9.36	6.11	3.25	2.36	0.89	8.79	5.19	3.60	1.40	2.20
STATES	Tamil Nadu					Andhra Pradesh				
Finance Commissions	TOTAL TRANSFERS	CENTRAL SHARED TAX	TOTAL GRANTS	PLAN GRANTS	NON-PLAN GRANTS	TOTAL TRANSFERS	CENTRAL SHARED TAX	TOTAL GRANTS	PLAN GRANTS	NON-PLAN GRANTS
11 TH FC (200004)	15.41	10.05	5.36	4.22	1.14	20.24	11.87	8.38	6.75	1.63
12 TH FC (200509)	5.25	3.10	2.16	1.28	0.88	9.25	5.61	3.64	2.68	0.96
13TH FC (201014)	4.95	2.96	1.99	1.33	0.66	10.04	6.22	3.83	2.68	1.15
14TH FC (201519) First year	7.66	3.78	3.88	2.79	1.09	29.55	15.76	13.79	6.88	6.91

Source: Authors compilation from the various documents of RBI state finances

The paper examines the extent of dependency of southern states on central transfers (Based on the methodology of Rao and Srivastava 2014) on different components of transfers from 11th finance commission to 13th finance commission. The southern states fall under the middle income category according to finance commission classification. The extent of dependency of southern states varies across the states and time. Among them Tamil Nadu (23.31%—11 FC) is having the lowest dependency on central transfers and has marginally increased to 25% in the 13 finance commission period. Andhra Pradesh (from 31 to 37%) is having the highest dependency on transfers followed by Karnataka and Kerala, which also have had a marginal increase in their dependency.

An index of dependence (D) is defined as: D = TR/RR_I. Where, TR = Transfers Received by a State on Revenue Account (TR is a sum of SCTR + STG + PT + OG) and RR = State's Total Revenue Receipts.

Where, SCTR = Share in central taxes, STG = Statutory Grants, PT = Plan Grants and OG = Other Grants

D is the sum of four components:

$$D = D1 + D2 + D3 + D4, \quad \text{where} \quad D1 = D * \text{SCTR}/\text{TR}; D2 = D * \text{STG}/\text{TR};$$
$$D3 = D * \text{PT}/\text{TR} \quad \text{and} \quad D4 = D * \text{OG}/\text{TR}$$

6.6 Summary

The southern states have been contributing a considerable share in the GDP. Southern states fiscal performance has significantly varied from one another and also over time. Tamil Nadu and Karnataka have enhanced their revenue generation power which largely relates to tax revenue; however a gradual decline in the Non-Tax Revenue can be noticed in the southern states except in Andhra Pradesh. The revenue buoyancy is higher in Karnataka, Tamil Nadu, Kerala and Andhra Pradesh but in the recent years gradual fall their revenue can be noticed. The size of revenue surplus has declined. While Andhra Pradesh has had a significant decline in the vertical fiscal gap, that of Tamil Nadu and Karnataka has increased significantly. Andhra Pradesh being the recipient of the largest share of central transfer of resources (both taxes and grants) among the southern states depicts the highest level of dependency on the central transfers which has also increased over time. Both with reference to Tamil Nadu and Karnataka which have had a large increase in the fiscal gap have had a much smaller dependence on the central transfers (although marginally on the increase). Kerala's situation with reference to dependence is more or less akin to that of Karnataka. This analysis hints at the need for a more detailed analysis of the state level fiscal implications of changing central transfers be it with reference to tax effort or composition of state level expenditure to understand the level of fiscal autonomy enjoyed by the states.

References

GOK (n.d.) Various Budget Documents. Government of Karnataka, Bengaluru

Hajra KS, Rakhe PB, Gajbhiye D (2009) Finances of Southern States: issues and concerns. In SD. al., Finance commission issues of the southern States. Madras School of Economics, Chennai, pp 111–130

MOSPI (n.d.) National Income Accounts report. GOI, New Delhi

Rao CB, Srivastava K (2014) Dependence of states on central transfers: state-wise analysis. Working paper No. 2014-137. National Institute of Public Finance and Policy, New Delhi

RBI (n.d.) Various Annual Reports of State Finances. RBI, Mumbai

Part II
Fiscal Decentralization for High Growth

Chapter 7
Fiscal Decentralization—A Case Study of Kerala State

Naseer Ahmed Khan and M.P. Muhammed Riyas

Abstract This work studies fiscal decentralisation at local level governments. It gives a critical narration to the empirical analysis in the fiscal decentralisation. The key components of fiscal decentralisation, fiscal autonomy has been given significant role while looking at the intergovernmental transactions between local governments with state and Centre. The aspects of fiscal responsibility also analysed.

Keywords Fiscal decentralisation · Fiscal autonomy · Fiscal responsibilities

Centralization is no more a catching slogan in the international polity. The age of concentration is fading fast. There is a distinct reception for the democratic decentralization. Liberal democracy, beyond its rhetoric, has failed to reach out into the poor and weak and failed to provide voice and choice in the decision-making process. In federal polity like India, where complex diversities exist, multi lingual and multi culture, democratic decentralization commands a natural appeal. Apart from the fact that it has the vehement potential to lower both transaction and coordination cost, it reduces inequality and it enhances equity. Fiscal decentralization is the subset of democratic decentralization is highly significant, because without which the idea becomes inoperative and meaningless. It calls for special attention when the fiscal responsibilities entrusted in the central, state and local self-government (LSG). In the public finance literature, it is broadly called as fiscal federalism or decentralized fiscal system.

India land marked its journey of 'fiscal federalism' through 73rd/74th amendment to its constitution in the year 1992 which inserted third tier of local government to its federal structure. The soul of the 73rd amendment was to reform and reconstruct rural India via Panchayat. It will be interesting to requite what the then Minister of State for Rural Development, Venal Swami said when forwarding the 73rd amendment to the constitution on 1 December 1992: 'the constitution (73rd) amendment bill cast a duty on the union as well as the states to establish and

N.A. Khan · M.P. Muhammed Riyas (✉)
School of Economics, University of Hyderabad, Hyderabad, India
e-mail: Mp.riyasbeeran@gmail.com

N.A. Khan (ed.), *Challenges and Issues in Indian Fiscal Federalism*,
India Studies in Business and Economics, https://doi.org/10.1007/978-981-10-6217-9_7

nourish the village Panchayat so as to make them effective self-governing institutions, we feel that unless the Panchayat is provided with adequate financial strength, it will be impossible for them to grow stature'. It was a vintage point from there the theory and praxis of the fiscal decentralization in India undergone a tremendous change.

Democratic decentralization is appreciated not only for its intrinsic value but also for the instrumental benefits it carries, i.e. efficient and equitable delivery of public services at the bottom level of people's participation. There are scholars who oppose decentralization the reason suggested is that fiscal decentralization will ruin the macroeconomic management and it make unviable to attain the macroeconomic objective. This is a purely an empirical query. A study conducted by Anwar Shah through the econometric analysis of the 24 countries stand strongly in defense of the decentralization with respect to macroeconomic management and what is required in the proper greater clarity in the role and functions of the various different layers transparency as well as immense care in the designing of the institutions. Shah critiques the decentralization and macro management of Chinese economy, which is the biggest unitary economy in the world, and argues otherwise.

What is fiscal decentralization? Before that it imperative to have an idea of what is decentralization all about. It is concept variously defined and differently understood by different people. That's why it has been abused by its usage many times. Sometimes it is used in limited sense of delegation or just de-concentration, i.e. unbundling of responsibilities or burden of the superior government officer to the bottom one. Democratic decentralization is a far reaching concept especially when it says strengthening the local levels of governance. We define the decentralization as the process of empowering the people through empowering the local self-government, in the rural context of India, empowering the Panchayat. So the fiscal decentralization means empowerment of Panchayat fiscally. It means devolution of fiscal powers such as taxing and spending powers to lower levels of governments. It is nothing less than local government should have adequate command over in term of its autonomy regarding the expenditure and revenue of its budget.

There is no single and universal pattern and objective of decentralization. The historical context or the temporal specification and the objective to be attained by the decentralization vary from country to country. In order to ensure more rational public finance in terms of efficiency and equity, a multi-level federal polity which aims to boost democratic decentralization has to address four basic questions. Those are being asked in the context of India as below (Oommen 2004).

Functional mapping: basically, it is a question of who should what? In a multi layered federal polity by considering the allocative efficiency which level of government should be done what is being decided. This is what is called principle of subsidiarity. India has been characterized as a quasi-federal system, it was the 73rd and 74th amendment was instrumental to reverse this to greater extend. Adding schedule XI for Panchayats and Schedule XII for the urban local bodies (ULBs) into the existing concurrence of centre and state will attract more confusion the role and responsibilities of different tiers. So the clear cut mapping of role assignment must take place.

Revenue assignment: the issue of financing the expenditure raises the equally important question of who should tax and what? Constitution envisaged a two tier system where more productive and elastic sources of taxes such as income tax, custom duties corporation tax, etc., were assigned to union list and land revenue, sales tax, stamp duties, etc., placed in state list.

Developing an efficient and an equitable transfer system: It basically means having an institutional arrangement to look after the both vertical and horizontal imbalances arising out of the intergovernmental fiscal relationship. Ideally, the expenditure requirement ad revenue acquirement must match. The vertical imbalances have to be addressed through proper arrangement.

Accountability mechanism: decentralized governance has been legitimized through proper mechanism of accountability. Their management of expenditure is critical, as the institution of Grama Sabha (Article 243A), the assembly of voters at village level having power to review the budget, hear audit report, and so on. The Panchayat raj amendment has taken the accountability institution into the door step people.

7.1 Objectives and Methodology

7.1.1 Introduction

Decentralization of governance has been widely acclaimed by the scholars and policy-makers as a way out from the melancholies of centralization. Democratic decentralization has been projected as the substitute to the centralized liberal democracy which utterly failed to give voice and choice to poor and other downtrodden sections of the society. Fiscal decentralization is having not only the intrinsic value but also numerous instrumental benefits too. Fiscal decentralization is important in order to operationalize the democratic decentralization. Fiscal decentralization is crucial not only in term of fiscal autonomy but also it ensures the financial health of the exchequer.

7.1.2 Research Problem

This is a case study of the state of Kerala. The broader intention is to understand the anatomy of the exchequer of the local self-government with emphasis on the Grama Panchayat in the state of Kerala. The spirit of decentralization is attained only when the local government having adequate financial or fiscal autonomy. The study is mainly interested in the structure and composition of the revenue as well as the expenditure.

7.1.3 *Objectives*

The following are the specific objectives of this study.

- To understand the structure and composition of receipt of Panchayat with respect fiscal autonomy.
- To critically evaluate pattern of expenditure with respect to financial health of the Grama Panchayat.
- To analyze the functioning of state finance commission.

7.1.4 *Methodology*

The study is analytical in nature and descriptive in form. The purpose of the study is to critically understand financing of the local governments especially Grama Panchayat. The aim of the study is to examine how far fiscal decentralization has been taking place. Report of the finance commission was the source in which study was depended more apart from the other government institutions like Information Kerala mission, website of the ministry of the Panchayat, etc., expert views and interactions with official in charge were harnessed for more information.

7.1.5 *Source of Data*

Mainly secondary data were used for the analysis. The report of the finance commissioner was the important reference for the data. In addition to other published sources like government publications especially ministry of the Panchayat, economic review, websites of the department of finance and Panchayat, the views and observations of the experts were taken into account as well as the practical experience of officers in charge.

7.2 Reviews of Related Literature

Various studies have been carried out by a large number of scholars with respect to different aspects of fiscal decentralization including the philosophical foundation of the idea called decentralization. A few among them are:

Fritz Breuss (2004) analyzed the question of fiscal decentralization and its relationship with that of economic growth. It was an enquiry to link between two. Even though theory indicates vehemently a positive impact of fiscal decentralization on economic growth due to efficiency gain, but there is no strong empirical work to completely endorse this argument, but support partially.

Akai et al. (2004) have presented new empirical evidence on this important issue. Having provided evidence that fiscal decentralization contributes to economic growth; this paper suggests that recent moves towards fiscal decentralization by developed countries may stimulate their economic growth.

Daniel Treisman's (2000) writings are interesting, which tries to answer why are some countries more fiscally decentralized than others? Scholars have attributed such differences to geographical, cultural, institutional and economic factors. Using a dataset of 66 countries, I test various hypotheses. The results suggest territorially larger—but not necessarily more populous—countries are more fiscally decentralized, etc.

7.3 Data Analysis and Interpretation on State Level

Table 7.1 depicts the structure and composition of receipts and gives the various components of revenue receipts of GPs. Own source revenue (own tax revenue + non-tax revenue) constitute only 12% of the total revenue. Lion share of the revenue comes through state transfer, i.e. 76% and central transfer along with made 85% of the revenue. We find a definite increase in the central transfers from the low of 8.3 in the year 2009–10 to 16.5% in 2013–14, an annual increment of 26%, is indeed high. The various flagship programmes of the central government in the

Table 7.1 Various components of revenue receipts of GPs

	2009–10	2010–11	2011–12	2012–13	2013–14	CAGR
Own tax revenue	118.4	123.8	152.0	160.4	160.1	7.8
	[6.9]	[6.4]	[7.9]	[7.2]	[6.4]	
Non-tax revenue	85.8	93.6	104.6	135.3	155.2	16
	[5]	[4.8]	[5.5]	[6]	[6.2]	
Own source revenue	204.2	217.3	256.7	295.7	315.4	11.5
	[12]	[11.2]	[13.4]	[13.2]	[12.6]	
State transfer	130.0	152.7	147.1	161.7	173.8	7.5
	[76.1]	[78.4]	[76.6]	[72.3]	[69.3]	
Central transfer	162.2	164.9	159.3	287.5	414.1	26.4
	[9.5]	[8.5]	[8.3]	[12.8]	[16.5]	
Borrowing	8.3	5.4	3.5	4.3	12.7	11.2
	[2]	[0.3]	[0.2]	[0.2]	[0.5]	
Other receipts	32.1	34.2	29.1	33.3	29.3	-2.3
	[1.1]	[1.8]	[1.5]	[1.5]	[1.2]	
Total receipts	1706.67	1948.60	1919.35	2237.99	2509.47	10.1

Rupees in Crore

Source Kerala State Finance Commission Report (2014)

recent years, which are implemented directly through LSG can explain this spur in central share to a large extend.

Table 7.1 gives the various components of revenue receipts of GPs. Own source revenue (own tax revenue + non-tax revenue) constitute only 12% of the total revenue. Lion share of the revenue comes through state transfer, i.e. 76% and central transfer along with made 85% of the revenue. We find a definite increase in the central transfers from the low of 8.3% in the year 2009–10 to 16.5% in 2013–14, an annual increment of 26%, is indeed high. The various flagship programmes of the central government in the recent years, which are implemented directly through LSG can explain this spur in central share to a large extend.

Table 7.2 gives us more precise analysis of the receipt by presenting it into per capita values. Per GP receipt increased from Rs. 1.85 crore to 2.72 crore during the period. Per capita receipt increased to Rs. 1023 from Rs. 696 with a 10.1 annual hike.

Table 7.2 Precise analysis of the receipt per capita values

	2009–10	2010–11	2011–12	2012–13	2013–14	CAGR
Per GP OTR	1,285,991	1,343,968	1,650,831	1,741,227	1,738,672	7.8
Per capita OTR	48	50	62	65	65	
Per GP NTR	931,251	1,015,801	1,135,907	1,469,198	1,685,571	15.6
Per capita NTR	35	38	43	55	63	
Per GP OSR	2,217,242	2,359,769	2,786,738	3,210,426	3,424,243	11.3
Per capita OSR	83	89	105	121	129	
Per GP state transfer	14,113,576	16,577,534	15,968,880	1,759,260	18,871,428	7.5
Per capita state transfer	530	623	600	660	709	
Per GP CSS	1,760,874	1,790,556	1,729,924	3,121,548	4,495,785	26.4
Per capita CSS	66	67	65	117	169	
Per GP borrowing	89,980	58,145	38,049	46,545	137,382	11.2
Per capita borrowing	3	2	1	2	5	
Per GP other receipt	348,962	371,449	316,230	361,810	318,401	−2.3
Per capita other receipt	13	14	12	14	12	
Per GP total receipt	18,530,633	21,157,453	20,839,822	24,299,589	27,247,239	10.1
Per capita total receipt	696	795	783	913	1023	

Source Kerala State Finance Commission Report (2014)

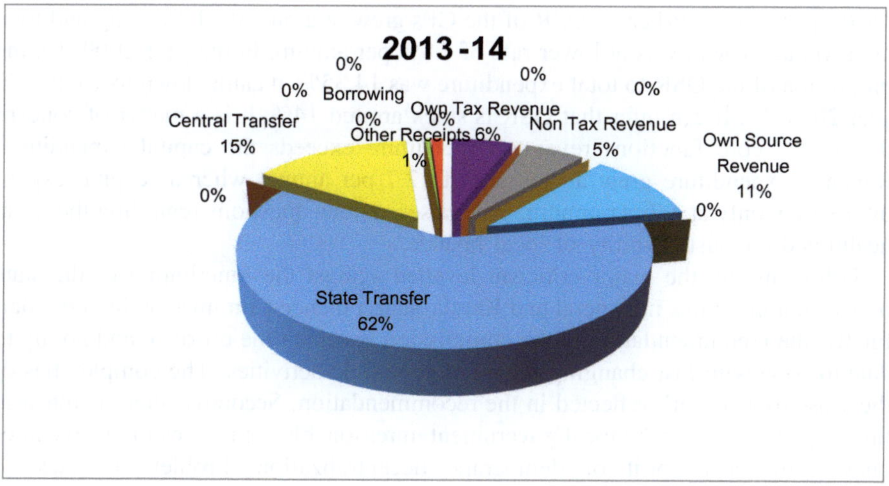

The expenditure

Expenditure is the integral part of the financing of local governance. For a sound public financing it is desirable to have rate of growth of OSR higher than that of public expenditure. Table 7.3 and gives the broad pattern of expenditure vis-a-vis OSR. Broadly, expenditure is for administration and for the core function which is consisting of revenue and capital expenditure. The total expenditure per GP has increased from Rs. 1.45 crore in 2009–10 to Rs. 2.58 crore in 2013–14, i.e. grew at

Table 7.3 Broad pattern of expenditure

	2009–10	2010–11	2011–12	2012–13	2013–14	CAGR 2009–10 to 2013–14
Onw source revenue	2,217,242	2,359,769	2,786,738	3,210,426	3,424,243	11.5
Expenditure on direction and administration	2,348,807	2,536,165	2,791,203	3,294,192	3,610,341	11.3
Expenditure on core functions (a + b)	1,457,345	1,797,338	1,992,026	1,998,567	2,170,206	10.5
a. Revenue	1,025,849	1,235,578	1,422,669	1,501,924	1,652,262	12.7
b. Capital	431,495	561,760	569,356	496,643	517,944	4.7
Total expenditure	14,529,691	16,445,771	18,651,997	21,518,818	25,771,047	15.4

Source Kerala State Finance Commission Report (2014)

15.4% per annum. Whereas OSR of the GPs grew at a rate of 11.5% only and total tax revenue growth was at lower rate of 7.8% per annum. In the year 2009–10, the proportion of the OSR to total expenditure was 14.35%, it came down to 13.29% in year 2013–14. It can infer that OSR is stuck around 14%. It is a matter of concern that in the core functions revenue expenditure exceeds the capital expenditure. Revenue expenditure grew at the rate of 12.7 per annum whereas capital expenditure grew only at 4.7 per annum. This raises serious questions regarding the fiscal health and the sustainability of local finance.

Following are the major criticism levelled against the functioning of the state finance commissions in general and Kerala State Finance Commission in particular. Firstly, the recommendation of the commission is some time obsolete and not up to date to cope with fast changing nature of economic activities. The complexities of the grass root weren't reflected in the recommendation. Secondly, there is intrinsic favoring of state over the local government unreasonable sometimes to the extent of questioning very spirit of democratic decentralization. Problem of lack of enforcement mechanism to get done the recommendation of the commission. Incompetent appointment of chairpersons and Lack of complete database containing the data related to every subject pertaining to economic activities in the Panchayat level, etc.

7.4 Finding of the Study

Local governments especially GPs overwhelmingly depended on the transfers from the higher government in order to finance their expenditure. Share of both centre and state will account for about the 85% of the total revenue of the GPs.

Own source revenue consists of two things. They are called as own tax revenue and non-tax revenue. Own tax revenues are those revenues collected by the GPs from the various items of taxes assigned by the state to local bodies. Non-tax revenues are those revenues earned by the local self-government through the sources other than taxation. In 2009–10, OSR was just 12% of the total revenue. Out of that OTR consist of 6.9% and NTR contributed 5.0% to the revenue.

Property tax, professional tax, entertainment tax, advertisement tax, etc., are the main sources of taxing revenues of the Panchayat. Property tax is the highest contributor to the total tax revenue of the Panchayat. In 2009–10, property tax contributed 53.8% of the tax revenue where as its share in 2013–14 even though declined to 47.4%, it continues to be the largest contributor into tax revenue of the Panchayat. During this period property tax registered only marginal annual growth rate of 4.5. And in 2009–10 per GP property tax was Rs. 637,549,417 whereas in 2013–14 it rose to Rs. 759,024,214. As per capita value, it was Rs. 26 in 2009–10 and Rs. 31 in 2013–14.

Expenditure on the core function is revenue and capital expenditure. As far as the financial/fiscal health is concerned the proportion of capital expenditure is important. But while revenue expenditure it has a growth rate of 12.7 per annum whereas capital expenditure has grown only at 4.7% per annum not only in the relative term in the absolute term also revenue expenditure has a leap compared to capital expenditure of the GPs in the state. Expenditure on core function together has a growth rate of 10.5 per annum during this period.

Per GP expenditure in 2009–10 was Rs. 14,529,691 and which gone up to Rs. 25,771,047 in 2013–14. And per capita expenditure in this period was 546 and 968 in the respective year.

In 2009–10, the percentage of expenditure for the welfare activities to the total expenditure was 37.2% and in 2013–14 it gone up to 47.5% in 2013–14, i.e. welfare expenditure is a significant component of expenditure of the Panchayat in the state. As far as equity aspects are concerned it is a desirable thing.

It is not a desirable trend with respect to developmental expenditure which comes down from 36.6 to 30% in the respective period. It poses uncomfortable signs of sustainability and fiscal health of the Panchayat. Expenditure on core functions of the Panchayat which includes both revenue as well as capital expenditure registered a declining trend from 10 to 8.4% from 2009–10 to 2013–14. Analysis by disintegrating will tell us, it was capital expenditure which declined drastically.

The expenditure for other activities too comes down from 16.1 to 13.9% during this period.

The structure and pattern of expenditure of Grama Panchayat is not desirable in some respect.

7.5 Conclusion

There is much greater appeal for democratic decentralization all over world regardless of their level of economic development. In order to operationalize democratic decentralization, fiscal decentralization is inevitable. Fiscal decentralization is important it leads to fiscal autonomy and ensures fiscal responsibility by the officials.

Kerala as a state is one who took pioneering steps of decentralized governance even before the Panchayat raj amendment. Kerala could manage quite good track record with respect to political and administrative devolution. In order to implement and sustain the decentralization, fiscal decentralization is crucial. Unfortunately in that respect, record of the state is not comfortable, especially regarding fiscal autonomy. Still, own source revenue of the GPs constitutes only 12% of the total revenue. The GPs could not grow to the expectation in making revenue finance its expenditure.

Own source revenue consists of own tax revenue as well as non-tax revenue. Property tax, professional tax, entertainment tax, and advertisement tax, etc., non-tax revenue consisting of fees, license charges, fines, rent, etc. The base and rate of the tax items and other revenue sources are not dynamic enough to cope up with spatial and temporal changes and ever changing economic relations. Expenditure on administration continues to be a major component of GPs expenditure. It must be brought down immediately for its sustainability. Out of the total expenditure, revenue expenditure out pass capital expenditure to the extent that formers growth rate is thrice that of latter. There are differences and exceptions to the average trend. There are exceptionally performing GPs too. Having power to borrow is imperative as far as fiscal autonomy is concerned, but GPs having negligible power for borrowing. The functioning of the state finance commission which is supposed to be the watch dog of the local bodies is not been satisfactory. Commission has always not been able to catch up to the required dynamism in dealing with decentralized exchequer.

In short, compared to the last report there is improvement in the fiscal position of the GPs in the state. But it is not at adequate pace. Kept aside the complete fiscal autonomy, finding half of that is a distant dream. There should be imaginative measures broaden the revenue base of the Panchayat through taxation and the sources other than taxation. Local bodies should rationalize their expenditure by focusing on the financial health and sustainability.

7.6 Recommendations

The following are the suggestions put forwarded in the light of analysis of the fiscal position of GPs in Kerala.

- Improve the revenue base of the Grama Panchayat both tax and non-tax base.
- Allow the GPs to fix their rate of the tax or else state government fix a reasonable range of rate with negotiation of the local government.
- Empower the state by devolving more taxing item through legislation.
- Stop the unilateral encroachment of state government into the existing tax base of the local government.
- Enlarge the non-taxing revenue of the local governments.
- Revise the rate, fees, fine, etc., periodically to meet cost of services.
- Rationalize and priorities the expenditure of the GPs.
- Bring down share of expenditure for the administration.
- Rationalize the revenue expenditure.
- Tally the rate of growth of total expenditure and rate of growth of own source revenue (OSR).
- Bestow the GPs with reasonable amount power to borrow from the market.
- Professionalize the accounting system of GPs.
- Professionalize the appointment of the members of the finance commission and improve the quality of the recommendation to cope with changes occurring on the ground.
- Put in place a mechanism to police or a structure of incentives to ensure the recommendation of the commission is being taken seriously.

References

Ahluwalia M (1998) Infrastructure development in India's reform. In: I.M.D. Little (ed.) Indian economic reforms and development: essays for Manmohan Singh. Oxford University Press, Delhi, Oxford and New York, pp 87–121

Akai N, Nishimura Y, Sakata M (2004) Fiscal decentralization, economic growth and economic volatility—theory and evidence from state-level cross-section data for the United States. Discussion paper series no. 03-F-2. The Center for International Trade Studies, Faculty of Economics, Yokohama National University

Bardhan P, Mookherjee D (2000) Decentralizing anti-poverty program delivery in developing countries. Working Paper, Institute for Economic Development, Boston University, J Public Econ (forthcoming)

Breuss F (2004) Fiscal decentralisation and economic growth: is there really a link? J Inst Comp 2 (1):3–9

Davoodi H, Zou H (1998) Fiscal decentralization and economic growth—a crosscountry study. J Urban Econ 43:244–257

Jha R (2007) Fiscal policy in developing countries: a synoptic view. ASARC Working Paper 2007/01, Australia South Asia Research Centre, The Australian National University, Canberra

Oates WE (1995) Comment on "Conflicts and dilemmas of decentralization" by Rudolf Hommes. In: Bruno M, Pleskovic B (eds) Annual World Bank conference on development economics, pp 351–353

Oommen MA (2004) Basic services, functional assignments and own revenue of panchayats: some issues in fiscal decentralisation for the consideration of the twelfth finance commission, ISS Occasional paper series-33. Institute of Social Sciences, New Delhi

Treisman D (2000) The causes of corruption: a cross-national study, J Public Econ (76):399–457

Chapter 8
Fiscal Deficit and Economic Growth Linkage in India: Impact of FRBM Act

Ranjan Kumar Mohanty

Abstract The major objective of the study is to examine the impact of fiscal deficit on economic growth in India using Autoregressive Distributed Lag (ARDL) approach. It also analyzes whether the execution of Fiscal Responsibility and Budget Management (FRBM) Act has any influence on the fiscal deficit-economic growth linkage in India. The ARDL Bounds Testing Approaches to Cointegration confirm the long-run relationship among the selected variables. The estimated results show that fiscal deficit has an adverse effect on economic growth in both the long run and short run in India. The Pre-FRBM Act regime analysis reveals that implementation of FRBM Act has influenced and weakens the relationship between fiscal deficit and economic growth in India. The Government should contain the fiscal deficit and should try to achieve the target set by the FRBM Act.

Keywords Fiscal deficit · Economic growth
Autoregressive distributed lag (ARDL) models · Bound testing approach

JEL Codes H62 · O40 · C32

8.1 Introduction

The impact of fiscal deficit on economic growth is one of the highly debated issues in all world economies. During the last four decades, gross fiscal deficit of the central government has increased from nearly 3% from 1970–1971 to more than 8% in mid-1980s and still remains more than 5% in 2012–2013 in India. The excessive fiscal deficit seems to be the major concern of academicians and policy makers in India. Fiscal Responsibility and Budget Management (FRBM) Act was enacted in August 2003 in order to improve the fiscal balance and revenue balance

R.K. Mohanty (✉)
National Institute of Public Finance and Policy (NIPFP), 18/2, Satsang Vihar Marg, Special Institutional Area, New Delhi 110067, India
e-mail: ranjanmohanty85@gmail.com; ranjan.mohanty@nipfp.org.in

N.A. Khan (ed.), *Challenges and Issues in Indian Fiscal Federalism*,
India Studies in Business and Economics, https://doi.org/10.1007/978-981-10-6217-9_8

position of the Central Government in India.[1] It imposes stringent fiscal discipline on the central government to maintain transparency in fiscal management, debt management, and long-term fiscal stability in the economy. Continuing high levels of fiscal deficit, in spite of adoption of FRBM Act, pose a serious threat to macroeconomic stability in India. Now, the question of interest is whether the persistence of fiscal deficit hampers economic growth in India? How has the increase in fiscal deficit impacted India's economic growth over the last four decades? Has the enactment of FRBM Act influenced the fiscal deficit-economic growth linkage in India? These crucial issues are addressed in this study.

Generally, there are three schools of thought concerning the economic effects of budget deficits on economic growth, i.e., Neoclassical, Keynesian, and Ricardian. The Neoclassicals views consider fiscal deficits are detrimental to investment and growth {Cebula (1995), Fischer (1993), Easterly and Rebelo (1993), etc.}. The Keynesians view stress that it constitutes a key policy prescription and has beneficial consequences on the economy when appropriately timed {Taylor et al. (2012), Eisner and Pieper (1984), etc.}. However, Ricardians consider deficits have a neutral effect on the growth of the economy {Daylop (2010), Tan (2006) etc.}.

A large and persistence of fiscal deficit would become an indication of several disturbing signs in the economy. Deficits are considered to be the major factors affecting the growth in the economy through increase in public debt burden and its repayment. Large public borrowing can also lead to crowding out of private investment, high interest payment, inflation, exchange rate fluctuations, etc. {Arora and Dua (1993), Karras (1994), Burney and Akhtar (1992), Darrat (2000) etc.}. However, if public and private investments are complementary and productive public investments increase, then the negative impact of high public borrowings on private investments and economic growth may be offset. Fiscal deficit used for creating infrastructure and human capital would have a different impact than if it is used for financing ill-targeted subsidies and wasteful recurrent expenditure. Therefore, the fear about high fiscal deficit is justified if the government incur deficit to finance its current expenditure rather than capital expenditure.

In this context, it is important to understand the consequences of rising fiscal deficit on the economic growth of Indian economy. Hence, the basic aim of the study is to examine both the short run and long run relationship between fiscal deficit and economic growth in India and also to verify whether the execution of FRBM Act does any influence on the fiscal deficit-economic growth linkage in India. The literature, in particular, the empirical part, on the relationship between fiscal deficit and economic growth is scarce. This study differs from existing literature in the following novel ways. First, it makes an attempt to examine the influence of FRBM Act on the fiscal deficit-growth linkage in India by using recently available time series data. For the best of knowledge, this issue has not studied earlier. Hence,

[1]FRBM Act (2003) came into effect from July 5, 2004 in India. Again the Government of India had set up a FRBM Review Committee on 2016 to evaluate the FRBM Act, 2003. It implies that mounting fiscal deficit is a serious concern for the economy.

policy makers find it useful for their policy formulation. Second, this study analyzed the impact of fiscal deficit on economic growth using ARDL model, which seems to be methodological addition to existing literature in Indian context.

8.1.1 Gross Fiscal Deficit and Growth Rate of Gross Domestic Product

Figure 8.1 plots the growth rate of Gross Domestic Product (GDP) against gross fiscal deficit (GFD) of the central government to GDP ratio for the period from 1970–1971 to 2012–2013. The gross fiscal deficit was increased from 3.04% of GDP in 1970–1971 to the peak of 8.37% in 1986–1987. During that period (1986–1987), growth rate of GDP was 4.31%. However, after 2003–2004 central governments contained the fiscal deficit from 4.48% of GDP to its all-time minimum of 2.54% in the year 2007–2008 but during that period growth rate of GDP was more than 9%. It is seen that the growth rate is lower when the GFD–GDP ratio of the Central government is higher and vice versa. This implies higher fiscal deficit may have detrimental effect on growth of Indian economy. However, this simple trend analysis is not sufficient for any valid inference. Therefore, the study has used the advanced econometric technique.

Apart from Sect. 1, Sect. 2 describes some empirical literature on fiscal deficit and economic growth. Section 3 presents the data source and methodology used in this study. Section 4 analyzes the empirical results and its interpretations and Sect. 5 concludes with a summary of the study and recommendations.

8.2 Review of Literature

In this section, some important empirical studies on fiscal deficit and economic growth have been reviewed.

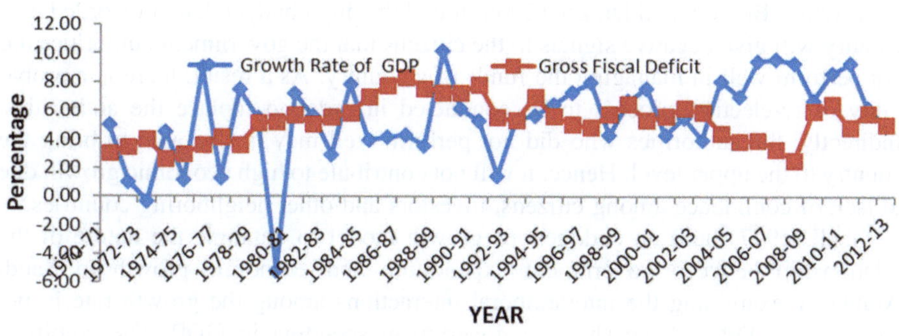

Fig. 8.1 Fiscal deficit and GDP growth rate

Keho (2010) examined the causal relationship between budget deficits and economic growth for seven West African countries over the period 1980–2005. The empirical evidence showed mixed results. In three countries, it did not find any causality between budget deficit and growth. In the remaining four countries, deficits had adverse effects on economic growth. Nelson and Singh (1994) used data on a cross section of 70 developing countries during two time periods, 1970–1979 and 1980–1989, to investigate the effect of budget deficits on GDP growth rates. This study concludes that the budget deficit had little or no significant effect on the economic growth of these nations in the 1970s and 1980s.

Avila (2011) analyzed the relationship between fiscal deficit, macroeconomic uncertainty, and growth of Argentina for the period 1915–2006 and concluded that the deficit hampered on per capita income growth in Argentina through the volatility in relative prices. Taylor et al. (2012) examined the interactions between the primary fiscal deficit, economic growth and debt for the period 1961–2011 of USA. It found a strong positive effect on growth of a higher primary deficit, even when possible increases in the interest rate are taken into account. Osinubi et al. (2010) examined the relationship between budget deficit and external debt in Nigeria from 1970 to 2003. They found the existence of debt Laffer curve and nonlinear effects of external debt on economic growth in Nigeria.

Dalyop (2010) examined the effectiveness of fiscal deficits on the growth rate of the real gross domestic product and found that fiscal deficit in the Nigerian economy is Ricardian. Fiscal deficits therefore had little effect on the level of economic activity. Adam and Bevan (2005) examined the relation between fiscal deficits and growth for a panel of 45 developing countries and found a possible non-linearity in the relation between growth and the fiscal deficit for a sample of developing countries. Cebula (1995) examined the impact of federal budget deficits on per capita real economic growth in the United States with quarterly data over the 1955–1992 periods. The empirical findings indicated that federal budget deficits, over time, reduce the rate of economic growth.

Fatima et al. (2011) aimed at verifying the impact of government fiscal deficit on investment and economic growth using time series of thirty years stretching between 1980 and 2009 and believed that fiscal profligacy has seriously undermined the growth objectives thereby adversely impacting physical and social infrastructure in the country. Brender and Drazen (2008) found that high budget deficit recorded by a country will give negative signals to the citizens that the government authorities did not perform well in managing the funds of a country. As a result, there is a probability of re-election process to be conducted in order to replace the authorities. Indirectly, the authorities who did not perform well may not be able to bring the country to the upper level. Hence, it will not contribute to high economic growth due to lack of confidence among citizens, investors and other neighboring countries.

Ghali (1997) built an endogenous growth model to untangle the nature of the relationship between government expenditure and economic growth in Saudi Arabia by examining the intertemporal interactions among the growth rate in per capita real GDP and the share of government spending in GDP. The empirical analysis found no consistent evidence that government spending can increase Saudi

Arabia's per capita output growth. Gupta et al. (2005) assessed the effects of fiscal consolidation and expenditure composition on economic growth in a sample of 39 low-income countries during the 1990s. The paper found that strong budgetary positions are generally associated with higher economic growth in both the short and long terms. Bose et al. (2007) examined the growth effects of government expenditure for a panel of thirty developing countries over the decades of the 1970s and 1980s and found that the share of government capital expenditure in GDP is positively and significantly correlated with economic growth, but current expenditure is insignificant.

Tan (2006) examined both the long and short-run relationship between fiscal deficit, inflation, and economic growth in Malaysian economy during 1966–2003. They found the absence of long-run relationship among these variables and also found that fiscal deficits appeared to have neither long nor short-run links with income. Eisner and Pieper (1984) reported a positive impact of cyclically and inflation-adjusted budget deficits on economic growth in the United States and other Organization for Economic Cooperation and development (OECD) countries. The negative impact of fiscal deficits on long-run growth has been empirically documented in several studies, such as Fischer (1993), Easterly and Rebelo (1993), Easterly, Rodriguez, and Schmidt-Hebbel (1994). Fischer (1993) found that larger budget surpluses were strongly associated with more rapid growth through greater capital accumulation and greater productivity.

8.3 Data and Methodology

This section presents the research questions, objectives, data source, and the methodology used in this study. The major questions are as follows: Does fiscal deficit affect gross domestic product (GDP) of the Indian economy? Does it significantly affect the growth of Indian economy in the long run? Is there any short-run relationship between fiscal deficit and GDP in India? Has the FRBM Act influenced on fiscal deficit-economic growth linkage in India? Thus, the broad objective of the study is to investigate both the short run and long run relationship between fiscal deficit and economic growth in the Indian economy and also to verify the impact of FRBM Act on the relationship between fiscal deficit and economic growth in Indian economy.

8.3.1 The Data

The study is entirely based on secondary data. The objectives of the study are being examined by using annual time series data covering period from 1970–1971 to 2012–2013. Relevant data for the study are obtained from Handbook of Statistics on Indian Economy from Reserve Bank of India. Variables are in 2004–2005 bases and measured in real terms by using GDP deflator. Gross domestic product at factor cost is used as the proxy for economic growth. Inflation rate is calculated from wholesale price index. Fiscal deficit[2] and gross domestic capital formation is used as the percentage of GDP at factor cost. Growth rate of employment is calculated from employment in the organized public and private sectors.[3] This study has examined the empirical relationship between fiscal deficit and economic growth in India using two different periods, i.e., 1970–1971 to 2012–2013 (whole period) and Pre-FRBM Act period from 1970–1971 to 2003–2004 (sub-period)[4] especially to analyze the influence of FRBM Act. The Autoregressive Distributed Lag (ARDL) bounds testing approaches to cointegration is used to analyze the objectives of the study.

8.3.2 Analytical Framework

Real Gross Domestic product at factor cost (GDPF) is used as the proxy for economic growth for this study. Sometime, large fiscal deficit (FSDF) can affect the country's economic growth adversely. A higher fiscal deficit implies high government borrowing and high debt servicing which forces the government to cut back in spending on relevant sectors like health, education, research and development, infrastructure, etc. It reduces growth of both physical and human capital, which has a long-term impact on economic growth. Fiscal deficit used for capital expenditure may have a different impact on the economy than if it is used for wasteful current expenditure like interest payment, subsidies, salaries, etc. Since the variable of interest is fiscal deficit; the study has used it in the analysis {Cebula (1995), Fischer (1993), Easterly and Rebelo (1993), Easterly et al. (1994), etc.}. It is widely believed that moderate and stable inflation rates enhance investment, creates favorable business environment, augment return to savers, and therefore, accelerates economic growth of the country. However, persistence of high inflation rates may lead to uncertainty about the future profitability of investment projects, reduce a country's international competitiveness by making its exports relatively more expensive, imposes negative externalities on the economy. Hence, persistence of high inflation affects the economy adversely and it hovers at high level during the study period. Therefore, the study has used inflation rate (INFLA) as an input in the

---

[2]Fiscal deficit of the central government is used here for several reasons. First, combined fiscal deficit data isn't available during the study period. However, it is available from 1980–1981 onwards. Second, policy makers give much more importance to fiscal deficit of the central government in India than other deficits. Third, FRBM Act (2003) was enacted to impose stringent fiscal discipline on the central government in its overall fiscal and macroeconomic management operations. Also one of the objectives of the study is to examine the influence of the FRBM Act. Fourth, FRBM Act isn't accepted by all the states in India. Hence, the study has used the fiscal deficit of the central government only.

[3]Time series data on employment in the unorganized sector is not available in India. Data constraint restricts to use organized employment for the proxy for employment in the analysis.

[4]However, Post-FRBM act period is not analyzed due to insufficient observation.

model to measure its impact on economic growth {Mallik and Chowdhory (2001), Faria and Carneiro (2001) etc.}. It is widely accepted that Capital formation and employment play crucial role in achieving economic growth and prosperity. Gross domestic capital formation (GDCF) & Employment in the organized sector (EMPL) are used as the proxy for capital stock and employment respectively.

Therefore, based on the literature, the present study has used the following model specification to analyze its objectives.

$$\mathrm{GDPF} = \mathrm{f(FSDF, GDCF, EMPL\ and\ INFLA)} \tag{8.1}$$

Theoretically, it is expected that the coefficients of GDCF and EMPL will be positively associated with economic growth. However, FSDF and INFLA could show ambiguous effect on growth, which need to be analyzed in the context of India. Because productive investments boost economic activity, whereas volatility in prices has an adverse consequence on the economy.

8.3.3 ARDL Model Specification

The autoregressive distributed lag (ARDL) model (Pesaran et al. 2001) is used here to check the existence of short and long-run relationship between the above selected variables. This model is used because of two reasons. First, the variables, included in the model, are mixture of both I (0) and I (1) order. Second, this approach is more suitable and provides consistent estimation for the small and finite sample data period (Pesaran et al. 2001). Hence, it adopts the ARDL modeling approach to cointegration analysis in this study. The following specification of ARDL model is used in this study.

$$\begin{aligned}\Delta \mathrm{LGDPF}_t = {} & \alpha + \theta T + \beta_1 \mathrm{LGDPF}_{t-1} + \beta_2 \mathrm{LFSDF}_{t-1} + \beta_3 \mathrm{LGDCF}_{t-1} + \beta_4 \mathrm{EMPLG}_{t-1} + \beta_5 \mathrm{INFLA}_{t-1} \\ & + \sum_{i=1}^{m} \delta_1 \Delta \mathrm{LGDPF}_{t-i} + \sum_{i=0}^{n} \delta_2 \Delta \mathrm{LFSDF}_{t-i} + \sum_{i=0}^{p} \delta_3 \Delta \mathrm{LGDCF}_{t-i} \\ & + \sum_{i=0}^{q} \delta_4 \Delta \mathrm{EMPLG}_{t-i} + \sum_{i=0}^{s} \delta_5 \Delta \mathrm{INFLA}_{t-i} + u_t \end{aligned} \tag{8.2}$$

where

LGDPF: Log of Gross Domestic Product at factor cost, LFSDF: Log of central government's fiscal deficit as a percentage of GDP, LGDCF: Log of Gross Domestic Capital Formation as a percentage of GDP, EMPLG: growth rate of employment in the organized sectors, and INFLA: inflation rate, Δ = the first difference operator, α is constant, θ, β_1, β_2, β_3, β_4, β_5, δ_1, δ_2, δ_3, δ_4, and δ_5 are coefficients and u_t is error term of the estimated equation.

8.3.4 Bound Testing Approach

After estimation of Eq. (8.2), the Wald test (F-statistic) can be conducted by imposing linear restrictions on the estimated long-run coefficients of one period lagged level of variables. The existence of long-run relationship among the variables can be found by testing null hypothesis of no cointegration against its alternative hypothesis of co-integrating relationship. The null and alternative hypotheses are as follows:

For Eq. (8.2)

$$\mathrm{H}_0 : \beta_1 = \beta_2 = \beta_3 = \beta_4 = \beta_5 = 0(\text{no long} - \text{run relationship});$$
$$\mathrm{H}_1 : \beta_1 \neq \beta_2 \neq \beta_3 \neq \beta_4 \neq \beta_5 \neq 0(\text{a long-run relationship exists})$$

The computed F-statistic value will be evaluated with the critical values tabulated in Table CI-(V) of Pesaran et al. (2001). According to these authors, the lower bound critical values assumed that the explanatory variables are integrated of order zero, i.e., I(0), while the upper bound critical values assumed as integrated of order one, i.e., I(1). Therefore, if the computed F-statistic is smaller than the lower bound value, then the null hypothesis of no cointegration cannot be rejected. Conversely, if the computed F-statistic is greater than the upper bound value I (1), then the null hypothesis of no cointegration is rejected. On the other hand, if the computed F-statistic falls between the lower and upper bound values, then the results are inconclusive.

Once it identifies the long-run relationship, the next step of ARDL model is to estimate the long-run coefficient from the equation, which is as follows:

$$\mathrm{LGDPF}_t = \alpha + \theta T + \sum_{i=1}^{m} \beta_1 \mathrm{LGDPF}_{t-i} + \sum_{i=0}^{n} \beta_2 \mathrm{LFSDF}_{t-i} + \sum_{i=0}^{p} \beta_3 \mathrm{LGDCF}_{t-i} + \sum_{i=0}^{q} \beta_4 \mathrm{EMPLG}_{t-i} + \sum_{i=0}^{s} \beta_5 \mathrm{INFLA}_{t-i} + u_t \quad (8.3)$$

In the final step, the short-run dynamic parameter by estimating an error correction model is obtained. This is as follows:

$$\Delta\mathrm{LGDPF}_t = \alpha + \sum_{i=1}^{m} \delta_1 \Delta\mathrm{LGDPF}_{t-i} + \sum_{i=0}^{n} \delta_2 \Delta\mathrm{LFSDF}_{t-i} + \sum_{i=0}^{p} \delta_3 \Delta\mathrm{LGDCF}_{t-i} + \sum_{i=0}^{q} \delta_4 \Delta\mathrm{EMPLG}_{t-i} + \sum_{i=0}^{s} \delta_5 \Delta\mathrm{INFLA}_{t-i} + \vartheta ECM_{t-1} + \varepsilon_t \quad (8.4)$$

where all the variables are previously defined. ε is error term and ϑ is the coefficients of speed of adjustment which is expected to have negative sign.

8.4 Empirical Analysis

The empirical results are disused in this section.

8.4.1 *Testing for Unit Roots*

The Augmented Dickey–Fuller (ADF) and Phillips Perron (PP), (details see Phillips and Perron 1988) tests are being exercised to check the order of integration of these variables.

Table 8.1 shows that the variables, i.e., LGDPF, LFSDF, and LGDCF are non-stationary at their levels. Because the null hypothesis of unit roots for these variables are rejected only at their first differences. Thus, these variables are stationary and integrated of same order, i.e., I (1), whereas the variables like EMPLG and INFLA are stationary at their levels, i.e., I (0) by both ADF and PP tests. The above results clearly reveal that these variables are of mixture of both I (0) and I (1). Hence, the present study employs the Autoregressive Distributed Lag Model (ARDL) bounds testing approaches to cointegration analysis, proposed by Pesaran et al. (2001), to examine the given objectives.

8.4.2 *Bounds Testing Approaches to Cointegration*

In order to test the presence of long-run relationship among the variables, the first step in the ARDL analysis is to estimate an Ordinary Least Square (OLS) regression for the first difference of both dependent and independent (Eq. 8.2) variables,

Table 8.1 Unit root test

Variables	ADF test				PP test			
	Level		First difference		Level		First difference	
	C	C&T	C	C&T	C	C&T	C	C&T
LGDPF	3.18 (1.00)	−1.96 (0.60)	−6.01 (0.00)	−7.52 (0.00)	3.51 (1.00)	−1.98 (0.59)	−6.04 (0.00)	−7.93 (0.00)
LFSDF	−2.81 (0.06)	−2.67 (0.25)	−6.98 (0.00)	−7.01 (0.00)	−2.79 (0.06)	−2.63 (0.26)	−7.88 (0.00)	−8.08 (0.00)
LGDCF	−0.67 (0.84)	−2.77 (0.21)	−8.29 (0.00)	−8.29 (0.00)	−0.22 (0.92)	−2.77 (0.21)	−9.78 (0.00)	−11.94 (0.00)
EMPLG	−4.14 (0.00)	−4.47 (0.00)	−7.89 (0.00)	−7.97 (0.00)	−4.13 (0.00)	−4.55 (0.00)	−12.68 (0.00)	−15.34 (0.00)
INFLA	−4.71 (0.00)	−4.97 (0.00)	−6.59 (0.00)	−5.25 (0.00)	−4.57 (0.00)	−4.97 0.00)	−14.96 (0.00)	−14.21 (0.00)

Note Brackets show MacKinnon (1996) one-sided *p*-values. *C* Constant and *T* Trend

Table 8.2 Results of bound test

ARDL Model: LGDPF = *f* (LFISDF, LGDCF, EMPLG, INFLA)		
Time period	Maximum lag	F-statistics
Whole period (1970–71 to 2012–13)	3	5.56**
Sub-period (1970–71 to 2003–04)	2	6.51*
Critical values	Lower Bound I(0)	Upper Bound I(1)
10% level	3.03	4.06
5% level	3.47	4.57
1% level	4.40	5.72

Note Case V: Unrestricted intercept and Unrestricted trend, Asymptotic Critical Value Bounds for *F*-Statistics by Pesaran et al. (2001)
* and ** denote one and 5% level of significance

and then using Wald test (*F*-statistic), the joint significance of the parameters of the lagged level variables added to the regression are tested. The *F*-statistic tests the joint null hypothesis that the coefficients of the lagged level variables are zero (i.e., no long-run relationship exists between them). Table 8.2 reports the results of the bound test.

The computed *F*-statistics, i.e., 5.56 and 6.51 for the given two periods, respectively, are higher than the upper bound critical value, i.e., 4.57 at 5% {Pesaran et al. (2001)}. Thus, the null hypotheses of no cointegration are rejected, implying long-run cointegration relationships among these variables. So, bounds testing approaches to cointegration support the long-run relationship among these selected variables.

8.4.3 Estimated Long-run Coefficients

After the confirmation of long-run relationship with the help of bounds test, Eq. (8.3) is estimated using the following ARDL (2,0,0,0,0) specification selected based on Schwarz Bayesian Criterion for the whole sample period, i.e., 1970–1971 to 2012–2013.

Table 8.3 states that during the whole period (1970–1971 to 2012–2013), 1% increase in fiscal deficit is likely to decrease gross domestic product (GDP) by 0.13% and this estimate is highly significant at 2%. Thus, it shows that in the long-run, there is a negative and significant relationship between fiscal deficit and GDP. In India, high fiscal deficit has a detrimental effect on the growth of the economy.

Table 8.3 Estimated long-run coefficient (1970–1971 to 2012–2013)

Dependent variable is LGDPF ARDL(2,0,0,0,0) selected based on Schwarz Bayesian Criterion			
Regressor	Coefficient	Standard Error	*T*-Ratio[Prob]
LFSDF	−0.127**	0.049	−2.597[0.014]
LGDCF	0.282***	0.159	1.783[0.084]
EMPLG	0.046*	0.013	3.545[0.001]
INFLA	−0.008**	0.003	−2.593[0.014]
Constant	7.911*	0.481	16.433[0.000]
Trend	0.059*	0.004	14.321[0.000]
LM Version Serial Correlation: 0.52846 [0.467] Functional Form: 2.0231[0.155] Normality: 0. 31491[0.854] Heteroscedasticity: 0.32016 [0.572] Arch Test: 1.1184[0.572]		**F Version** Serial Correlation: 0.41784[0.523] Functional Form: 1.6610[0.207] Heteroscedasticity: 0.30693[0.583] Arch Test: 0.43468[0.651]	

[ ] shows *p*-value
Note *, ** and *** denote 1, 5, and 10% level of significance respectively

During the last four decades capital expenditure to GDP ratio has declined from 5.62% in 1970–1971 to 1.77% in 2012–2013. The share of non-developmental expenditure to total expenditure has increased from 43.34% in 1980–1981 to nearly 52% in 2012–2013 in India. This implies that resources generated through fiscal deficit are used more on unproductive manner which has a detrimental effect on the growth rate of the economy. Similarly, gross domestic capital formation has a positive and significant impact on GDP. There is also a positive and significant relationship exists between employment in the organized sector and GDP. Hence, it implies higher capital formation and employment will lead to higher growth to the economy. However, inflation rate has a significant and negative impact on GDP.

The sub-period analysis from 1970–1971 to 2003–2004 (Table 8.4) shows that there exists a negative and highly significant relationship between fiscal deficit and GDP. During this period, It implies that 1% increase in fiscal deficit leads to 0.16% decrease in GDP. Similarly, capital formation has positive and significant impact on GDP and inflation rate has negative & significant impact on GDP, consistent with the earlier findings. However, employment growth has a negative impact contrary to the expected result, but the estimated coefficient is insignificant. During these periods, highly volatile or even negative employment growth in some period might be the possible reason for the insignificant effect on GDP.

But one interesting result has come out, when the study examined the pre-FRBM Act sub-period (1970–1971 to 2003–2004). The negative impact of fiscal deficit is more on GDP in case of sub-period (−0.16) than the whole sample period (−0.13).

Table 8.4 Estimated long-run coefficient (1970–71 to 2003–04)

Dependent variable is LGDPF
ARDL(1,0,0,1,0) selected based on Schwarz Bayesian Criterion

Regressor	Coefficient	Standard Error	*T*-Ratio[Prob]
LFSDF	−0.156*	0.026	−5.958[0.000]
LGDCF	0.235**	0.099	2.383[0.025]
EMPLG	−0.013	0.009	−1.371[0.183]
INFLA	−0.007*	0.002	−4.256[0.000]
Constant	8.167*	0.291	28.099[0.000]
Trend	0.048*	0.002	22.803[0.000]

LM Version	F Version
Serial Correlation: 1.3074[0.253] Functional Form: 0.79569 [0.372] Normality: 3.4077[0.182] Heteroscedasticity: 0.0040137 [0.949] Arch Test: 0.062330[0.803]	Serial Correlation: 0.99005[0.330] Functional Form: 0.59298[0.449] Heteroscedasticity: 0.0037709[0.951] Arch Test: 0.045416[0.833]

Note *, ** and *** denote 1, 5 and 10% level of significance respectively, [ ] shows *p*-value

After the implementation of FRBM Act (2003–2004), central government tried to reduce fiscal deficit as a percentage of GDP from 4.7 in 2003–2004 to its all-time low 2.76 in 2007–2008. Again fiscal deficit has been increased to overcome the ill effects of global financial crisis (2008). This implies enactment of FRBM Act has influenced and weakens the fiscal deficit-economic growth linkage. This is a crucial and novel finding for India. As a whole, the cointegration results show there is long-run relationship among these variables and fiscal deficit has negative impact on economic growth in India.

8.4.4 Estimated Short-run Coefficients

The results of the estimated error correction models are summarized in Tables 8.5 and 8.6, respectively. The coefficient of ECM_{t-1} term for the whole time period (1970–1971 to 2012–2013) suggests that approximately 22% of adjustment proceeds toward the long-run equilibrium after one year. For the sub-periods (1970–1971 to 2003–2004), the coefficient of ECM_{t-1} is −0.46, which is statistically significant and comparatively high speed of adjustment process to correct the disequilibrium of the previous year's shock adjust back to the long-run equilibrium in the current year. Both the coefficients of ECM_{t-1} are negative and highly significant at one % level. This implies long-run causality from the selected variables to the GDP.

In the short run, the coefficients of fiscal deficit (both in whole and sub-period) are negative and highly significant, which also supports that high fiscal deficit has a

Table 8.5 Error correction model (1970–71 to 2012–13)

Dependent variable is DLGDPF
ARDL(2,0,0,0,0) selected based on Schwarz Bayesian Criterion

Regressor	Coefficient	Standard Error	*T*-Ratio[Prob]
DLGDPF(-1)	−0.449*	0.116	−3.889[0.000]
DLFSDF	−0.028**	0.011	−2.589[0.014]
DLGDCF	0.063	0.039	1.622[0.114]
DEMPLG	0.011*	0.002	4.369[0.000]
DINFLA	−0.002*	0.63E−3	−3.106[0.004]
Constant	1.771*	0.369	4.787[0.000]
ECM(-1)	−0.224*	0.048	−4.702[0.000]

Note *, ** and *** denote 1, 5 and 10% level of significance respectively, [ ] shows *p*-value

Table 8.6 Error correction model (1970–71 to 2003–04)

Dependent variable is DLGDPF
ARDL(1,0,0,1,0) selected based on Schwarz Bayesian Criterion

Regressor	Coefficient	Standard Error	*T*-Ratio[Prob]
DLFSDF	−0.072*	0.0161	−4.465[0.000]
DLGDCF	0.109**	0.048	2.244[0.034]
DEMPLG	0.003	0.003	1.009[0.322]
DINFLA	−0.003*	0.725E−3	−4.243[0.000]
Constant	3.776*	0.705	5.356[0.000]
ECM(-1)	−0.462*	0.085	−5.428[0.000]

Note *, ** and *** denote 1, 5 and 10% level of significance respectively, [ ] shows *p*-value

detrimental effect on the growth of the economy. The inflation rate has a negative and highly significant effect in both these periods in the short run. The result also reveals that employment and capital formation have positively affected the growth in short run. It also confirms that enactment of FRBM Act has influenced the given linkage less adversely, while comparing Pre-FRBM Act regime (−0.07) against whole regime (−0.03).

8.4.5 Diagnostic Tests and Stability Test

The robustness of the estimated models has been carried out by several diagnostic tests such as serial correlation, Jacque-Bera normality test and Ramsey RESET specification test, Heteroscedasticity test and ARCH test. All these models pass these tests. To make the results more robust, the plot of the stability test results (CUSUM and CUSUMSQ) of the ARDL models are given in Figs. 8.2 and 8.3, respectively, which clearly shows that the critical values are not exceeded the bounds of 5% level of significance. Hence, the results reported are valid for reliable interpretation.

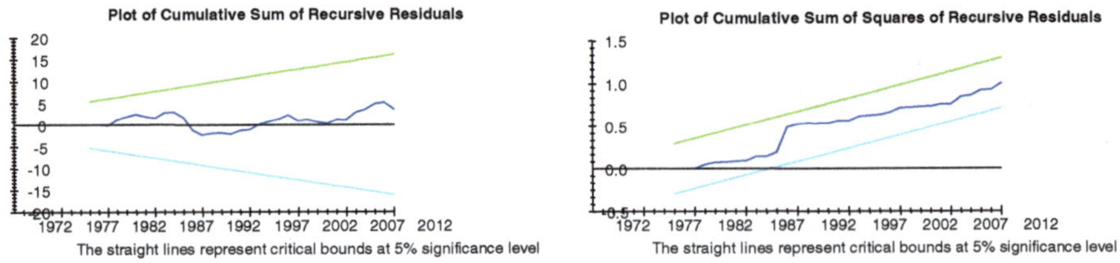

Fig. 8.2 CUSUM and CUSUMSQ test results for whole period

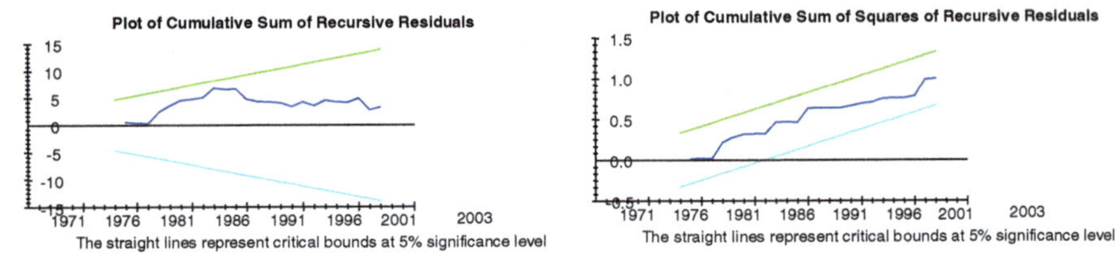

Fig. 8.3 CUSUM and CUSUMSQ test results for sub-period

8.5 Conclusion and Policy Implications

This paper has analyzed the impact of fiscal deficit on economic growth by addressing some other crucial control variables in case of India by using annual data from 1970–1971 to 2012–2013. The analysis is carried out for two different periods, i.e., whole sample period (1970–1971 to 2012–2013) and sub-sample period (1970–1971 to 2003–2004) especially to analyze the influence of execution of FRBM Act on the fiscal deficit-growth linkage in India. The ARDL Bounds Testing approaches to cointegration support the long-run relationship among the selected variables. The finding indicates that in the long run, fiscal deficit has a negative and significant effect on economic growth of the Indian economy. One percent increase in fiscal deficit is likely to decrease gross domestic product by 0.13% and this estimate is highly significant at 2% for the whole period. The negative impact of fiscal deficit is more on GDP in case of Pre-FRBM Act sub-period (−0.16) than the whole sample period (−0.13). This implies that implementation of FRBM Act has influenced and lessens fiscal deficit-economic growth linkage in India. This is a crucial finding for the policy makers of India.

Error Correction models support the short-run relationship between fiscal deficit and economic growth. In the short run, the coefficients of fiscal deficit in all these periods are negative and highly significant. The magnitude of ECM term is higher in the sub-period (−0.46) than the whole sample period (−0.22). In the short run, the coefficients of fiscal deficit are also higher in case of sub-period (−0.07) than the whole period (−0.02), which also supports the earlier finding, i.e., FRBM Act has influenced less adversely to the fiscal deficit-economic growth linkage. Hence, it is clear that fiscal deficit has a detrimental effect both in the short and long run in India. It supports Neoclassical theory, which holds that fiscal deficits lead to a fall in the Gross Domestic Product. The Government should contain the fiscal deficit and should try to achieve the target set by FRBM Act. Necessary steps should be taken to control high inflation as it hampers growth of the economy.

Appendix 1

Autoregressive Distributed Lag Estimates for Whole Period (1970–1971 to 2012–2013)

ARDL(2,0,0,0,0) selected based on Schwarz Bayesian Criterion
Dependent variable is LGDPF

Regressor	Coefficient	Standard Error	T-Ratio[Prob]
LGDPF(-1)	0.327	0.123	2.662[0.012]
LGDPF(-2)	0.449	0.116	3.889[0.000]
LFSDF	−0.028	0.011	−2.589[0.014]
LGDCF	0.063	0.039	1.622[0.114]
EMPLG	0.011	0.002	4.369[0.000]
INFLA	−0.002	0.6369E−3	−3.105[0.004]
Constant	1.770	0.369	4.787[0.000]
Trend	0.0132	0.002	5.375[0.000]

R-Squared: 0.99, R-Bar-Squared: 0.99, F-stat. F(7, 33):8995.9[0.000]
Akaike Info. Criterion: 105.594 Schwarz Bayesian Criterion; 98.740
DW-statistic; 1.757

Appendix 2

Autoregressive Distributed Lag Estimates for Sub-period (1970–1971 to 2003–2004)

ARDL(1,0,0,1,0) selected based on Schwarz Bayesian Criterion
Dependent variable is LGDPF

Regressor	Coefficient	Standard error	T-Ratio[Prob]
LGDPF(-1)	0.538	0.085	6.312[0.000]
LFSDF	−0.072	0.016	−4.466[0.000]
LGDCF	0.109	0.048	2.244[0.034]
EMPLG	0.003	0.003	1.009[0.323]
EMPLG(-1)	−0.009	0.003	−3.266[0.003]
INFLA	−0.003	0.7255E−3	−4.243[0.000]

(continued)

(continued)

C	3.776	0.705	5.356[0.000]
T	0.0221	0.004	5.396[0.000]

R-Squared: 0.99, R-Bar-Squared: 0.99, F-stat. F(7, 25): 3884.0[0.000]
Akaike Info. Criterion: 85.289 Schwarz Bayesian Criterion: 79.303
DW-statistic: 2.321, Durbin's h-statistic 1.058[0.290]

References

Adam CS, Bevan DL (2005) Fiscal deficits and growth in developing countries. J Public Econ 89:571–597

Arora H, Dua P (1993) Budget deficits, domestic investment, and trade deficits. Contemp Policy Issues 11:29–44

Avila J (2011) Fiscal deficit, macro-uncertainty, and growth in Argentina. Available at http://www.ucema.edu.ar/publicaciones/download/documentos/456.pdf. CEMA. Working Papers no-456

Bose N, Haque ME, Osborn DR (2007) Public expenditure and economic growth: a disaggregated analysis for developing countries. The Manchester School 75:533–556

Brender A, Drazen A (2008) How do budget deficits and economic growth affect reelection prospects? Evidence from a large panel of countries. Am Econ Rev 98:2203–2220

Burney NA, Akhtar N (1992) Government budget deficits and exchange rate determination: evidence from Pakistan. Pak Dev Rev 31:871–882

Cebula RJ (1995) The impact of federal government budget deficits on economic growth in the United States: an empirical investigation, 1955-1992. Int Rev Econ Financ 4:245–252

Dalyop GT (2010) Fiscal deficits and the growth of domestic output in Nigeria. Jos J Econ 4: 153–173

Darrat AF (2000) Are budget deficits inflationary? A reconsideration of the evidence. Appl Econ 7:633–636

Easterly W, Rebelo S (1993) Fiscal policy and economic growth: an empirical investigation. J Monet Econ 32:417–458

Easterly W et al (1994) Public sector deficits and macroeconomic performance. Oxford University Press for the World Bank, Oxford and New York

Eisner R, Pierper PJ (1984) A new view of the federal debt and budget deficits. Am Econ Rev 74:11–29

Faria JR, Carneiro FG (2001) Does high inflation affect growth in the long and short run? J Appl Econ 4:89–105

Fatima et al (2011) Fiscal deficit and economic growth: an analysis of Pakistan's economy. Int J Trade Econ Financ 2:501–504

Fischer S (1993) The role of macroeconomic factors in growth. J Monet Econ 32:485–512

Ghali KH (1997) Government spending and economic growth in Saudi Arabia. J Econ Dev 22:165–172

Gupta S et al (2005) Fiscal policy, expenditure composition, and growth in low-income countries. J Int Money Financ 24:441–463

Karras G (1994) Macroeconomic effects of budget deficits: further international evidence. J Int Money Financ 13:190–210

Keho Y (2010) Budget deficits and economic growth: causality evidence and policy implications for AEMU countries. Eur J Econ Financ Adm Sci 18:99–104
Mallik G, Chowdhury A (2001) Inflation and economic growth: evidence from four South American countries. Asia-Pacific Dev J 8:123–133
Nelson MA, Singh RD (1994) The deficit-growth connection: some recent evidence from developing countries. Econ Dev Cult Change 43:167–191
Osinubi TS, Dauda ROS, Olaleru OE (2010) Budget deficits, external debt and economic growth in Nigeria. Singap Econ Rev 55:491–521
Pesaran MH et al (2001) Bound testing approaches to the analysis of level relationship. J Appl Econ 16:289–326
Phillips PC, Perron P (1988) Testing for unit root in the time series regression. Biometrika 75:335–346
Tan EC (2006) Fiscal deficits, inflation and economic growth in a successful open developing economy. Rev Appl Econ 2:129–139
Taylor L et al (2012) Fiscal deficits, economic growth and government debt in the USA. Camb J Econ 36:189–204

Author Biography

Ranjan Kumar Mohanty The author is immensely grateful to the participants of 4th international conference on Applied Econometrics, IBS Hyderabad, India (2014), Prof. P. Chaudhury, Prof. N.R. Bhanumurthy, Prof. T. Tripathy, Prof. A.K. Das, Dr. Dinesh kumar Nayak, Dr. Bhabesh Hazarika and Dr. Amandeep Kaur for their valuable guidance and constructive suggestions. Errors and omissions, if any, are my own doing.

Chapter 9
Grants-in-Aid and State Domestic Product: An Empirical Analysis in India

Sajad Ahmad Bhat, Aadil Ahmad Ganaie, Naseer Ahmed Khan and Bandi Kamaiah

Abstract The smooth transfer of the finances keeping in view the objectives and the requirements of the different levels of the government is an indicator of the healthy federal system. Further, it demarcates the degree of decentralization that exists within a federation. This study examines the relationship between Grants-in-Aid taken as a measure of fiscal decentralization and state domestic product in case of India using panel data for 14 non-specialized states for the period 1981–2014. The results showed that long-run equilibrium relationship exists between the two. The estimates from FMOLS, and dynamic OLS (DOLS) framework revealed that Grants-in-Aid have a positive and significant impact on the state domestic product. So from this angle, it is centralization that is growth enhancing, not decentralization. However, the study failed to detect the true nature of the causation between these two.

Keyword Grants-in-Aid · GSDP · DOLS · India

9.1 Introduction

The strength of the federal structure of an economy much depends on the way fiscal transfers are managed between the centre and the states. The smooth transfer of the finances keeping in view the objectives and the requirements of the different levels of the government is an indicator of the healthy federal system. Further, it demarcates the degree of decentralization that exists within a federation. The heavy dependence on the transfers from the centre gives a clear indication about the centralized type of system, that damages the autonomic characteristic of the states to generate own revenues and utilize the funds that suit the local requisites.

S.A. Bhat · A.A. Ganaie (✉) · N.A. Khan · B. Kamaiah
School of Economics, University of Hyderabad, Hyderabad, Telangana 500046, India
e-mail: aadilganaie77@gmail.com

S.A. Bhat
e-mail: sajadeco@gmail.com

N.A. Khan (ed.), *Challenges and Issues in Indian Fiscal Federalism*,
India Studies in Business and Economics, https://doi.org/10.1007/978-981-10-6217-9_9

To manage vertical and horizontal fiscal inequalities, intergovernmental transfers play an important role, besides affecting the stability of regional and local economy (Boadway and Shah 2007). The importance grew further when there exist substantial divergences on the economic front among different regions as are experienced in India. The nature and the current state of regional inequality reflect the large structural differences in the economy of the states. It increases the task of both local as well as national governments to draw the road map for a balanced and robust federal structure that besides solving the economic problems will strengthen the bond between the two considering the political integrity of the country.

The intergovernmental transfers in the case of India happen through three different channels like, sharing of taxes, disbursement of loans and the allocation of grants. In fact, the corresponding response of the output growth of the states to these transfers does not emerge same. Much depends on the efficient utilization of these transfers by the individual states. However, institutional factors can drive largest variations in the responsibility that state governments may get accustomed with while behaving with the transfers from the centre and the resources generated by full authority and autonomy. So, these may either harm the local economy by generating disincentives or may fuel the growth when received as a complimentary resource.

In this paper, we tried to deal with only one part of the intergovernmental transfers, i.e. Grants-in-Aid. The sole purpose is to dig out the effect of decentralization on the state economy via the mechanism of unconditional transfers. Considering the widening gap in terms of the resources and the requirements of the different regions, the Article 275(1) of the constitution of India clearly mentions about the provision of Grants-in-Aid from the centre to the states. There are various measures that have been used in the literature to represent the index of decentralization. However, we presume that to look it through the prism of grants may provide a better picture about the degree of dependence and decentralization. Further, it may highly influence the behaviour of the local governments with respect to the measures they will adopt to proceed for the higher stages of growth and development. The present study mainly focuses on to explore the mode Grants-in-Aid to states from centre affect the state gross domestic product. We have taken grants-in-aid in general, the share of grants-in-aid in the total revenue receipts and ratio of grants-in-aid to that of state's own tax revenue as the indicators of decentralization. Besides that we have taken into account other factors like capital stock, population and expenditure on social services as a proxy for human development expenditure that affects state gross domestic product. The results from the study reveal that grants-in-aid and state gross domestic product are cointegrated and former has a positive effect on Later. However, we failed to detect the true nature of the causation between the variables.

9.2 Review of Literature

As the study is mainly concerned about to explore the effect of decentralization, the review is focused to include some main studies that deal with the subject. The theoretical background about effects of fiscal decentralization on economic growth takes its legacy from the model of Tiebout (1956), Oates (1972, 1999, and 2005) and Musgrave (1983). However, as far as empirical literature is considered there is no consensus on the relationship between the two, despite the attention it received in the literature. There are almost many studies that find evidence for a positive, negative, or no relationship. A comprehensive review of the studies is beyond the scope of this paper. Therefore, the main focus will be on some recent studies that too on developing countries in particular with context to India.

9.2.1 Studies Against Decentralization

Davoodi and Zou (1998) using the panel data set of 46 countries over the period 1970–1989 studied the relationship between fiscal decentralization and economic growth. The study found a negative relationship between the two in the case of developing countries while for developed countries there exist no relationship. Another study by Davoodi et al. (1998) examined the above relation in the context of United States. The study found that further decentralization may be detrimental to growth. Woller and Phillips (1998) examined the relationship between the level of fiscal decentralization and economic growth rates across a sample of 23 LDCs from 1974 to 1991. The study failed to find any systematic relationship among two for the given sample of LDCs.

Jin and Zou (2005) examined how fiscal decentralization affected provincial economic growth in China. By using a panel data set for China's 30 provinces for the period from 1979 to 1993 and 1994 to 1999 separately, the results of this study suggest that in both time periods, expenditure and revenue decentralization levels should further diverge to benefit provincial growth. Similarly, Zhang and Zou (1998) using annual data for 28 provinces of China, from 1980 to 1992 examined the given relationship. The results of this study also corroborate with the above studies. Tarigan S (2003) uses a pooled data set of 34 countries from the period 1979 to 1999 including India, China and Indonesia analyses the relationship between fiscal decentralization and economic development. The study also found a negative but insignificant relationship.

9.2.2 Studies in Favour of Decentralization

Lin and Liu (2000) uses province level panel data for 28 provinces of China for the period 1970–1993. The study finds that fiscal decentralization has made a significant contribution to economic growth, which is consistent with fiscal decentralization hypothesis. Zhang and Zou (2001) examined the relationship between fiscal decentralization and economic growth based on the panel data from 1970 to 1994 for 16 major Indian states. The results reveal that fiscal decentralization is positively and significantly associated with state economic growth. Akai and Sakata (2002) using new panel data set for the United States covering 1992 to 1996 period, finds a positive relationship between fiscal decentralization and economic growth. The positive results are somewhat attributed to the inclusion of historical and cultural factors.

Limi (2005) using the Instrumental Variables technique with latest cross-country data for the period from 1997 to 2001, the study found that fiscal decentralization has a positive and significant impact on growth rate of GDP. From the above brief review of the literature, it is clear regarding the fiscal decentralization hypothesis that results are ambiguous in nature. As pointed out by Akia and Sakata (2002) cross-country studies have the disadvantage of pooling countries with substantial differences in history, politics, institution and culture, which if not taken into consideration gives rise to blur in the relationship between the fiscal decentralization and growth (Jin and Zou 2005). With these viewpoints in due consideration, this study attempts to analyze fiscal decentralization and growth nexus with reference to India.

9.3 Data and Methodology

The panel includes 14 states[1] of Indian Federation for the period 1981–2014. To study the relationship, our main variables include State Gross domestic product (Gsdp) and three indicators (lnGr, Gr_OR and Gr_TRR) and of fiscal decentralization constructed on the basis of revenue data for states and centre. Besides that we have used gross fixed capital of industries as a proxy for capital stock of the states (GC), population (Pop) and expenditure on social services (lnhdx) as the proxy for human development expenditure as control variables. For data, we have relied on the RBI Handbook on Indian economy and EPW Research Foundation. All the variables are used in natural logarithm form.

To observe the effect of different indicators of fiscal decentralization on economic growth, we have used a simple model based on Cobb-Douglas Production function. The basic model runs as,

[1]Andhra Pradesh, Bihar, Gujarat, Haryana, Karnataka, Kerala, Rajasthan, Madhya Pradesh, Maharashtra, Orissa, Punjab, Tamil Nadu, Uttar Pradesh, West Bengal.

$$Y_{it} = A_{it} L_{it}^{\alpha} K_{it}^{\beta} H_{it}^{c} \quad (1)$$

where *Y*, *L*, *K* and *H* denotes state gross domestic product (Gsdp), the population, physical capital stock and human development expenditure, respectively. While *A* is used to represent the technological factors, in this study we have taken it to reflect the effect of fiscal decentralization measures besides other unobservable factors. Transforming Eq. (1) into logarithmic form to allow for linear estimation, we have

$$\ln(Y_{it}) = \ln(A_{it}) + \alpha.\ln(L_{it}) + \beta.\ln(K_{it}) + c.\ln(H_{it}) \quad (2)$$

$$y_{it} = \theta_{it} + \alpha.l_{it} + \beta.k_{it} + c.h_{it} \quad (3)$$

Further decomposing θ_{it} (or $\ln(A_{it})$) into observable shocks to represent fiscal decentralization (fd_{it}) and unobservable factors to denote error term (ε_{it}), the model can be framed as

$$y_{it} = \vartheta.fd_{it} + \alpha.l_{it} + \beta.k_{it} + c.h_{it} + \varepsilon_{it} \quad (4)$$

Accordingly, the panel regression model we will estimate can be showed as

$$\text{lnGsdp}_{it} = \beta_i + \beta_{1i} fd_{it} + \beta_{2i}\text{lnGC}_{it} + \beta_{3i}\text{lnPop}_{it} + \beta_{4i}.\text{ln}h_{it} + \varepsilon_{it} \quad (5)$$

where i = 1, ………,14 and t = 1981,…………, 2014.

To carry out the estimation, first we have checked the stationarity of the data with the help of both first- and second-generation Unit Root tests. The long-run equilibrium between the variables is detected with the help of Pedroni (2004) cointegration test.

In order to estimate the cointegrated variables, we have used Fully Modified Ordinary Least Squares (FMOLS) by Pedroni (2001). It provides consistent estimates while taking care of endogeneity and serial correlation. The general representation for the model follows as:

$$\theta_i^* = (z_i' z_i)^{-1} \left(z_i' y_i^* - T\gamma^+ \right) \quad (6)$$

where $\theta_i^* = (\alpha, \beta^*)$, y_i^* is the transformation of endogenous variable that takes care of endogeneity and γ^+ is the adjustment parameter to treat autocorrelation.

For robustness of long-run coefficients we further used on Dynamic Ordinary Least Squares (DOLS) estimator of Stock and Watson (1993) extended by Kao and Chiang (1999, 2001) for panel estimation. The DOLS estimator uses both lags and leads of the independent variables to take care of endogeneity and serial correlation in the series. The basic DOLS regression can be represented as

$$Y_{it} = \alpha_i + X'_{it}\beta + \sum_{j=-k}^{k} \Phi_{ij}\Delta X_{it+j} + \varepsilon_{it} \tag{7}$$

where X includes all the explanatory variables. Φ_{ij} represents coefficients of current, lead and lag differences.

Given the existence of cointegration between the variable of discussion along with their long-run coefficients estimated using FMOLS and DOLS, we have resorted to panel causation test in order to ensure the direction of causation. For that purpose, we have used granger Causality test adopted by Dumitrescu-Hurlin (2012). This approach fetches advantage to the previous ones by making utmost contrary assumption about the coefficients, permitting them to differ across panel groups. The general representation is as follows:

$$y_{i,t} = \alpha_{0,i} + \alpha_{1,i}y_{i,t-1} + \cdots + \alpha_{l,i}y_{i,t-1} + \beta_{1,i}x_{i,t-1} + \cdots + \beta_{l,i}x_{i,t-1} + \epsilon_{i,t} \tag{8}$$

$$x_{i,t} = \alpha_{0,i} + \alpha_{1,i}x_{i,t-1} + \cdots + \alpha_{l,i}x_{i,t-1} + \beta_{1,i}y_{i,t-1} + \cdots + \beta_{l,i}y_{i,t-1} + \epsilon_{i,t} \tag{9}$$

In the equations above t represents time dimension and i represents cross section of the panel.

The heterogeneity of coefficients across groups is represented as

$$\alpha_{0,i} \neq \alpha_{0,j}, \alpha_{1,i} \neq \alpha_{1,\mathrm{j}}, \ldots, \alpha_{l,i} \neq \alpha_{l,\mathrm{j}}, \forall i,j \tag{10}$$

$$\beta_{1,i} \neq \beta_{1,j}, \ldots, \beta_{1,i} \neq \beta_{1,j}, \forall i,j \tag{11}$$

The test gives Wbar statistic which is basically the average of the Granger Causality regressions run for every individual cross section.

9.4 Empirical Analysis

To validate the stationarity of the variables, unit root tests employed and results are reported in Table 9.1. We have used first generation test (Maddala and Wu 1999 and the results reveal that variables are stationary at first difference. However, this test suffers from the problems associated with cross-sectional dependency. To overcome this issue, we have used a second-generation cross-sectional augmented test developed by Im, Pesaran and Shin (2007). The results corroborate the earlier results. Thus, we may conclude that all variables are first difference stationary involving both constant as well trend.

As discerned by results of unit root test that all variables are stationary at first difference. Cointegration test, for ensuring long-run relationship developed by Pedroni (2004) has been employed. This test gives values of six statistics, out of which four are associated across the groups with pooling autoregressive coefficients

Table 9.1 Unit root tests

Variables at levels								
Maddala and Wu (1999) **panel unit root test (MW)**								
Deterministic: constant								
Lags	lnGsdp	(*p*)	lnPoP	(*p*)	lnGC	(*p*)		
0	0.280	1.000	200.547	0.000	17.228	0.944		
1	0.228	1.000	70.835	0.000	10.865	0.998		
2	0.156	1.000	50.782	0.005	8.111	1.000		
3	0.267	1.000	47.996	0.011	10.670	0.999		
4	0.291	1.000	47.465	0.012	9.082	1.000		
	lnhdx	(*p*)	lnGr	(*p*)	Gr_OR	(*p*)	Gr_TRR	(*p*)
0	1.710	1.000	2.027	1.000	64.880	0.000	78.299	0.000
1	1.504	1.000	1.598	1.000	48.210	0.010	51.225	0.005
2	1.070	1.000	0.929	1.000	28.570	0.435	36.282	0.136
3	1.191	1.000	0.774	1.000	21.738	0.793	28.844	0.420
4	0.913	1.000	0.359	1.000	14.359	0.984	16.857	0.951
Deterministic: constant and trend term								
	lnGsdp	(*p*)	lnPoP	(*p*)	lnGC	(*p*)		
0	35.006	0.170	19.467	0.883	58.529	0.001		
1	16.520	0.957	12.169	0.996	26.696	0.535		
2	22.211	0.771	12.087	0.996	17.832	0.930		
3	28.974	0.414	13.345	0.991	30.274	0.350		
4	17.561	0.937	11.541	0.997	39.172	0.078		
	lnhdx	(*p*)	lnGr	(*p*)	Gr_OR	(*p*)	Gr_TRR	(*p*)
0	36.759	0.124	62.848	0.000	66.920	0.000	68.087	0.000
1	45.175	0.021	34.056	0.199	43.096	0.034	39.855	0.068
2	30.461	0.342	22.180	0.773	24.770	0.640	25.522	0.599
3	45.683	0.019	23.068	0.730	27.250	0.505	29.412	0.392
4	30.863	0.323	7.771	1.000	11.428	0.998	11.312	0.998
Pesaran (2007) **panel unit root test (CIPS)**								
Deterministic: constant								
	lnGsdp	(p)	lnPoP	(p)	lnGC	(p)		
0	−4.159	0.000	2.600	0.995	−8.628	0.000		
1	−0.773	0.220	2.766	0.997	−4.049	0.000		
2	0.656	0.744	2.923	0.998	−0.896	0.185		
3	−0.456	0.324	3.700	1.000	−0.649	0.258		
4	−1.424	0.077	3.255	0.999	1.180	0.881		
	lnhdx	(*p*)	lnGr	(*p*)	Gr_OR	(*p*)	Gr_TRR	(*p*)
0	−2.822	0.002	−7.246	0.000	−4.035	0.000	−4.530	0.000
1	−2.282	0.011	−4.107	0.000	−1.407	0.080	−1.928	0.027
2	0.118	0.547	−3.001	0.001	0.875	0.809	−0.108	0.457
3	0.231	0.592	−1.676	0.047	2.825	0.998	1.355	0.912

(continued)

Table 9.1 (continued)

Variables at levels								
4	0.709	0.761	−0.634	0.263	2.966	0.998	1.696	0.955
Deterministic: constant and trend term								
	lnGsdp	(*p*)	lnPoP	(*p*)	lnGC	(*p*)		
0	−4.058	0.000	3.356	1.000	−9.035	0.000		
1	−0.516	0.303	2.723	0.997	−4.550	0.000		
2	0.941	0.827	1.899	0.971	−0.418	0.338		
3	−0.590	0.278	2.508	0.994	−0.410	0.341		
4	−1.233	0.109	1.760	0.961	0.787	0.784		
	lnhdx	(*p*)	lnGr	(*p*)	Gr_OR	(*p*)	Gr_TRR	(*p*)
0	−3.344	0.000	−6.663	0.000	−6.204	0.000	−6.377	0.000
1	−3.415	0.000	−3.184	0.001	−3.518	0.000	−2.841	0.002
2	−0.853	0.197	−2.919	0.002	−1.130	0.129	−1.264	0.103
3	−1.758	0.039	−3.258	0.001	0.074	0.530	−0.851	0.197
4	−2.322	0.010	−2.279	0.011	0.312	0.622	−1.517	0.065
Variables at first difference								
Maddala and Wu (1999) **panel unit root test (MW)**								
Deterministic: constant								
Lags	lnGsdp	(*p*)	lnPoP	(*p*)	lnGC	(*p*)		
0	601.113	0.000	270.983	0.000	606.748	0.000		
1	198.476	0.000	111.7	0.000	282.362	0.000		
2	83.814	0.000	69.727	0.000	117.516	0.000		
3	80.73	0.000	50.533	0.006	75.726	0.000		
4	85.764	0.000	37.566	0.107	63.154	0.000		
	lnhdx	(*p*)	lnGr	(*p*)	Gr_OR	(*p*)	Gr_TRR	(*p*)
0	497.021	0.000	593.502	0.000	527.432	0.000	562.768	0.000
1	264.256	0.000	235.747	0.000	221.562	0.000	233.002	0.000
2	137.536	0.000	128.189	0.000	141.247	0.000	137.901	0.000
3	119.849	0.000	138.159	0.000	143.006	0.000	149.583	0.000
4	94.259	0.000	101.14	0.000	98.98	0.000	103.753	0.000
Deterministic: constant and trend term								
	lngsdp	(*p*)	lnPoP	(*p*)	lnGC	(*p*)		
0	554.055	0.000	299.185	0.000	507.63	0.000		
1	181.267	0.000	122.449	0.000	215.202	0.000		
2	63.952	0.000	82.469	0.000	75.318	0.000		
3	58.027	0.001	61.897	0.000	41.74	0.046		
4	57.955	0.001	45.731	0.019	31.769	0.284		
	lnhdx	(*p*)	lnGr	(*p*)	Gr_OR	(*p*)	Gr_TRR	(*p*)
0	429.838	0.000	508.947	0.000	450.036	0.000	481.275	0.000
1	231.73	0.000	180.768	0.000	167.697	0.000	178.364	0.000
2	100.616	0.000	85.412	0.000	97.415	0.000	94.027	0.000

(continued)

Table 9.1 (continued)

Variables at levels								
3	86.077	0.000	97.757	0.000	102.072	0.000	107.382	0.000
4	75.889	0.000	73.227	0.000	73.713	0.000	77.044	0.000
Pesaran (2007) **panel unit root test (CIPS)**								
Deterministic: constant								
	lnGsdp	(*p*)	lnPoP	(*p*)	lnGC	(*p*)		
0	−17.23	0.000	−6.975	0.000	−17.572	0.000		
1	−11.912	0.000	−2.538	0.006	−15.401	0.000		
2	−4.957	0.000	−1.408	0.080	−9.807	0.000		
3	−2.927	0.002	0.646	0.741	−6.678	0.000		
4	−3.069	0.001	0.973	0.835	−4.201	0.000		
	lnhdx	(*p*)	lnGr	(*p*)	Gr_OR	(*p*)	Gr_TRR	(*p*)
0	−16.197	0.000	−17.210	0.000	−17.098	0.000	−17.304	0.000
1	−11.875	0.000	−12.092	0.000	−12.000	0.000	−12.526	0.000
2	−6.774	0.000	−8.293	0.000	−8.936	0.000	−8.45	0.000
3	−4.305	0.000	−6.125	0.000	−5.359	0.000	−5.291	0.000
4	−3.726	0.000	−4.582	0.000	−4.029	0.000	−4.413	0.000
Deterministic: constant and trend term								
	lnGsdp	(*p*)	lnPoP	(*p*)	lnGC	(*p*)		
0	−16.831	0.000	−9.592	0.000	−17.028	0.000		
1	−10.277	0.000	−4.383	0.000	−14.353	0.000		
2	−3.036	0.001	−2.881	0.002	−8.136	0.000		
3	−1.265	0.103	−0.257	0.399	−5.236	0.000		
4	−1.486	0.069	0.423	0.664	−2.638	0.004		
	lnhdx	(*p*)	lnGr	(*p*)	Gr_OR	(*p*)	Gr_TRR	(*p*)
0	−15.494	0.000	−16.728	0.000	−16.640	0.000	−16.716	0.000
1	−10.901	0.000	−10.355	0.000	−10.297	0.000	−10.781	0.000
2	−5.594	0.000	−6.376	0.000	−7.096	0.000	−6.536	0.000
3	−2.823	0.002	−3.918	0.000	−3.229	0.001	−3.061	0.001
4	−2.085	0.019	−2.406	0.008	−2.210	0.014	−2.472	0.007

Null for MW and CIPS tests: series is I(1). MW test assumes cross-sectional independence
CIPS test assumes cross-section dependence is in the form of a single unobserved common factor

referred as within dimension while other three are concerned with heterogeneity averages and are named as group specific or between dimension tests. The results for all the models used in the study are reported in Table 9.2. As revealed by results null of no cointegration for most of the cases gets rejected at 1 and 5%, respectively.

In order to apprehend the effect of decentralization on state domestic product, a panel data model is constructed using state domestic product as proxy for well-being, gross fixed capital of industries as a proxy for capital stock being one of the fundamental factor influencing GDP, developmental expenditure on social services, population along with different measures of decentralization. The

Table 9.2 Cointegration tests

M	Statistics of panel tests				Statistics of group tests		
	V statistics	Rho statistics	pp statistics	Adf statistics	Rho statistics	pp statistics	Adf statistics
M1	7.550[a]	−1.724[b]	−6.739[a]	−7.200[a]	0.901	−4.513[a]	−5.526[a]
	(0.000)	(0.042)	(0.000)	(0.000)	(0.816)	(0.000)	(0.000)
M2	10.991[a]	−1.522[c]	−6.545[a]	−5.707[a]	0.999	−4.395[a]	−4.669[a]
	(0.000)	(0.064)	(0.000)	(0.000)	(0.841)	(0.000)	(0.000)
M3	11.062[a]	−1.483[c]	−6.540[a]	−7.040[a]	1.044	−4.360[a]	−5.369[a]
	(0.000)	(0.069)	(0.000)	(0.000)	(0.852)	(0.000)	(0.000)

Note [a, b,], [c] refers to rejection of null of no cointegration at 1, 5 and 10% level of significance respectively. Values in parenthesis are *P*-values

Table 9.3 Estimates from FMOLS and DOLS

Var/Model	FMOLS			DOLS		
	M1	M2	M3	M1	M2	M3
lnGr	0.076[a]			0.088[a]		
	0.018			0.027		
	0.000			0.001		
Gr_OR		0.168[a]			0.121[b]	
		0.059			0.057	
		0.005			0.035	
Gr_TRR			0.493[a]			0.535[b]
			0.150			0.232
			0.001			0.022
lnGC	0.030[a]	0.040[a]	0.038[a]	0.035[a]	0.049[a]	0.047[a]
	0.009	0.009	0.009	0.013	0.008	0.011
	0.002	0.000	0.000	0.007	0.000	0.000
lnPoP	−0.284[a]	−0.290[a]	−0.284[a]	−0.274[a]	−0.286[a]	−0.289[a]
	0.088	0.090	0.089	0.095	0.065	0.096
	0.001	0.001	0.002	0.004	0.000	0.003
lnhdx	0.042[a]	0.053[a]	0.048[a]	0.041[a]	0.052[a]	0.046[a]
	0.010	0.010	0.010	0.013	0.008	0.012
	0.000	0.000	0.000	0.002	0.000	0.000
Adj. R Sq.	0.992	0.992	0.992	0.992	0.992	0.992

Note [a], [b] indicate 1 and 5% level of significance, respectively

coefficients of FMOLS interpreted as growth for decentralization measures while as elasticity's for other independent variables as they are in logarithmic form are reported in Table 9.3. Most glaring fact from the above-estimated results in all models is positive and statistically significant coefficient of different versions of decentralization. There by implying that with increase in total grants from Centre to

State or in other words with decrease in decentralization growth in income of states follows the same projection. Thus, the above results indicate state economic growth is positively associated with centralization while as negatively associated with decentralization. More in-depth and through analysis are inferred from reported results while looking for different models separately.

Model 1 captures the effect of total grants from centre as measure of decentralization along with other control variables such as gross capital formation, human development index and population on income. The coefficient of control variables are on expected line and statistically significant. While as coefficient of decentralization measure reveals that as centralization increases GSDP also increases. Model 2 captures the effect of total grants from Centre to state as percentage of states own revenue as a measure of decentralization along with above-mentioned control variables on income. Regarding the coefficient of control variables they are on expected lines with statistically significant in nature and coefficient of decentralization measure corroborates the above findings. Model 3 in which ratio of total grants from Centre to state upon states total revenue receipts as measure for decentralization along with above-mentioned control variables to comprehend the effect of these variables on income mimic the above-mentioned models.

Further to check the robustness and sensitiveness of our results, we have applied another estimation methodology which also takes care of issue of endogeneity namely Dynamic ordinary Least Squares (DOLS). The results are also reported in Table 9.3. The findings corroborate with previous one.

Panel Granger Causality:

Having established the existence of long-run relationship between various measures of fiscal decentralization along with some control variables to that of income, pairwise Dumitrescu-Hurlin (2012) causality test were employed to examine the direction of causality between these variables. In case of Model 1 there exists bidirectional causation between grants from Centre to state and gross state domestic product. Similarly, between lnGSDP and lnhdx bidirectional causation exists while as lnGC is found to granger cause lnGSDP and lnGSDP granger cause lnpop. The results are reported in Table 9.4. For model 2, results of pairwise panel causality test are reported in Table 9.5, which endorse with model 1 except bidirectional causation between gross state domestic product and measure of decentralization. For model 3, results are reported in Table 9.6. The results reveal that neither lnGSDP causes GR_TRR nor GR_TRR causes lnGSDP. Direction of causation between other pairs follows with the above two models.

Table 9.4 Panel Granger causality results for model 1

Results of pairwise Dumitrescu-Hurlin (2012) panel causality test	
$lnGr_{it} -/\rightarrow lnGSDP_{it}$	3.119[a]
$lnGSDP_{it} -/\rightarrow lnGr_{it}$	10.03[a]
$lnGC_{it} -/\rightarrow lnGSDP_{it}$	1.014
$lnGSDP_{it} -/\rightarrow lnGC_{it}$	6.374[a]
$lnpop_{it} -/\rightarrow lnGSDP_{it}$	12.479[a]
$lnGSDP_{it} -/\rightarrow lnpop_{it}$	1.704
$lnhdx_{it} -/\rightarrow lnGSDP_{it}$	2.075[b]
$lnGSDP_{it} -/\rightarrow lnhdx_{it}$	7.204[a]

Note Reported values are of W-Statistic. The null hypothesis of Dumitrescu-Hurlin (2012) causality test that x does not homogeneously cause y. [a], [b] indicate 1 and 5% level of significance, respectively

Table 9.5 Panel Granger causality results for model 2

Results of pairwise Dumitrescu-Hurlin (2012) panel causality test	
$Gr\_OR_{it} -/\rightarrow lnGSDP_{it}$	3.592
$lnGSDP_{it} -/\rightarrow Gr\_OR_{it}$	4.643[c]
$lnGC_{it} -/\rightarrow lnGSDP_{it}$	4.230
$lnGSDP_{it} -/\rightarrow lnGC_{it}$	5.166[b]
$lnpop_{it} -/\rightarrow lnGSDP_{it}$	5.228[b]
$lnGSDP_{it} -/\rightarrow lnpop_{it}$	3.108
$lnhdx_{it} -/\rightarrow lnGSDP_{it}$	5.499[a]
$lnGSDP_{it} -/\rightarrow lnhdx_{it}$	10.453[a]

Note Reported values are of W-Statistic. The null hypothesis of Dumitrescu-Hurlin (2012) causality test that x does not homogeneously cause y. [a], [b], [c] indicate 1%, 5% and 10% level of significance, respectively

Table 9.6 Panel Granger causality results for model 3

Results of pairwise Dumitrescu-Hurlin (2012) panel causality test	
$Gr\_TRR_{it} -/\rightarrow lnGSDP_{it}$	3.305
$lnGSDP_{it} -/\rightarrow Gr\_TRR_{it}$	4.315
$lnGC_{it} -/\rightarrow lnGSDP_{it}$	4.209
$lnGSDP_{it} -/\rightarrow lnGC_{it}$	5.166[b]
$lnpop_{it} -/\rightarrow lnGSDP_{it}$	5.228[b]
$lnGSDP_{it} -/\rightarrow lnpop_{it}$	3.107
$lnhdx_{it} -/\rightarrow lnGSDP_{it}$	5.500[a]
$lnGSDP_{it} -/\rightarrow lnhdx_{it}$	10.452[a]

Note Reported values are of W-Statistic. The null hypothesis of Dumitrescu-Hurlin (2012) causality test that x does not homogeneously cause y. a , b indicate 1 and 5% level of significance, respectively

9.5 Conclusion

The strength of the federal system of an economy depends on the nature and the process intergovernmental transfers happen between the centre and the states. These transfers play an important role in curing the horizontal and vertical imbalances of the economy. Considering the widening gap between the different regions of India, it is a hard choice to decide about the perfect degree of decentralization. Though a higher degree of centralization is criticized lot for hampering the progress of the states, it is not easy to determine the real effect of the decentralization. The study has tried to investigate the effect of decentralization on the state economy via the mechanism of unconditional transfers. Using panel data cointegration and causality techniques we have tried to explore the effect of Grants-in-Aid on the state domestic product. The results reveal that there exists a long-run relationship between the two. The estimates from the study show that grants-in-aid have a positive effect on the states output. However, the study failed to explain the nature of causation between the variables. Besides that results showed that while capital stock and human development expenditure affects positively state domestic product, population has a negative impact.

References

Akai N, Sakata M (2002) Fiscal decentralization contributes to economic growth: evidence from state-level cross-section data for the United States. J Urban Econ 52(1):93–108

Boadway R, Shah A (2007) Intergovernmental fiscal transfers: principles and practice. Washington, DC, World Bank

Davoodi H, Zou HF (1998) Fiscal decentralization and economic growth: a cross-country study. J Urban Econ 43(2):244–257

Dumitrescu EI, Hurlin C (2012) Testing for Granger non-causality in heterogeneous panels. Econ Model 29(4):1450–1460

Iimi A (2005) Decentralization and economic growth revisited: an empirical note. J Urban Econ 57 (3):449–461

Jin J, Zou HF (2005) Fiscal decentralization, revenue and expenditure assignments, and growth in China. J Asian Econ 16(6):1047–1064

Kao C, Chiang MH (1999) On the estimation and inference of a cointegrated regression in panel data. Available at SSRN 1807931

Kao C, Chiang MH (2001) On the estimation and inference of a cointegrated regression in panel data. In: Nonstationary panels, panel cointegration, and dynamic panels . Emerald Group Publishing Limited, pp 179–222

Lin JY, Liu Z (2000) Fiscal decentralization and economic growth in China*. Econ Dev Cult Chang 49(1):1–21

Maddala GS, Wu S (1999) A comparative study of unit root tests with panel data and a new simple test. Oxford Bull Econ Stat 61(S1):631–652

Musgrave RA (1983) Public finance, now and then. FinanzArchiv/Public Finance Analysis, (H. 1), pp 1–13

Oates W (1972) Fiscal decentralization. Harcourt Brace Javanovich, New York

Oates WE (1999) An essay on fiscal federalism. J Econ Lit 37(3):1120–1149

Oates WE (2005) Toward a second-generation theory of fiscal federalism. Int Tax Pub Finance 12 (4):349–373

Pedroni P (2001) Fully modified OLS for heterogeneous cointegrated panels. Advances in Econometrics 15:93–130

Pedroni P (2004) Panel cointegration: asymptotic and finite sample properties of pooled time series tests with an application to the PPP hypothesis. Econometric Theory 20(03):597–625

Pesaran MH (2007) A simple panel unit root test in the presence of cross-section dependence. J Appl Econometrics 22(2):265–312

Stock JH, Watson MW (1993) A simple estimator of cointegrating vectors in higher order integrated systems. Econometrica: J Econometric Soc 783–820

Tarigan MS (2003) Fiscal decentralization and economic development: a cross-country empirical study

Tiebout CM (1956) A pure theory of local expenditures. J Polit Econ 416–424

Woller GM, Phillips K (1998) Fiscal decentralisation and IDC economic growth: an empirical investigation. J Dev Stud 34(4):139–148

Zhang T, Zou HF (1998) Fiscal decentralization, public spending, and economic growth in China. J Pub Econ 67(2):221–240

Zhang T, Zou HF (2001) The growth impact of intersectoral and intergovernmental allocation of public expenditure: with applications to China and India. China Econ Rev 12(1):58–81

Part III
Emerging Issues

Chapter 10
Public Debt and Economic Growth in India: Evidence from Granger Causality Test

Nityasundar Manik and Naseer Ahmed Khan

Abstract In the eve of inconclusive controversy over the "cause-effect" relationship between public debt and economic growth, this paper tries to examine this dynamic relationship empirically for the Indian economy over the period of 1980–1981 to 2015–2016. This paper applies the time-series techniques like unit root test, VAR lag selection criteria, Johansen cointegration test, VECM, VEC granger causality test, impulse response function, and variance decomposition function. The application of Johansen test on first order integrated series shows the presence of long-run cointegration among variables like domestic debt, external debt, and economic growth. The VECM model found the statistically significant and negative coefficient of error correction term in external debt equation expressing the restoration of the long-run equilibrium at the rate of 6.83% every year between growth, domestic debt, and external debt. The infliction of the VEC Granger causality test noticed that there is no feedback relationship among the variables in short run, but there exists the unidirectional causality from economic growth and domestic debt to external debt in long run. The result of impulse response function and variance decomposition function also confirms the long-run causality from growth and domestic debt to external debt. Therefore, these empirical results suggest that reliance on debt for development purposes is not a safe option, even though the presence of no feedback relationship among the said variables in short runs. So, Indian economy should ensure higher growth rate while accumulating public debt and should extend its efforts to increase the revenue to finance the development expenditure.

JEL Classification H63 · O40 · E43 · F34

Keywords Public debt · Economic growth · Domestic debt · External debt

---

N. Manik (✉) · N.A. Khan
School of Economics, University of Hyderabad, Hyderabad, Telangana 500046, India
e-mail: nitya.baban@gmail.com

N.A. Khan
e-mail: drkhan58@gmail.com

N.A. Khan (ed.), *Challenges and Issues in Indian Fiscal Federalism*,
India Studies in Business and Economics, https://doi.org/10.1007/978-981-10-6217-9_10

10.1 Introduction

Nowadays, it has been seen that one of the thought provoking issue, that is, "what is the relationship between public debt and economic growth?" has been entrapping a noticeable consideration of the researchers, academicians, as well as policy makers. Before addressing the said burning issue, one question remained unsolved is that between debt and economic growth, "which one is the cause? And which one is the effect?". Some literature like Amoateng et al. (1996), Karagol (2000), Butts (2009), Ferreira (2009), Egbetunde (2012), Wadad (2012) advocated that the debt is a cause of the economic growth. The causation of the public debt to the economic growth may be positive (Jayaraman et al. 2008; Putunoi et al. 2013; Barik 2012; Fincke and Greiner 2014) or adverse (Lin 2000; Schclarek 2004; Mohamed 2005; Akram 2011, Rais et al. 2012; Georgiev 2012; Bal and Rath 2014) depending upon the nature of expenditure of debt amount. On contrast, some literature like Dritsaki (2013), Ahmed et al (2000) were of the view that public debt is an effect of the economic growth. Higher or lower economic growth may necessitate the lower or higher incurring of public debt, respectively. Hence, there is no concrete idea on this issue so far. Therefore, the "cause-effect" puzzle between the said variables is un-simplified and inconclusive. This inconclusive issue for the world economy in general and of the Indian economy, in particular, creates a huge debate among the intellectuals, researchers, academicians, and policy makers. Keeping this issue in consideration, the brief statistical description of the growth trajectory of total public debt (TPD), domestic debt (DD), external debt (ED) and GDP at market price (a proxy for economic growth) evidences the background of the emergence of the causal issue in Indian economy since 1980.

10.1.1 Statistical Evidence

Getting a better insight of the statistical evidence on the current issue for the Indian economy, the whole period of study is, on the basis of Fig. 10.2, segregated into four different phases viz. 1980–1981 to 1990–1991 entitled as pre-economic reforms, 1991–1992 to 1996–1997 as immediate economic reforms, 1997–1998 to 2002–2003 as post economic reforms and 2003–2004 to 2015–2016 as post-FRBM Act.[1] During the first 30 years of independence spanning from 1950 to 1980, the fiscal position of the central, as well as the state governments, was under comfortable level. In that period, the country witnessed some sort of revenue surplus and moderate fiscal and primary deficit. However, in 1979–1980, the revenue surplus turned into the deficit and fiscal condition of both governments went into a

[1]The FRBM act brought the formalization in the fiscal discipline through the mechanism of slashing down the deficit in fiscal indicators like revenue deficit, fiscal deficit and primary deficit and, thereby, maintaining the sustainability and transparency in fiscal discipline.

fiscal stress due to heavy automatic monetization of the fiscal deficit by Reserve Bank of India (RBI) and reckless expenditure of both the government (Kaur et al 2012). Because of these, the debt/GDP ratio started rising from 46.48 to 68.85% in pre-reform periods. In the same period, the compound annual growth rate (CAGR) of the TPD, DD, and ED displayed in Table 10.6 reported at 18.17, 17.77, and 20.24%, respectively, which are substantially higher than the growth rate of GDP (13.27%). However, the question remains whether the higher growth of debt variables causes a lower growth of GDP or vice versa. But, in the immediate economic reform phase, the drastic deterioration in the annual average growth rate of TPD, DD and ED to 12.59, 14.05 and 06.49% correspondingly and mild increase of the CAGR of GDP had brought down the debt/GDP ratio to 64.37%. The credit of the desirable change in the said variable are, along with LPG (Liberalization, Privatization and Globalization), a plethora of fiscal reforms like simplification of tax procedures, stimulus to strengthen the contribution of direct tax to the total tax revenue, conversion of excise into a VAT and improvement in tax administration, etc. (Rao and Rao 2006). However, this improvement could not be sustained thereafter because of industrial slowdown, poor public sector performance, Fifth Pay Commission award and lower performance of tax buoyancy etc. (Rao and Rao 2006). The sharp decrease in growth rate of GDP to 9.33% and meager increment in growth rate during post-reform phase instigated the debt/GDP ratio to soar from 66.29% in 1997–1998 and reached at second highest of 82.86% in 2002–2003 (highest 83.23% in 2003–2004). A sincere effort was made in 2003–2004 in the field of fiscal discipline, i.e., the introduction of Fiscal Responsibility and Budget Management (FRBM) Act in 2003–2004, which slashed down the growth rate of the debt variables and facilitated the GDP to witness a higher growth of 13.83%. Since the growth rate of GDP is higher than the growth rate of TPD (11.63%), DD (11.91%) and ED (7.07%), the debt/GDP ratio degenerated sharply to about 66% in 2015–2016.

Here, the major finding from the annual growth rate analysis follows that there has been an inverse relationship between growth rate of public debt and growth rate of GDP. But, nowhere this inverse relationship mentions about the causality of both the variables, i.e., higher or lower growth of public debt leads to lower or higher GDP growth rate (economic growth), respectively, as well as the reverse causality, i.e., low or high growth rate of GDP, is likely to induce or to deduce incurring of public debt. Therefore, the question of "cause-effect" between the concerned variables for India is yet to be answered, and this paper addresses this question by evaluating its two objectives. Namely,

I. To investigate the causal relationship between domestic debt and economic growth
II. To examine the causal relationship between external debt and economic growth.

The paper has been organized into 5 sections. Besides Sect. 10.1 of introduction, Sect. 10.2 deals with the review of the literature focused on nature of the relationship between public debt and economic growth. Section 10.3 is about the brief description about the variable, data sources and proposed methodology used in the analysis. The results of the empirical analysis are explained in Sect. 10.4. Lastly, the Sect. 10.5 concerns with the conclusion and implication of the results.

10.2 Literature Reviews

Over last three decades, numerous studies have been conducted on the relationship between public debt and economic growth. But, scanty literature is available in the present context of an Indian economy. The brief overview of the relevant literature is summarized below. To have a better insight into the same compatibility, the whole study of the literature is segregated between theoretical reviews and empirical reviews (based on causal, linear, and nonlinear nature of the relationship).

10.2.1 Theoretical Reviews

Classical[2] and Neoclassical economist viewed the role of public debt in the area of economic growth differently on the basis of their faith in the role of the government in the economy. Classical as well as the Neoclassical economists considered debt as the degenerative aspects of the economic growth. Because of the debt amount, which could have been used for productive purposes, was spume offered for unproductive in an exaggerating manner. Going by this Frame, Diamond (1965) postulated that both types of public debts (internal and external) make the reduction in the available lifetime consumption of taxpayers, as well as, their savings and, in turn, agitate capital stock and, then, economic growth adversely. Prof Buchanan (1958) in his book "Public Principles of Public Debt" holds that so long as the burden of debt can be transferred from the present generation, who subscribes the debt voluntarily, to the future generation, who pays taxes compulsorily to its return, public debt has a negative impact on the economy. Modigliani (1961), redefining the Buchanan's contribution, wrangled that posterity will be no longer a burden if the debt finance could bequeath to the real income of future generation. Elmendorf and Mankiw (1999), as an adherent to the crowding–out hypothesis, noticed that higher long-term interest rates, resulting from higher debt financed for government budget deficits, can crowd-out private investment and, thus, dampen the potential economic growth.

Completely different opinion proposed by Keynes expounded that the accumulation of public debt did not put any infliction on the path of the economic

[2]Classical economists like J.B. Say, Adam Smith, Ricardo, Malthus, J.S. Mill, Bastable, Paul Leroy–Beaulieu, etc.

growth rather boosted the tempo of economic growth. According to him, through debt creation, the government can stimulate saving streams, put the unemployed resources into mobilization, and, thus, raise their productivity and capital formation, which ultimately increases the national income. This surplus national income, in turn, facilitates in tax collection to treat the debt. In a similar vein, A.P. Lerner (1948) advocated that an internal debt does not create any burden on the future generation because of the transfer of incomes from one group to another within an economy. Therefore, it is rightly remarked as "the right hand owes to the left hand." Nevertheless, in the case of external debt, if used productively, it puts no more burdens to the further generation and becomes a stimulus to the economic growth and vice versa.

In the Ricardian Equivalence or Ricardo-De Viti-Barro Equivalence theorem Barro (1979), the ascendancy of government debt on the economy is neutral. Because, if the government will go for deficit financing through debt creation in the current period, consumers, acknowledging to be rational and far-sighted, can predict the imposition of higher taxation on them in future. Accordingly, they start saving in such a way that the present value of saving is equivalent to discounted future tax and thereto, discounted value of deficit financing through debt. Because of which there is no change in level saving and investment in the economy. So, this leads to a neutral impact on national income.

10.2.2 Empirical Reviews

The empirical analysis starts with the discussion of the linear nature of the relationship between debt and economic growth. Lin (2000), by analyzing the debt and economic growth nexus in both steady state equilibrium and comparative steady state equilibrium framework, remarked that the government debt will retard the growth rate of per capita output if the growth rate is less than the real interest rate and reverse explanation is also true. The empirical study of Mohamed (2005) and Akram (2011) for Sudan and for Pakistan specifically found that public debt (internal and external) and debt servicing treated the economic growth and investment adversely through twin debt problem of "debt overhang"[3] and "crowding out."[4] Similarly, Schclarek (2004) and Rais et al. (2012) got negative and statistical

[3]**Debt overhang** is the condition of an organization (for example, a business, government, or family) that has existing debt so great that it cannot easily borrow more money, even when that new borrowing is actually a good investment that would more than pay for itself. Simply, it asserts that if there is a possibility that countries' future debt will be more than its repayment abilities.

[4]The **crowding out effect** is an economic theory stipulating that rises in public sector spending drive down or even eliminate private sector spending. Again, if govt will go for higher ED and if the greater share of public debt (foreign capital) is used to treat the debt obligations, then very little would remain available to finance investment and growth; this cannel is also known as the "crowding out effect" of ED.

significant bearing of both domestic and external debts on the economic growth. To boot, the outcome of Georgiev (2012) reveals a negative, significant, and indirect link between the concerned variables through the instrument of crowding out investment due to higher interest rate and higher debt servicing cost. On the other hand, some of the literatures like Jayaraman et al. (2008), Putunoi et al. (2013), Fincke and Greiner (2014) argued a significant and positive correlation between the debts to GDP. This result was so because the emerging market economies are on the transition path of high growth rates due to heavy public investment in growth-enhancing public sectors like infrastructure.

Some of the literature was of the view that there is, often, a nonlinear nexus between the questioned variables with a threshold level of debt to GDP ratio, beyond which the reverse relation persists. Balassone et al. (2010), covering the study period in Italy over 1961–2009, discovered a negative link between debt and growth with threshold level at above 100 % of debt to GDP ratio. Checherita and rother (2010) made an empirical study in 123 euro area countries over a period of about 40 years of 1970–2008 and realized a nonlinear concave link with a threshold at 90–100% of GDP. Cecchetti et al. (2011), practicing the new data set on debt levels in 18 OECD countries from 1980 to 2010, came with a nonlinear nexus of debt-growth with the doorway at 85–90% of GDP. Again, Reinhart and Rogoff (2010) exhibited that average post-World War II economic growth was dramatically declining in advanced economies, once the debt to GDP ratio was above a 90% threshold level. Kumar and Woo (2010) also admitted same threshold level at 90% of GDP for the advanced and emerging economies.

Another contesting view is that of ‘causal” relationship between debt variables and economic growth. The literature of Butts (2009) on panel data of 27 Latin American countries and Caribbean countries, Ferreira (2009) on OECD countries, Egbetunde (2012) on Nigeria inquired into the “cause and effect” nexus between public debt and economic growth and found the bidirectional causality between them. This bidirectional causality resembles the circumstances that the higher debt leads to lower economic growth and lower economic growth influence the evolution of higher debt. The research work of Karagol (2000) on Turkey for the period of 1956–1996 and Dritsaki (2013) on Greece over the vintage of 1960–2011, however, stumbled on unidirectional causality from debt to growth and from growth to debt, respectively. Again, Choudhury (1994) and Tasos (2014) worked on Greece counted no causality between two concerned variables. In the case of ED, the scholars noticed the mix results. Wadad (2012), Amoateng et al. (1996) and Ahmed et al (2000) recognized the bidirectional, unidirectional (from ED to growth) and no feedback between ED and growth correspondingly.

In an Indian context, Singh (1999) investigated the link between the domestic debt and economic growth in India by exercising cointegration test and Granger causality test for the period of 1959–1995. The study fortified the Ricardian Equivalence Hypothesis (neutral effect) between them. Barik (2012) determined the positive relationship between the public debt and economic growth, in India, through its (debt) potential impact on induced investment covering the period of 1981–2011. Kaur et al (2012) found that there is a statistically significant nonlinear relationship between public debt and economic growth in India with threshold level at 61% of GDP implying its negative impact on economic growth at a higher level. Bal and Rath (2014) examined the both short run and long-run effect of public debt on economic growth in India during 1980–2011. The finding of the study pointed out the significant negative relationship between the concerned variables.

After discussing both theoretical and empirical literature, it can be concluded that there is no concrete link between the concerned variables rather it differs with the different countries, period, and instrumental variables like sociopolitical, institutional, and economic variables taken in the literature.

10.3 Variables, Data Sources, and Methodology

The present study is exclusively based on a secondary source of annual time-series data for India spanning from 1980–1981 to 2015–2016. The data on GDP,[5] TPD,[6] DD,[7] ED[8] are sourced from Hand Book of Statistics (RBI), Indiastat, Budget Document (GoI). Debt (DD or ED) to GDP ratio, contemplated as the important variable to judge the relationship between public debt and economic growth, represents the amount of GDP required to be liquidated for the repayment of the debt. It should be noted that TPD, i.e., Combined total liabilities of the center & states and DD, i.e., Combined domestic liabilities of Center and States have been revised to include "reserve funds," "deposits and advances," and "contingency fund" of State Governments. ED is evaluated at current exchange rate. Besides, Data in respect of TPD are inclusive of securities/treasury bills under Market Stabilization Scheme (MSS) and exclusive of NCT Delhi from 2005–2006 onwards.

[5]GDP at the current price at market price is used as a proxy for economic growth. Because all other variables such as TPD, DD, ED are expressed in current price.

[6]The vibrant concept 'public debt' plays a pivotal role in the traditional as well as modern or contemporary public finance. Literarily, public debt demonstrates the loans or liabilities raised by the government with a corresponding commitment to the repayment within a stipulated time period. Total Public Debt (TPD) is the combination of Domestic Debt (DD) and External Debt (ED).

[7]Domestic Debt (DD), otherwise termed as National Debt, refers to the loans or borrowings raised by the public authorities within the legal jurisdiction of the economy. DD is not only composed of internal debt but also of small savings, provident funds & other accounts and reserve funds & deposits. The main internal sources from which the government can amass funds are individuals, non-banking financial institutions, commercial banks and central banks of the concerned economy.

[8]A debt is said to be external debt (ED) if/when a loan is floated outside the country. Its main sources are foreign financial institutions, foreign governments, and foreign multinationals and international organization such as IMF, IBRD, and ADB etc.

10.3.1 Specification of Methodology

In this section, this paper proposes different methodologies to be appreciated for the empirical analysis of the stipulated objectives. As the paper is completely contingent upon the time-series data, it generally applies various time-series techniques like unit root test for checking the stationarity property of the interested series; lag selection criteria for determining the maximum lag in the series; Johansen–Juselius (JJ) cointegration test to verify long-run relationship between the series; Vector Error Correction Model (VECM) to correct short run dynamics heading to long-run equilibrium; VEC Granger causality test owing to access the direction of causality; and impulse response function and variance decomposition function to capture innovation accounting in endogenous variables in future forecasting horizons.

10.3.1.1 Unit Root Test

The result derived from the non-stationary series can't be used for generalization and can't be reliable for the prediction. Hence, it is customary to ascertain the stationarity property of the time series with a view to avoid spurious or redundant results. There are both informal tests like time-series plots and correlogram as well as formal tests like Dickey–Fuller test, Augmented Dickey–Fuller test (ADF), Phillips-Perron test (PP), Kwiatkowski test, etc., available for testing the stationarity of the series. But, this paper engages both ADF and PP test to identify the order of integration of the underlying series.

The ADF unit root test procedure requires the estimation of the following equation,

$$\Delta X_t = \Upsilon + \alpha X_{t-1} + \sum_{i=1}^{k} \beta i \Delta X_{t-1} + \varepsilon_t \tag{10.1}$$

Where,

X_t is time series (here LNGDP_t or LNDDR_t or LNEDR_t)
Υ is the drift parameter
k is that lag value which ensures ε_t white noise series,
Δ is difference operator,
α and β are parameters to be estimated.

The Phillips-Perron unit root test requires the estimation of the following equation (without trend)

$$X_t = \Upsilon + \alpha X_{t-1} + u_t \tag{10.2}$$

Where, t = 1,2,3,…..T.

u_t is the random error term

The null and alternative hypothesis for the existence of unit root in the series X_t in Eqs. (10.1) and (10.2) is $H_0 : \alpha = 0$ against $H_1 : \alpha < 0$. If the test statistic is not statistically significant, i.e., $\alpha = 0$, then X_t is non-stationary while otherwise (i.e., $\alpha < 0$) is statistically proved, it will be inferred that the said series is stationary and can validly be used for any time-series applications. However, the PP test has been undertaken as a preference to ADF test in the line of two reasons. First, it (PP test) does not require an assumption of homoscedasticity of the error term and; second, it rectifies the serial correlation and autoregressive heteroscedasticity of the error term.

10.3.1.2 Lag Selection Criteria

The inevitable application, either directly or indirectly, of a famous time-series technique termed as Auto regressive (AR) in the time-series analysis necessitates the exercise of determination of the lag length of the time series. To have the determination satisfied, many lag selection criteria, such as Aikaike's Information Criteria (AIC), Schwarz Information Criteria (SIC), Hannan–Quinn Criteria (HQ), Final prediction error (FPE), Bayesian Information Criteria (BIC) are to be used in the present. By Guideline, the test selects the maximum lag at which either the majority of tests should be statistically significant or AIC & FPE should be significant at 5% level of significance (Liew 2004).

10.3.1.3 Johansen and Juselius (JJ) Cointegration Test

Abstractly, JJ cointegration test not only verifies long-run compatibility among the non-stationary variables but also explains the extent of deviation of the series from long-run equilibrium. Here, the equilibrium relationship may be causal, behavioral or simply a reduced form affiliation among similar trending variables.

The specification of the test may, symbolically, be written as follows.

If $\mathrm{LNGDP}_t \sim \mathrm{I}(0)$, $\mathrm{LNDDR}_t \sim \mathrm{I}(0)$ and $\mathrm{LNEDR}_t \sim \mathrm{I}(0)$, then the linear combination of these series can be inscribed as

$$\mathrm{LNGDP}_t = \beta_0 + \beta_1 \mathrm{LNDDR}_t + \beta_2 \mathrm{LNEDR}_t + u_t \qquad (10.3)$$

The concept of cointegration includes the following cointegration test procedures.

Firstly, estimation of the unknown parameters in Eq. (10.3)

Secondly, test to find out whether the estimated residuals $\hat{u}_t$ appears to be I(0) or not by running

$$\text{ADF test on } \Delta\hat{u}_t = \alpha\hat{u}_{t-1} + \sum_{i=0}^{k} \beta i\, \Delta\hat{u}_{t-1} + \mathrm{e}_t$$

Thirdly, if $\hat{u} \sim \mathrm{I}(0)$ is proved, there exists cointegration among LNGDP_t, LNDDR_t and LNEDR_t.

Lastly, detection of the number of co integrating vectors through both trace statistics and maximum likelihood statistics.

Briefly, JJ cointegration test ascertains the imperative theoretical framework for analyzing the dynamics of instantaneous changes in a pair of the concerned variables along with their valuable long-run information.

10.3.1.4 Vector Error Correction Model (VECM)

The cointegration theory provides a proper theoretical justification for error correction framework that short-run dynamics are influenced by the deviation from long-run equilibrium. So, the "Granger Representation Theory" states that once cointegration of one set of variables is conformed, there exists a valid error correction representation of the data and the reverse is true. Hence, two different sorts of equations arise

Long-run equation which is the similar with the long-run cointegrating equation, i.e., Eq. (10.3).

The short-run model or the vector error correction equations.

$$\begin{aligned}\Delta\mathrm{LNGDP}_t = \alpha_1 + \sum_{i=1}^{k} \Upsilon_{1i}\, \Delta\mathrm{LNGDP}_{t-i} + \sum_{i=1}^{k} \delta_{1i}\, \Delta\mathrm{LNDDR}_{t-i} \\ + \sum_{i=1}^{k} \xi_{1i}\, \Delta\mathrm{LNEDR}_{t-i} + \theta_1\, \mathrm{ECT}_{t-1} + \mathrm{e}_{1t}\end{aligned} \tag{10.4}$$

$$\begin{aligned}\Delta\mathrm{LNDDR}_t = \alpha_2 + \sum_{i=1}^{k} \Upsilon_{2i}\, \Delta\mathrm{LNGDP}_{t-i} + \sum_{i=1}^{k} \delta_{2i}\, \Delta\mathrm{LNDDR}_{t-i} \\ + \sum_{i=1}^{k} \xi_{2i}\, \Delta\mathrm{LNEDR}_{t-i} + \theta_2\, \mathrm{ECT}_{t-1} + \mathrm{e}_{2t}\end{aligned} \tag{10.5}$$

$$\begin{aligned}\Delta\mathrm{LNEDR}_t = \alpha_3 + \sum_{i=1}^{k} \Upsilon_{3i}\, \Delta\mathrm{LNGDP}_{t-i} + \sum_{i=1}^{k} \delta_{3i}\, \Delta\mathrm{LNDDR}_{t-i} \\ + \sum_{i=1}^{k} \xi_{3i}\, \Delta\mathrm{LNEDR}_{t-i} + \theta_3\, \mathrm{ECT}_{t-1} + \mathrm{e}_{3t}\end{aligned} \tag{10.6}$$

where

Δ shows the difference operator, k is the number of lags, e_{it} (i runs from 1 to 3) is the stochastic error term with zero mean and constant variance.

ECT_{t-1} $= LNGDP_t - \beta_0 - \beta_1 LNDDR_t - \beta_2 LNEDR_t$, i.e., one period lagged value of the error derived from the estimated Eq. (10.3).

θ_s required to be negative and significant depicts the speed of adjustment of short-run dynamics tending to the long-run equilibrium.

Thus, VECM reconciles the short-run behavior of an economic variable with its long-run behavior.

10.3.1.5 VEC Granger Causality Test

Granger causality test, as a statistical hypothesis test for forecasting the time series from another time series, is going to be applied in the present study with a view to recognizing the 'Cause and Effect" nexus among the $LNGDP_t$, $LNDDR_t$, and $LNEDR_t$. It is said that once cointegration is conformed, causality must exist in at least one direction and the reverse is also true. The VEC Granger causality test, otherwise known as Block Exogeneity Wald Test, is contemplated as an amplified and comprehensive test of causality than standard causality test because the VEC approach to Granger causality incorporates the valuable information from the cointegrating properties of the variable of interest.

10.3.1.6 VECM Impulse Response Function

The VECM model has the scope for innovation accounting, where the impact of cross-equation shocks can be analyzed. Particularly, the model presented here consists of three endogenous variables and, therefore, considers three types of shocks, which are to be transmitted through LNGDP channel, LNDDR channel, and LNEDR channel. The impulse response function, otherwise known as 'Innovation accounting' traces the effect of one of the innovations on current and future values of the endogenous variables. Therefore, the impulse response function may be used in the VECM system to describe the dynamic behaviors of the whole system with respect to innovations.

10.3.1.7 Variance Decomposition Analysis

Again, the 'variance decomposition' separates the variations in an endogenous variable into some component shocks. The variance decomposition provides information about the relative importance of each random innovation in the matter of affecting the variables. These may provide better insight into interrelations between the endogenous variables.

10.4 Result of Empirical Analysis

This section deals with the results of the empirical analysis applied on the series of $LNGDP_t$, $LNDDR_t$, and $LNEDR_t$ owing to address the stipulated objectives of the paper. The inferences drawn from each test already illustrated in the previous section are analyzed below.

10.4.1 Results of Unit Roots

As evident from Table 10.1, the ADF test and PP test failed to reject the null hypothesis of "presence of unit root" in the $LNGDP_t$, $LNDDR_t$, and $LNEDR_t$ series at the level. Because their respective *p*-value in both ADF test and PP test stand higher than the conventional significance level of 0.01 (1%) and 0.05 (5%). Hence, the testing of the series will be processed to its first difference in both tests. Then, at the first difference, the both tests rejected the null hypothesis at 5% level of significance for $LNGDP_t$ and $LNDDR_t$. However, in case of the series $LNEDR_t$, ADF test, and PP test reject the null hypothesis at 1% level of significance. In nutshell, the unit root test says that all the series are integrated at their first difference.

10.4.2 Result of Lag Selection Criteria

The findings of lag selection criterion depicted in Table 10.2 substantiate the information that, at lag 2, LR test, FPE test, AIC test, and HQ test are statistically significant at 5% level of significance. It implies the selection of lag 2 as the maximum lag in the series. Along with following the usual guideline of selecting optimum lag, that is majority of significant criterions, FPE criterion and AIC test reckoned as superior criterions are also significant at lag 2.

Table 10.1 Result of unit root test

Variables	ADF statistics		PP statistics	
	t-Statistics	*P*-Values	Adj *t*-Statistics	*P*-Values
LNGDP	−0.6149	0.8542	−0.8430	0.7941
ΔLNGDP	−3.1051**	0.0356	−3.1649**	0.0311
LNDDR	−2.8779*	0.0585	−2.4150	0.1451
ΔLNDDR	−3.5252**	0.0133	−3.5576**	0.0122
LNEDR	0.4602	0.9828	0.2836	0.9740
ΔLNEDR	−5.6584***	0.0000	−5.7252***	0.0000

Note ***denotes 1% level of significance. ** encrypts 5% level of significance. *P*-value depicts MacKinnon (1996) one-sided *p*-values. Δ is the first difference operator. *Source* Author's estimation

Table 10.2 Result of lag selection criteria

Lag	LogL	LR	FPE	AIC	SC	HQ
0	−12.66891	NA	0.000552	1.010898	1.149671	1.056134
1	187.1852	348.1331	2.49e-09	−11.30227	−10.74718**	−11.12133
2	201.3886	21.99225**	1.81e-09**	−11.63797**	−10.66656	−11.32132**
3	204.9599	4.838566	2.70e-09	−11.28774	−9.900006	−10.83537
4	213.3443	9.736668	3.09e-09	−11.24802	−9.443968	−10.65994
5	222.1821	8.552740	3.68e-09	−11.23755	−9.017186	−10.51377

**indicates lag order selected by the criterion
LR: sequential modified LR test statistic (each test at 5% level)
FPE: Final prediction error
AIC: Akaike information criterion
SC: Schwarz information criterion
HQ: Hannan–Quinn information criterion

10.4.3 Result of JJ Cointegration Test

The first order integration of the concerned series and stationarity of the derived error term at level head to the use of Johansen and Juselius(JJ) technique of cointegration with Trace test and Maximum Likelyhood test in order to track the long-run relationship among the series.

Empirical results from Table 10.3 reveals that at $r = 0$, both the trace statistics (31.4751) and max-eigen statistics (22.5482) exceed their corresponding critical vales of 29.7971 and 21.1316. The result evidences the rejection of the null hypothesis of no cointegrating equations. But, both test became failure to reject the "presence of at least one cointegrating equation" and, hence, are insignificant at $r \leq 1$. So, both tests authenticate one cointegrating equation in the series at 5% level of significance. Thus, it can be reckoned that the long-run relationship exists between $LNGDP_t$, $LNDDR_t$, and $LNEDR_t$

Table 10.3 Result of JJ cointegration test

Null hypothesis	Eigen value	Statistics		5% critical value	
LNGDP, LNDDR, LNEDR ($K = 3$)		Trace test	Max-Eigen	Trace test	Max-Eigen
$r^{**} = 0$	0.4848	31.4751 (0.0317)	22.5482 (0.0314)	29.7971	21.1316
$r \leq 1$	0.1752	8.9269 (0.3722)	6.5487 (0.5438)	15.4947	14.2646
$r \leq 2$	0.0676	2.3782 (0.1230)	2.3782 (0.1230)	3.8414	3.8415

Note **indicates rejection of null hypothesis at 5% level of significance. Figures in the parenthesis show MacKinnon–Haug–Michelis (1999) p-values. *Source* Author's estimation

10.4.4 Result of Vector Error Correction Model (VECM)

Once the determination of a number of cointegrating equations is accomplished, and if a set of variables are found to have one or more cointegrating vectors, then VEC model is the suitable estimation technique to identify both the short and long-run association between the variables and also ascertain the rate of adjustment of deviations to the equilibrium. In this analysis, as cointegrating equation is one, the utilization of VEC model is inevitable.

The result of the VECM Eqs. (10.4), (10.5), and (10.6) is documented below.

$$\begin{aligned}\Delta \text{LNGDP} = {} & 0.0539 + 0.6198\,\Delta \text{LNGDP}_{t-1} - 0.0381\,\Delta \text{LNGDP}_{t-2} + 0.0597\,\Delta \text{LNDDR}_{t-1} \\ & - 0.0586\,\Delta \text{LNDDR}_{t-2} + 0.0675\,\Delta \text{LNEDR}_{t-1} \\ & + 0.0036\,\Delta \text{LNEDR}_{t-2} - 0.0004\,\text{ECT}_{t-1}\end{aligned} \tag{10.7}$$

$$\begin{aligned}\Delta \text{LNDDR} = {} & 0.1136 - 0.5857\,\Delta \text{LNGDP}_{t-1} - 0.1729\,\Delta \text{LNGDP}_{t-2} + 0.0912\,\Delta \text{LNDDR}_{t-1} \\ & - 0.1189\,\Delta \text{LNDDR}_{t-2} + 0.0675\,\Delta \text{LNEDR}_{t-1} \\ & + 0.0461\,\Delta \text{LNEDR}_{t-2} - 0.0078\,\text{ECT}_{t-1}\end{aligned} \tag{10.8}$$

$$\begin{aligned}\Delta \text{LNEDR} = {} & 0.1017 - 0.5532\,\Delta \text{LNGDP}_{t-1} - 0.3968\,\Delta \text{LNGDP}_{t-2} + 1.3473\,\Delta \text{LNDDR}_{t-1} \\ & - 0.6100\,\Delta \text{LNDDR}_{t-2} + 0.1957\,\Delta \text{LNEDR}_{t-1} \\ & + 0.0291\,\Delta \text{LNEDR}_{t-2} - 0.0683^{***}\,\text{ECT}_{t-1}\end{aligned} \tag{10.9}$$

Note: *** denotes 1 percent level of significance Source: Author's estimation Where, $\text{ECT}_{t-1} = \text{LNGDP}_{t-1} + 5.2512\ \text{LNDDR}_{t-1} + 1.0995\ \text{LNEDR}_{t-1} - 33.3936$, i.e., cointegrating equation

The results of the Eqs. (10.7), (10.8), and (10.9) establish the fact that since the coefficient of ECT_{t-1} is not equal to zero in all equations, it can be inferred that the model is not out of the equilibrium. But, the statistically significant and negative coefficient of ECT_{t-1} in ΔLNEDR helps in restoring the long-run equilibrium at the rate of 6.83% every year between LNGDP_t, LNDDR_t, and LNEDR_t.

10.4.5 Result of VEC Causality Test

Having conformed to the stationarity and presence of cointegration among LNGDP_t, LNDDR_t, and LNEDR_t, it is said that there must exist causal relationship in at least one direction. Here, testing of causal relationship will be made between one dependent variable with an independent variable jointly with its current as well as its lagged value. The analysis of the short causality depicted in Table 10.4

Table 10.4 Results of VEC Granger causality

Dependent variables	Sources of causality			
	Short-run causality			Long-run causality
	Chi-square statistics (Prob)			*t*-statistics
	ΔLNGDP	ΔLNDDR	ΔLNEDR	ECT_{t-1}
ΔLNGDP	–	0.1224 (0.9406)	0.0661 (0.9675)	−0.0776
ΔLNDDR	1.4360 (0.4877)	–	1.9226 (0.3824)	−1.0530
ΔLNEDR	0.2004 (0.9046)	2.0360 (0.3613)	–	−2.9846***

Note *** indicates rejection of null hypothesis at 1% level of significance. *Source* Author's estimation

reports that there is no causality in either of direction among the variables. So far as long-run causality is concerned, the significant t-statistics of the coefficients for the ECT_{t-1} in ΔLNEDR conforms the long-run causality from $LNGDP_t$, $LNDDR_t$ to $LNED_t$. Briefly, the VEC Granger causality test unveils the statistics that there is no causal relationship between debt variables and economic growth but there exists the unidirectional causality from economic growth and domestic debt to external debt in long run.

10.4.6 Result of VECM Impulse Response Function

In Fig. 10.1, it can be observed that the LNGDP doesn't respond to the innovation transmitted through the LNDDR and LNEDR in short run as well as in long run. In case of LNDDR, the shock of innovation in LNDDR will dominate over shocks of the innovation in LNGDP in a bid to influence the LNDDR in future. The LNEDR responds immediately to the innovations transmitted through LNEDR channel by rising above base line. However, this transmission in short lived because its influence lowers in long future. It is the innovations channelized through LNGDR which will bring change in the LNEDR in the medium term, and will dominate the influence of LNEDR in long run, in brief, economic growth affects external debt in long run.

10.4.7 Result of Variance Decomposition Analysis

Table 10.5 shows that the shocks transmitted through the LNGDP channel accounted for the entire variation in LNGDP in the initial period. The impact of this

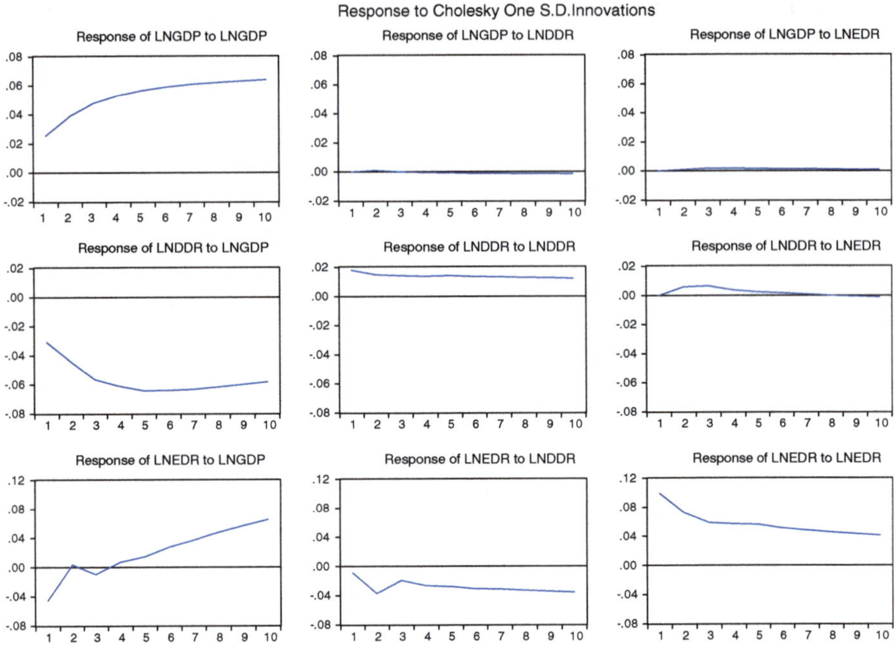

Fig. 10.1 Result of VECM impulse response function, *Source* Author's estimation

Table 10.5 Result of variance decomposition

Var. Decom. of LNGDP				
Period	S.E.	LNGDP	LNDDR	LNEDR
1	0.0255	100.000	0.0000	0.0000
2	0.0466	99.9170	0.0410	0.0418
3	0.0669	99.8754	0.0199	0.1045
4	0.0854	99.8687	0.0154	0.1158
5	0.1025	99.8801	0.0158	0.1039
6	0.1183	99.8903	0.0174	0.0922
7	0.1330	99.8977	0.0202	0.0820
8	0.1468	99.9036	0.0233	0.0730
9	0.1597	99.9083	0.0264	0.0651
10	0.1720	99.9120	0.0294	0.0585
Var. Decom. of LNDDR				
Period	S.E.	LNGDP	LNDDR	LNEDR
1	0.0355	74.6603	25.3396	0.0000
2	0.0591	83.4220	15.5980	0.9798
3	0.0833	88.0794	10.7878	1.1326
4	0.1043	90.5271	8.63317	0.8396

(continued)

Table 10.5 (continued)

5	0.1233	91.8585	7.50389	0.6375
6	0.1397	92.6900	6.79961	0.5102
7	0.1539	93.2326	6.34443	0.4229
8	0.1663	93.6011	6.03668	0.3621
9	0.1773	93.8583	5.82169	0.3199
10	0.1870	94.0428	5.66581	0.2913
Var. Decom. of LNEDR				
Period	S.E.	LNGDP	LNDDR	LNEDR
1	0.1095	16.9880	0.6159	82.3959
2	0.1364	11.0168	7.6709	81.3122
3	0.1501	9.4939	8.0127	82.4933
4	0.1628	8.2560	9.4061	82.3377
5	0.1750	7.8286	10.6288	81.5425
6	0.1870	9.0797	11.9878	78.9323
7	0.1991	11.5063	13.0345	75.4591
8	0.2124	15.1780	13.8897	70.9322
9	0.2268	19.5924	14.4893	65.9181
10	0.2423	24.4435	14.8679	60.6884

Source Author's estimation

shock remained same in the subsequent periods. The shocks from LNDDR and LNEDR don't impact on the variation in the LNGDP in 10 forecast horizon. LNGDP and LNDDR accounted the 74.66 and 25.33% variation in LNDDR in initial periods. However, the share of LNGDP increased to 94.04% in 10 period forecasting horizons. In case of LNEDR, the share of LNGDP and LNDDR in the variation of LNEDR increased substantially. But, the variation is predominated by LNEDR. It can be concluded that the external debt has long-run association with economic growth and domestic debt.

10.5 Conclusion and Implication of the Results

Investigation of the causal relationship among LNDDR, LNEDR, and LNGDP for Indian economy over more than three decades starting from the fiscal year 1980–1981 to 2015–2016 follows a series of empirical tests like unit root test, lag selection criteria, Johansen cointegration test, VECM, VEC Granger causality test, VECM impulse response function, and finally variance decomposition function. The result of unit root tests like ADF test and PP test confirms the integration of these variables at their first difference. With regard to the selection of maximum lag, the study chooses the optimum of lag 2 through VAR model by following LR, FPE, AIC and HQ criterion. Then Johansen cointegration test authenticates one cointegrating equation in the series and, thus, there is the long-run relationship existing between LNGDP, LNDDR, and LNEDR. Besides, the finding of the VECM reveals that the statistically significant and negative coefficient of ECT_{t-1} in ΔLNEDR helps in restoring the long-run equilibrium at the rate of 6.83% every year between LNGDP, LNDDR and LNEDR. The infliction of the VEC Granger causality test found that there is no feedback relationship among the variables in short run, but there exists the unidirectional causality from economic growth and domestic debt to external debt in long run. The result of impulse response function and variance decomposition function also confirms the long-run causality from growth and domestic debt to external debt.

The result of unidirectional causality from economic growth to external debt is supported by the findings of the literatures of Choudhury et al. (1994), Amoateng et al. (1996) and Karagol (2000). Hence, it can be inferred that causality running from economic growth to external debt may head to two circumstances, where either higher economic growth leads to lower the need for external debt accumulation (inverse relationship) or higher growth stimulates the heavy incurring of ED for the strategic investment (positive relationship). Moreover, another finding, i.e., no joint feedback between domestic debt and economic growth is in confinement with the findings of Singh (1999), and Tasos (2014). Therefore, it cannot be just said that there is no evidence of "debt has an influence on the economic growth in India", rather it could be viewed that there is the evidence of "debt has no influence on economic growth in India". It does not mean that Indian economy can sustain any level of public debt. Again, the reliance on debt, either DD or ED for financing deficits should not be considered as a risk-free option. Therefore, this paper recommends that both fiscal and monetary authority should take care of debt accumulation and its productive utilization so that the debt accumulation paves a path of economic growth rather than dampens the tempo of economic growth.

Appendix

See Figure 10.2 and Table 10.6.

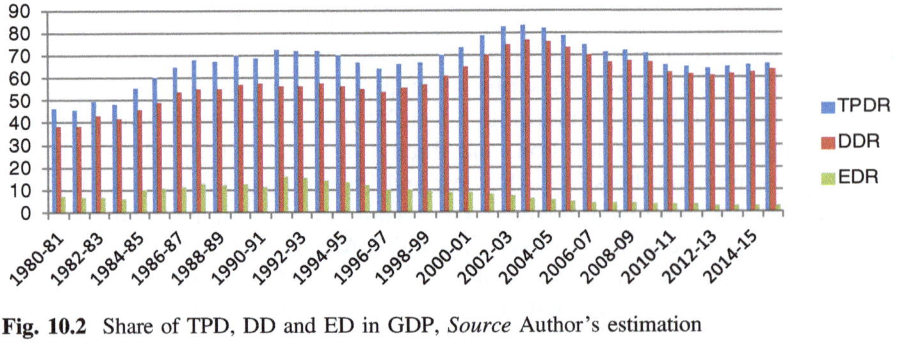

Fig. 10.2 Share of TPD, DD and ED in GDP, *Source* Author's estimation

Table 10.6 Result of compound annual growth rate

Periods → Variables ↓	1980–2015 (%)	1980–1990 (%)	1991–1996 (%)	1997–2002 (%)	2003–2015 (%)
GDP at MP	12.94	13.27	15.04	09.33	13.83
TPD	13.72	18.17	12.59	14.02	11.63
DD	14.25	17.77	14.05	15.46	11.91
ED	09.15	20.24	06.49	03.81	07.07

Source Author's estimation

References

Ahmed Q, Butt M, Sabihuddin M, Shaista A (2000) Economic growth, export and external debt causality: the case of Asian countries. Pak Dev Rev 34(4):591–608

Akram Naeem (2011) Impact of public debt on the economic growth of Pakistan. Pak Dev Rev (Pakistan Institute of Development Economics) 50(4):599–615

Amoateng K, Amoako-Adu B (1996) Economic growth, export and external debt causality: the case of African countries, Appl Econ 28(1):21–27

Bal DP, Rath BN (2014) Public debt and economic growth in India: a reassessment. Econ Anal Policy 44(3):292–300

Balassone F, Francese M, Pace A (2010) Public debt and economic growth in Italy, Preliminary version

Barik A (2012) Government debt and economic growth in India, Punjab University Paper

Barro RJ (1979) On the determination of the public debt. J Polit Econ 87(5, Part 1):940–971

Buchanan JM (1955) Public Principles of Public Debt: a Defense and Restatement. vol 2. Homewood Ill, Richard D. Irwin

Butts HC (2009) Short-term external debt and economic growth—Granger causality: evidence from latin America and the Caribbean. Rev Black Polit Econ 36:93–111

Cecchetti SG, Mohanty MS, Zampolli F (2011) The real effect of debt, BIS working paper 352. Basel, Switzerland: Bank for International Settlement

Checherita C, Rother P (2010) The impact of high and growing government debt on economic growth: an empirical investigation for the Euro area, European Central Bank working paper series no. 1237

Chowdhury K (1994) A structural analysis of external debt and economic growth: some evidence from selected countries in Asia and the Pacific. Appl Econ 26(12):1121–1131

Diamond P (1965) National debt in a neoclassical growth model, Am Econ Rev 55(5):1126–1150

Dritsaki C (2013) Causal nexus between economic growth, exports and government debt: the case of Greece. Procedia Econ Finance 5:251–259

Egbetunde T (2012) Public debt and economic growth in Nigeria: evidence from Granger causality, Am J Econ 2(6):101–106

Elmendorf D, Mankiw N (1999) Government debt. In: Taylor J, Woodford M (eds) Handbook of macroeconomics, vol 1C. North-Holland, pp 1615–1669

Ferreira C (2009) Public debt and economic growth: a Granger causality panel data approach, working paper (ISEG-UTL), ISSN no. 0874-4548

Fincke B, Greiner A (2014) Public debt and economic growth in emerging market economies, working paper in economics and management, no. 08–2014

Georgiev B (2012) Implications of public debt on economic growth and development: a European study, Bachelor thesis, department of economics and business, Aarhus University

Jayaraman TK, Lau E (2008) Does external debt lead to economic growth in Pacific Island countries. J Policy Model 31:272–288

Karagöl (2000) The causality analysis of external debt service and GNP: the case of Turkey. Cent Bank Rev 2(1):39–64
Kaur B, Mukherjee A (2012) Threshold level of debt and public debt sustainability: the Indian experience, Reserve Bank of India occasional papers, vol 33, no. 1&2
Kumar MS, Woo J (2010) Public debt and growth, International Monetary Fund working paper, 174: 1–45 Cambridge, Cambridge University Press
Lerner AP (1948) The Burden of the National Debt. In: Lloyd A. Metzler et al. (eds) Income, employment and public policy, Essays in Honour of Alvin Hanson, W. W. Norton, New York, 255–275
Liew VKS (2004) Which lag length selection criteria should we employ? Econ Bull 3(33):1–9
Lin S (2000) Government debt and economic growth in an overlapping generations model. South Econ J 66(3):754–763
MacKinnon JG (1996) Numerical distribution functions for unit root and cointegration tests. J Appl Econ 11:601–618
MacKinnon JG, Haug AA, Michelis L (1999) Numerical distribution functions of likelihood ratio tests for cointegration. J Appl Econ 14:563–577
Modigliani F (1961) Long-run implications of alternative fiscal policies and the burden of the national debt. Econ J 71(284):730–755
Mohamed MAA (2005) The impact of external debt on economic growth: an empirical assessment of the Sudan 1978–2001. Eastern Afr Soc Sci Res Rev 21(1):53–66
Putunai GK, Mutukh CM (2013) Domestic debt and economic growth nexus in Kenya. Curr Res J Econ Theory 5(1):1–10
Rao N, Govinda R, Rao K (2006) Trends and issues in tax policy and reform in India, India Policy Forum, NCAER
Rais SI, Anwar S (2012) Public debt and economic growth in Pakistan: a time series analysis from 1972 to 2010. Acad Res Int 2(1):535–544
Reinhart C, Rogoff K (2010) Growth in a time of debt. Am Econ Rev: Pap Proc 100(2)
Schclarek A (2004) Debt and economic growth in developing and industrial countries, working papers 2005:34, Lund University, Department of Economics
Singh C (1999) Domestic debt and economic growth in India. Econ Polit Wkly 34(23):1445–1453
Tasos S (2014) Debt and economic growth: is there any causal effect? An empirical analysis with structural breaks and Granger causality for Greece, Theor Appl Econ XXI 1(590):51–62
Wadad S (2012) Causality between economic growth, export, and external debt servicing: the case of Lebanon. Int J Econ Finance 4(11):134–143

Chapter 11
Efficiency and Adequacy of Public Health System in Improving Health Outcomes: A Stochastic Frontier Analysis for Indian States

J.V.M. Sarma and Pradeep Kamble

Abstract State governments plays important role in ensuring health of its residence by making them available affordable and quality health services. However, states in India largely differ in their achievements in crucial health indicators like IMR, CMR and MMR. These wide differences in improvement in these health indicators can be attributed to either inadequate public investment in the health sector or inefficiency of utilising these resources or both. The present study mainly focuses on these two aspects namely efficiency of public resources in improving health indicators and adequacy of current level of health inputs in achieving maximum improvement in health indicators. Using Stochastic Frontier Analysis, the study has measured efficiency of major Indian states for the period 2003–2004 to 2012–2013. The efficiency analysis indicates that the states have achieved lower levels of improvements in health indicators than their potential levels. On the other hand, the analysis of adequacy of health inputs indicates that most of the states will not achieve higher improvement of health indicators by mere improving in efficiency. These states, particularly low income states need to increase health inputs drastically in order to improve health indicators further. The study also finds that spread of rural health infrastructure and manpower (spread of sub-centres and health workers) will improve health indicators substantially.

Keywords Health indicators · State public health expenditure
Stochastic frontier analysis

11.1 Introduction

Universal Health Coverage (UHC) is an important aspect of ensuring health of citizens in a country. Universal Health Coverage includes various aspect of public health like citizen's access to promotive, preventive and curative health services;

J.V.M. Sarma · P. Kamble (✉)
School of Economics, University of Hyderabad, Hyderabad, India
e-mail: kamblepradeep25@gmail.com

N.A. Khan (ed.), *Challenges and Issues in Indian Fiscal Federalism*,
India Studies in Business and Economics, https://doi.org/10.1007/978-981-10-6217-9_11

affordable and quality health services to all sections of society; and government's role as grantor and enabler of health and health related services (Planning Commission 2011). The major aspect of UHC in ensuring health of citizens is adequacy of health related infrastructure and skilled health workforce. Considering the role of government in granting and enabling health related services, governments need to ensure adequate level of health infrastructure and health workforce in circumstances where citizens do not have access to private healthcare provider or at an affordable level. Especially, in case of developing countries like India where considerable population lives in poverty, government's intervention in health is crucial in ensuring Universal Health Coverage to all its citizens.

However, government's intervention in health sector in developing country is constrained by the availability of resources at government's disposal. Therefore, in order to ensure health of population by UHC, it is important to not only have adequate resources devoted to the health sector but also efficient use of available resources. Efficient use of resources by some regions that have achieved maximum health of population can free resources for use by other regions where maximum health of population is not yet achieved. In other words, if all regions use resources efficiently in provision of health services, then there will be more resources available to health sector as whole to improve public health further. As pointed out by Chisholm and Evans (2010), attainment of highest possible health out of given level of resources can be seen as efficient use of resources. Efficient use of resources by all regions is very important from the point of view of UHC in case of developing country like India. Therefore, two important aspects for ensuring UHC could be adequacy of health infrastructure and efficient use of it.

Apart from importance of efficiency in ensuring universal access to health services and thereby improving overall public health of all regions, efficient use of resources by a particular region also ensures improved health outcome in that particular region. This is because some regions may provide adequate resources to health sector but failure of using it efficiently may result in lower achievement in health status of its residence. Thus, provision of adequate health infrastructure and its efficient use is important from the point of view of ensuring UHC by freeing resources from one region to others and ensuring improvement in public health in a particular region.

Universal Health Coverage in case of India seems to be still distinct goal reflected in diverse achievements in crucial indicators of health like CMR,[1] MMR,[2] and IMR.[3] Lack of UHC in terms of spread of quality health services at affordable level across the regions has resulted in differences in achievement of these major indicators of health across the states. For example, states like Bihar, Madhya Pradesh, Rajasthan, Uttar Pradesh, Odisha, Jharkhand, and Chhattisgarh have reported very high level of CMR, MMR, and IMR in the country (Table 11.1).

[1]Child Mortality Rate (CMR 0–4) is measured in terms of death of number of children (0–4 years) taking place per 1000 children (0–4 year's age).

[2]Maternal Mortality Ratio (MMR) is defined as the number of maternal deaths per 100,000 live births.

[3]Infant Mortality Rate (IMR) refers to the number of deaths of children in the age 0–1 year per thousand live births.

Table 11.1 State-wise health indicators, health expenditure, and health infrastructure in India

State				PC real expenditure on health		Per 100,000 rural population			Per 100,000 total population		
	CMR	MMR	IMR	Pub[a]	PVT	PHC	Sub-Centre	Health worker	Hosp	Bed	Doc
Andhra Pr	10	92	39	360	2088	3.0	22.1	43.5	0.5	42.8	9.5
Bihar	22	208	42	122	1000	2.0	10.1	19.4	1.3	10.6	4.6
Chhattisgarh	16	221	46	256	1032	3.9	25.5	39.4	2.4	45.1	3.8
Gujarat	14	112	36	471	1760	3.3	20.6	36.0	0.6	44.6	5.6
Haryana	15	127	41	337	1939	2.7	15.1	39.1	0.6	29.2	10.5
Jharkhand	17	208	37	194	1409	1.3	15.2	30.9	1.6	15.8	5.0
Karnataka	9	133	31	357	2218	5.9	24.4	38.4	1.0	80.7	7.3
Kerala	3	61	12	611	4715	5.0	27.8	69.0	3.8	111	15.1
Madhya Pr	22	221	54	253	1533	2.1	16.1	32.9	0.6	34.9	5.6
Maharashtra	7	68	24	352	2833	2.9	16.9	46.2	0.9	45.9	3.6
Orissa	15	222	51	225	1180	3.6	18.7	32.5	4.1	38.7	7.5
Punjab	7	141	26	385	3254	2.4	16.8	33.0	0.8	41.5	12.4
Rajasthan	22	244	47	279	1237	3.9	27.0	36.1	4.4	65.4	10.5
Tamil Nadu	5	79	21	432	2040	3.6	23.1	26.5	1.1	86.5	9.7
Uttar Pr	22	285	50	237	1845	2.2	12.8	25.1	0.4	27.2	4.7
West Bengal	9	113	31	247	2250	1.4	16.4	35.9	1.7	83.5	10.1

[a]Public expenditure on health includes expenditure on medical and public health and family welfare (see National Health Account Cell (NHAC 2013), Ministry of Health and Family Welfare)

Source CMR, MMR, and IMR- Sample Registration System, Public Expenditure-State Finances: A Study of Budget, Private Expenditure- Household Consumption Expenditure Survey, NSSO, Health infrastructure data-National Health Profile and Rural Health Statistics

These are the states which also lie at the bottom of ranking in terms of real per capita GSDP. These low income states with lower achievement s in health indicators have not able to spent sufficiently on health sector. Real per capita public expenditures on health of these states are below the average of major states taken together. Not only in case of public expenditure but per capita private expenditures of these states on health are also below average. However, in case of health infrastructure the scenario is different. Some of these states that have reported lower achievement in health indicators like Odisha, Rajasthan, Chhattisgarh, Jharkhand, and Bihar have reported relatively higher number of hospitals per 100,000 populations. However, in case of bed per 100,000 population, except for Rajasthan and Chhattisgarh, all other above mentioned states have reported relatively lower number than others. Similarly, in case of number of doctors per 100,000 populations, except for Rajasthan and Odisha, all other above mentioned states have reported lower number. This implies that although the spread of government hospitals in these regions have been achieved, it lacks other complementary infrastructure like beds and skilled manpower. In other words, low performing states in terms of health indicators, have relatively well equipped with past investment in infrastructure like Hospitals but not well equipped with other physical medical inputs like beds and doctors.

Since majority of population resides in rural area, rural health infrastructure is also very important from the point of view of improving overall public health. State-wise Primary Health Centres (PHC) per 100,000 populations indicates that, except Rajasthan, Chhattisgarh, and Odisha, all other states in the class of low achievement in health indicators have reported lower number or lower spread of PHCs. In case of spread of sub-centres as well we can see the same pattern.

In contrast to these states with lower achievements in health indicators, Kerala is leading state with significant achievements in terms of health indicators. Kerala has able to perform well in health sector mainly because of wide spread of public health infrastructure, particularly, rural health infrastructure (Table 11.1). Kerala has reported not only higher level of public expenditure in the country but also highest private expenditure on health. These high levels of public and private expenditure are likely to be resulted in considerable improvements in health indicators of Kerala. This further put emphasis on the importance of public intervention in health where majority of population cannot afford private health care due to lower income. Therefore, low income states that have lower achievements in health need special attention.

The above discussion suggests that some states have not achieved improvement in indicators of health due to lower public and private expenditure on health and lower health infrastructure. Moreover, in case of other states that have achieved better health indicators differs in their health inputs. For example, in case of Gujarat and Tamil Nadu, their public expenditure on health and health infrastructure is very close to each other but their achievement in health indicators differs considerably.

This indicates that there are differences in utilisation of resources by the states that have resulted in differential achievements in health indicators. Therefore, there is need to assess efficiency of states in utilisation of their health inputs like public expenditure on health and/or health infrastructure for achieving better public health. This exercise will enable us to see potential improvements in health indicators that existing public resources in health sector can achieve.

Some of the previous studies have measured the efficiency of public health system of the Indian states. Out of these studies some studies have used non-parametric method (Data Envelopment Analysis) while others have used parametric method (Stochastic Frontier Analysis) to measure efficiency of states in improving health indicators. Chakrabarti and Rao (2007), Parachita and Shanmugam (2012), and Kathuria and Sankar (2005) have measured efficiency of major Indian states in health sector by using Stochastic Frontier Analysis (SFA) method. All these studies have used IMR as output as an indicator of public health. According to Kathuria and Sankar (2005), IMR was considered as measure of public health since it represents efforts in terms of providing appropriate health services in ensuring survival of child at the beginning of his or her life. In their efficiency model, these studies have used inputs indicating crucial health infrastructure like Primary Health Centre (PHC), Sub-Centres, Doctors, Beds, Hospitals, government health expenditure, etc. In case of inefficiency model, these studies have included female literacy and rural population in order to take into account of states-specific factors determining inefficiency of health system. According to Jain (1985), female education is likely to reflect improved health education, child care, hygienic conditions, and overall social development. Therefore, it is likely to reduce inefficiency in utilisation of health services. The efficiency measured in these studies differ mainly because of difference in time period, variables used, form of variables used (e.g. use of total number of PHC or population per PHC), etc. However, most of these studies found that variables like public health expenditure, PHC, doctors, beds, etc., are important inputs for improving health indicators.

Some studies have used Data Envelopment Analysis to measure efficiency of heath system across the states. These studies include Tigga and Mishra (2015) and Shetty and Pakkala (2010).

The present study is using SFA for measurement of efficiency of the health system in case of Indian states. However, the present study differs from previous studies on the following grounds. First, previous studies have used only one indicator of public health namely IMR. However, the present study will use index of health constituting IMR, MMR, and CMR. These mortality indicators reflects adequacy of promotive, preventive, and curative health services at child birth and after birth of child up to 4 years. They also represents measures taken by the governments in ensuring mother's and children's survival at the beginning of child's life.

Second, using parametric method the study also tries to isolate some of the most crucial inputs that are responsible for improving health index. This will be important from the policy perspective since it will give direction in which these health indicators can be reduced drastically.

Third, as it is mentioned above, most of the low income states have reported lower public expenditure on health as well as lower health infrastructure. Considering the crucial inputs determined in the SFA, the study will determine how much increase in these inputs that each state requires in order to achieve improvement in the health indicators that of the best state.

Against this backdrop, an endeavour of study is summarised as follows. (A) measurement of efficiency of public health system in improving the health outcome indicated by health index consisting major health indicators, (B) determination of potential health outcome of each state at given level of inputs, (C) finding out crucial infrastructural variables that help in improving health index, and (D) determining level of these crucial inputs that each state require to achieve health index of best performing state in terms of achievement in health indicators.

The article is structured as follows. Section 2 deals with the concept of efficiency and methodology of its measurement across the cross-section units. Section 3 gives input and output variables considered for the analysis. It gives methodology of measuring health index based on some crucial health indicators. It further discusses empirical model used in the study along with data sources. Section 4 discusses results and analysis of empirical model. Section 5 assesses required levels of inputs for each state so that they can achieve level of improvements of health indicators of Kerala. Section 6 concludes the study.

11.2 Concept of Efficiency and Methodology of Its Measurement

11.2.1 Definition of Efficiency

Efficiency can be divided into two types, technical efficiency and allocative efficiency. Technical efficiency is nothing but getting maximum output from given level of inputs or minimising inputs for given level of output. In case of health, it refers to achieving highest improvement in public health with given level of investment in health sector. On the other hand, allocative efficiency in health sector refers to mix of health services that maximises public health or health improvement, within a particular health service (preventive vs curative services) as well as across the services (what types of health services can improve overall public health the most) (Chisholm and Evans 2010). In the present study, the focus is on the measurement of technical efficiency. In other words, assessing how much states have improved its health indicators as compared to its potential level, given the resources devoted to public health sector.

11.2.2 Model Specification[4]

Stochastic frontier production function can be written as

$$Y_{it} = x_{it}\beta + V_{it} - U_{it},$$

where Y_{it} is production of ith firm in tth period, x_{it} is vector of inputs of production of ith firm in tth period, β is vector of unknown parameters, V_{it}s are random errors with iid N (0, σ_v^2). U_{it}s are non-negative random variables representing technical inefficiency of production and assumed to be independently distributed, such that U_{it} is obtained by truncation (at zero) of the N(m_{it}, σ_U^2) distribution where,

$$m_{it} = z_{it}\delta$$

z_{it} is a vector of variables influencing efficiency of a firm and δ is a vector of parameters to be estimated.

The technical inefficiency U_{it} can be written as

$$U_{it} = z_{it}\delta + W_{it},$$

where W_{it}, is random variable N(0, σ_W^2) and $W_{it} \geq -z_{it}\delta$. This assumption will ensure U_{it} being non-negative.

The method of maximum likelihood can be used to estimate parameters of the stochastic frontier and model of the technical inefficiency. The likelihood function is expressed in terms of the variance parameters, $\sigma^2 = \sigma_V^2 + \sigma_U^2$ and $\gamma = \sigma_U^2/(\sigma_V^2 + \sigma_U^2)$.

γ represents proportion of inefficiency variance to the total variance of the model and it lies between 0 and 1. In case γ is zero, it indicates that σ_U^2 is zero and inefficiency term, U_{it}, can be removed from the model and parameters of the model can be consistently estimated by using OLS.

11.3 Input and Output Variables

As pointed out earlier, unlike previous studies where only IMR has been considered as an indicator of public health, the present study is constructing a health index by considering IMR, CMR, and MMR. The health index is constructed as follows. First, all these three indicators' index has been measured using the following formula:

---

[4]See for more details Battese and Coelli (1995) and Coelli (1996).

$$\text{IMR Index} = (\text{IMR}_{\max} - \text{IMR}_{it})/(\text{IMR}_{\max} - \text{IMR}_{\min})$$

$$\text{CMR Index} = (\text{CMR}_{\max} - \text{CMR}_{it})/(\text{CMR}_{\max} - \text{CMR}_{\min})$$

$$\text{MMR Index} = (\text{MMR}_{\max} - \text{MMR}_{it})/(\text{MMR}_{\max} - \text{MMR}_{\min})$$

where max and min are maximum and minimum values of these indicators over the time and across the states. '*it*' is value of a indicator of *i*th state in *t*th year.

$$\text{Health Index} = (1/3 * \text{IMR Index}) + (1/3 * \text{CMR Index}) + (1/3 * \text{MMR Index})$$

The value of health index lies between 0 and 1 and higher the value higher is the achievement in reducing these mortality indicators. The health index has been considered as output variable for the frontier analysis that will be related to various input variables.

Various input variables can be considered for the analysis including monetary variables and physical variables. Physical variables like number of government hospitals, beds, PHCs, Sub-Centres, etc., reflect past investment in health sector by the government. On the other hand, government expenditure on health represents current efforts of government in improving public health. The study is also including manpower variable like number of doctors, health workers, health assistance, etc. However, expenditure on these variables is included in the public expenditure on health. As the study is intended to find out crucial inputs that can improve health indicator significantly, these variables are considered for the analysis. Finding of such variables will give direction to the states in terms of allocation of resources on those inputs that have higher impact on indicators of health. In case of inefficiency model, variables like female literacy and proportion of rural population in total population are used.

The empirical model of stochastic frontier production function in Cobb-Douglas form is as follows,

$$\ln(\text{Hindex})_{it} = \beta_0 + \sum \beta_j \ln x_{jit} + V_{it} - U_{it}$$

Inefficiency model is given as,

$$U_{it} = \delta_0 + \sum \delta_k z_{kit} + W_{it}$$

Data on IMR and CMR is collected from the Sample Registration System (SRS) Statistical Report of various years and MMR from MMR Bulletin, SRS of various years published by Ministry of Home Affairs, Government of India. Data on health infrastructure is collected from National Health Profile and Rural Health Statistics of various years published by Central Bureau of Health Intelligence, Government of India and Ministry of Health, respectively. Data on public expenditure on health is collected from State Finances: A Study of Budget, various years,

Reserve Bank of India. State Domestic Product is collected from Data Table, Planning Commission and data on population and literacy is collected from Census of India, 2001 and 2011.

Data for the analysis consists of panel of 16 major states observed for 10 years (2003–04 to 2012–13). These particular years has been selected since data on newly formed states are available around 2003–2004 and 2012–2013 is the latest data available.

11.4 Empirical Results

As pointed our earlier, the study has considered many variables for Stochastic Frontier Model. However, the model with only significant variables is shown in Table 11.2. The per capita public expenditure on health in 2004–2005 prices has significant and positive impact on health index. The elasticity of health index with respect to public expenditure on health is 0.23. Population per bed (Lnbed) and population per health worker (Lnhework) have significant and negative impact on health index as expected. Since, higher the number of beds and health workers, lower will be these ratios and higher will be improvement in health indicators. Both of these variables have elasticity around −0.10.

In case of inefficiency model, female literacy (Lnfimlit) has negative and significant impact on inefficiency while proportion of rural population in total population (Lnrur) has significant positive impact on inefficiency. The results indicate

Table 11.2 Estimation results of Stochastic frontier model dependant variable: index of health indicator (log of health index)

Frontier model	Coefficient	Sigma-squared	0.387 (2.911)***
Constant	0.215 (0.404)	Gamma	0.996 (464.124)***
Lnpcpubxs	0.229 (5.347)***	Log likelihood function	−11.342
Lnbed	−0.108 (−3.004)***	LR test of the one-sided error	134.021
Lnhework	−0.104 (−2.405) **	Number of iterations	27
Inefficiency Model	coefficient	Total number of observations	160
Constant	2.060 (0.293)	Mean efficiency	0.688
Lnfemlit	−3.117 (−3.263)***		
Lnrur	2.451 (2.021)**		

Note *** indicates 1% significance level and ** represents 5%

that states with higher female literacy and higher urbanisation have shown better efficiency in terms of use of resources in health sector.

The results also show that Gamma is significantly different from zero indicating that inefficiency term should be included in the model since variance of inefficiency is significantly different from zero. Value of Gamma is 0.996 and it represents variation caused by inefficiency out of total variation in performance. The mean efficiency of all states taken together is 68.8%. It implies that the current level of output or improvements in the health indicators is 31.2% lower that the potential output. This result indicates that the current level of health output is much lower than its potential and with the same level of inputs it can be increased considerably.

State-wise and year-wise efficiency scores in improving health indicators are shown in Table 11.3. As it can be seen from the table, Maharashtra state is most efficient states among the selected states in terms of use of resources and improvement in health index during the period under consideration. Kerala, Tamil Nadu and West Bengal have also per performed well in terms of efficiency scores. On the other hand, Uttar Pradesh is least efficient state followed by Madhya Pradesh, Rajasthan and Odisha. The efficiency score of these states are lower that 50% during most of the years under consideration.

As depicted in Table 11.3, for all states, there is a possibility of improving current level of health index with existing level of inputs if these states improve on their efficiency. If all states show maximum efficiency in utilising available resources then the resulting potential level of health index of each state is shown in Table 11.4.

Table 11.3 State-wise year-wise efficiency scores

State	2004	2005	2006	2007	2008	2009	2010	2011	2012	2013
Andhra Pr	70.1	67.3	67.0	70.6	71.8	75.0	76.4	77.4	77.3	80.4
Bihar	80.5	69.8	69.8	80.0	71.0	82.2	94.3	96.0	75.2	78.9
Chhattisgarh	44.0	38.3	44.1	55.4	53.3	56.0	60.3	65.7	59.4	59.5
Gujarat	71.0	66.6	66.4	69.6	73.1	72.6	74.5	61.1	71.6	70.8
Haryana	64.0	61.3	64.7	72.2	78.4	74.6	72.0	78.1	72.9	72.7
Jharkhand	79.2	68.6	61.0	72.5	65.3	69.1	77.1	82.3	75.5	79.6
Karnataka	69.8	65.3	66.5	70.1	67.6	68.9	75.1	75.8	77.2	77.6
Kerala	98.6	97.5	96.7	97.0	96.6	95.8	95.5	96.4	91.2	83.3
Madhya Pr	14.3	20.2	22.2	32.8	36.4	41.8	48.6	51.3	46.3	47.7
Maharashtra	93.7	90.8	95.1	97.3	98.2	95.4	95.4	94.9	95.5	93.9
Orissa	29.4	29.8	32.6	41.9	43.9	47.2	53.8	58.5	61.4	61.5
Punjab	76.2	76.2	76.7	80.9	84.7	85.9	86.8	90.5	87.9	88.3
Rajasthan	24.5	24.7	22.5	36.0	38.0	41.7	51.1	56.6	43.7	45.0
Tamil Nadu	88.6	89.0	82.8	92.1	94.8	92.5	92.3	93.0	97.4	92.6
Uttar Pr	12.9	11.4	12.7	27.2	31.0	37.4	45.4	51.6	45.8	46.6
West Bengal	91.2	90.8	90.8	92.9	94.4	96.9	92.7	89.7	85.8	87.3

Source Author's own computation

Table 11.4 State-wise potential health index

State	2004	2005	2006	2007	2008	2009	2010	2011	2012	2013
Andhra Pr	0.76	0.78	0.78	0.80	0.82	0.84	0.89	0.91	0.94	0.92
Bihar	0.43	0.42	0.46	0.46	0.58	0.56	0.56	0.58	0.57	0.57
Chhattisgarh	0.66	0.69	0.68	0.70	0.74	0.77	0.81	0.80	0.83	0.85
Gujarat	0.74	0.78	0.79	0.80	0.80	0.82	0.87	1.11	0.92	0.97
Haryana	0.69	0.72	0.74	0.74	0.70	0.78	0.85	0.83	0.84	0.86
Jharkhand	0.56	0.59	0.69	0.68	0.76	0.75	0.74	0.72	0.71	0.69
Karnataka	0.79	0.82	0.83	0.85	0.89	0.93	0.92	0.97	0.96	0.97
Kerala	0.90	0.94	0.96	0.98	1.00	1.02	1.03	1.02	1.10	1.21
Madhya Pr	0.65	0.69	0.69	0.71	0.70	0.68	0.75	0.77	0.78	0.81
Maharashtra	0.78	0.81	0.77	0.77	0.75	0.84	0.88	0.92	0.90	0.93
Orissa	0.66	0.72	0.67	0.70	0.71	0.73	0.75	0.76	0.77	0.79
Punjab	0.77	0.80	0.80	0.78	0.77	0.79	0.84	0.84	0.89	0.91
Rajasthan	0.76	0.77	0.74	0.77	0.78	0.82	0.84	0.81	0.87	0.89
Tamil Nadu	0.80	0.84	0.90	0.84	0.85	0.90	0.95	0.96	0.90	0.99
Uttar Pr	0.50	0.53	0.64	0.68	0.66	0.65	0.70	0.70	0.69	0.75
West Bengal	0.75	0.77	0.77	0.76	0.77	0.75	0.85	0.87	0.88	0.89

Source Author's own computations

During the period under consideration, Kerala has reported lowest IMR, CMR and MMR among the states. Kerala's health index during the study period is almost 1. It can be noted from Table 11.4 that even if all states show maximum efficiency; almost all of them are not going to achieve health index of value 1. Only state that may achieve health index of Kerala in 2013 is Tamil Nadu. If Tamil Nadu utilises the existing health resources efficiently then without increasing inputs it can achieve maximum health output. However, for all other states improving just efficiency of existing resources will not help them to achieve health index of Kerala. The problem is very acute in case of low income states like Bihar, Jharkhand, Uttar Pradesh, and Odisha since their potential health index, given inputs, is very low. This implies that these states need to invest extensively in health sector in order to improve health index.

11.5 Assessment of Required Level of Infrastructure and Public Expenditure

The present study has assessed some crucial health inputs that have significant influence on the health index of states. These variables are per capita public expenditure on health in 2004–2005 prices, total population per bed of government hospitals, and rural population per health worker in sub-centre. Health worker is staff of sub-centre in rural areas. Health worker includes both male health worker and female health worker (Auxiliary Nurse Midwife). Sub-centres are the first point of contact between the primary health care system provided by the government and residence of rural areas. The sub-centres are intended to bring about behaviour changes and provide services related to maternal and child health, family welfare, nutrition, and control of various diseases. As per the norm, two health workers (one male and one female) are required for each sub-centre.[5] Considering this norm, study has also calculated required number of sub-centres consistent with required number of health workers to improve health index.

Following Table 11.5 gives required per capita public expenditure in 2004–2005 prices, required number of beds, and required number of health workers to improve health index of each state to Kerala's index in 2012–2013. The required level is the percentage increase in the above-mentioned variables from their respective level in the year 2012–13.

It can be seen from Table 11.5 that state like Tamil Nadu has to increase its level of inputs to just 5% from its level in 2012–2013 in order to achieve health indicator of Kerala. On the other hand, states like Bihar, Uttar Pradesh, Jharkhand, Odisha, Madhya Pradesh, etc., require huge investment in health sector in order to improve their health outcome. These states need to increase spread of hospitals and sub-centres (in accordance with required number of beds and health workers) in order to improve public health.

Table 11.5 also shows per lakh requirement of beds and health workers. For example, in case of Bihar, the existing beds and health workers per lakh population are 11 and 19, respectively. As per the proposed model of the present study, these ratios should be increased to 38 beds and 70 health workers.

Considering the norm for number of health workers in the sub-centres, Table 11.6 represents required number of sub-centres consistent with required number of health workers. The table also shows number of villages covered per sub-centre. As it can be seen from the table, two states, Bihar and Uttar Pradesh, required very large number of increase in number of sub-centres. Some states like Gujarat, Karnataka, Rajasthan, and Tamil Nadu have greater number of existing sub-centres than required. These states just need to increase in their manpower in sub-centres in order to achieve better health outcome. In case of number of villages per sub-centres, the existing ratio is around four villages per sub-centre. States like Jharkhand, Odisha, Madhya Pradesh, Uttar Pradesh, and Bihar have reported over five villages per sub-centre, however, the required ratio is around 2–3 villages. In case of Bihar and Uttar Pradesh the required ratio is 1.3 and 2.8, respectively.

[5]See Rural Health Care System in India, Rural Health, Statistics, National Health Mission, Ministry of Health and Family Welfare (2014); and Indian Public Health Standards Guidelines for Sub-Centres, Ministry of Health and Family Welfare (2012).

Table 11.5 Required level of health inputs to achieve health index of Kerala

	2013 level			Improvement	Required level			2013 Level		Required level	
State	pcpubx	Bed	Work	in %	pcpubx	Bed	Work	Bed	Work	Bed	Work
Andhra Pr	360	2337	2301	25	450	1870	1841	43	43	53	54
Bihar	122	9429	5154	260	439	2619	1432	11	19	38	70
Chhattisgarh	256	2215	2540	45	371	1528	1752	45	39	65	57
Gujarat	471	2243	2777	10	518	2039	2525	45	36	49	40
Haryana	337	3430	2560	45	489	2366	1766	29	39	42	57
Jharkhand	194	6345	3241	130	446	2759	1409	16	31	36	71
Karnataka	357	1239	2606	10	393	1126	2370	81	38	89	42
Madhya Pr	253	2865	3040	70	430	1685	1788	35	33	59	56
Maharashtra	352	2177	2166	20	423	1814	1805	46	46	55	55
Orissa	225	2583	3072	70	383	1519	1807	39	33	66	55
Punjab	385	2412	3033	25	481	1930	2426	41	33	52	41
Rajasthan	279	1530	2773	30	362	1177	2133	65	36	85	47
Tamil Nadu	432	1156	3772	5	453	1101	3592	86	27	91	28
Uttar Pr	237	3677	3980	90	450	1935	2095	27	25	52	48
West Bengal	247	1198	2782	30	321	922	2140	83	36	109	47

Source Author's own computations

Table 11.6 State-wise required number of sub-centres

States	Sub-centre		Number of villages per sub-centre	
	2013	Required	2013	Required
Andhra Pr	12,522	15,361	2.2	1.8
Bihar	9729	33,680	4.6	1.3
Chhattisgarh	5161	5783	3.9	3.5
Gujarat	7274	6994	2.5	2.6
Haryana	2542	4764	2.7	1.4
Jharkhand	3958	9214	8.2	3.5
Karnataka	9264	8020	3.2	3.7
Madhya Pr	8764	15,200	6.3	3.6
Maharashtra	10,580	17,395	4.1	2.5
Orissa	6688	9893	7.7	5.2
Punjab	2951	3628	4.3	3.5
Rajasthan	14,407	12,500	3.1	3.6
Tamil Nadu	8706	5248	1.8	3.0
Uttar Pr	20,521	38,318	5.2	2.8
West Bengal	10,356	14,747	3.9	2.7

Source Author's own computations

11.6 Conclusion

Universal Health Coverage (UHC) to all citizens in India is still a distinct goal. It can be seen from wide differences in health indicators as well as health infrastructure across the states. Health facilities provided by the government are crucial in terms of providing quality health services at affordable level to all citizens. Therefore, adequacy of public investment in health sector is important from the point of view of UHC. Considering limited resource availability in developing country like India, efficient use of resources is also important in ensuring UHC. The present study has dealt with these two issues of UHC namely adequacy of public resources in health sector and efficiency of use of these resources.

Analysis of efficiency of public health services in achieving improved health outcome using Stochastic Frontier Analysis (SFA) indicates that per capita public expenditure on health in 2004–2005 prices, population per beds, and population per health workers have significant influence on health performance index. This indicates that spread of government hospitals (reflected in population per beds variable) and spread of manpower in rural areas (indicated by population per health workers) are the most important policy variables along with public expenditure on health for improvement in health indicators.

Efficiency scores vary across states and over the period of time. Maharashtra state continued to be most efficient states during the period under consideration among the selected states while Rajasthan is most inefficient state. States like

Rajasthan, Uttar Pradesh and Madhya Pradesh have large scope to improve their health indicators with the given level of health inputs since their efficiency scores are less than 50%. Overall, efficiency scores suggest that states have been performing lower than their potential in improving health indicators, given the existing level of health inputs.

The second part of the present study focused on the adequacy of the health inputs in achieving level of health indicators of best performing state like Kerala. The study showed that even if states improve their efficiency at maximum the resulting potential output, i.e., health index will be lower than that of Kerala. In other words, in order to achieve health index of Kerala state, mere improvement in efficiency is not enough and states need to increase their health inputs. Analysis of required level of inputs indicates that state like Bihar and Jharkhand need special attention in health sector since the required increase in health inputs are remarkably high. These states falls into low income state category. Other low income state category states like Uttar Pradesh, Madhya Pradesh and Odisha also require huge increase in health inputs.

The present study has also highlighted importance of spread of sub-centres and health workers in rural areas in order to improve health indicator. Especially, in case of low income states like Bihar, Jharkhand, Madhya Pradesh, Uttar Pradesh and Odisha required to reduce villages covered per sub-centre substantially from the existing level. In case of Bihar, almost each village should have one sub-centre in order to improve health indicators substantially.

Overall, states in India differ in their achievements in health indicators. Improvements in efficiency as well as increase in health inputs are required to ensure improvements in health indicators. Considering the huge requirements of health inputs of low income states, special attention need to be given to these states in order to ensure UHC and thereby improvement in overall health of citizens of the nation.

Appendix 1

State-wise actual health index

States	2004	2005	2006	2007	2008	2009	2010	2011	2012	2013
Andhra Pr	0.53	0.53	0.53	0.56	0.59	0.63	0.68	0.70	0.72	0.74
Bihar	0.35	0.29	0.32	0.37	0.42	0.46	0.53	0.57	0.43	0.45
Chhattisgarh	0.29	0.26	0.30	0.39	0.39	0.43	0.49	0.53	0.49	0.50
Gujarat	0.52	0.52	0.52	0.55	0.58	0.59	0.64	0.67	0.66	0.68
Haryana	0.44	0.44	0.48	0.53	0.55	0.58	0.61	0.64	0.61	0.62
Jharkhand	0.45	0.40	0.42	0.49	0.49	0.52	0.57	0.59	0.53	0.55
Karnataka	0.55	0.53	0.55	0.59	0.60	0.64	0.69	0.73	0.74	0.75
Kerala	0.96	0.95	0.94	0.97	0.98	0.98	0.98	0.99	1.00	1.00

(continued)

(continued)

States	2004	2005	2006	2007	2008	2009	2010	2011	2012	2013
Madhya Pr	0.09	0.14	0.15	0.23	0.25	0.28	0.36	0.39	0.36	0.38
Maharashtra	0.73	0.74	0.74	0.77	0.78	0.81	0.84	0.88	0.86	0.87
Orissa	0.19	0.22	0.22	0.29	0.31	0.35	0.40	0.44	0.47	0.49
Punjab	0.59	0.60	0.61	0.63	0.65	0.68	0.72	0.76	0.78	0.80
Rajasthan	0.19	0.19	0.17	0.28	0.30	0.34	0.43	0.46	0.38	0.40
Tamil Nadu	0.71	0.74	0.74	0.77	0.81	0.83	0.87	0.89	0.90	0.91
Uttar Pr	0.06	0.06	0.08	0.18	0.20	0.24	0.32	0.36	0.32	0.35
West Bengal	0.68	0.70	0.70	0.71	0.73	0.75	0.79	0.78	0.76	0.77

Source Authors' own calculations

References

Battese GE, Coelli TJ (1995) A model for technical inefficiency effects in a Stochastic frontier production function for panel data. Empir Econ 20:325–332

Chakrabarti A, Rao DN (2007) Efficiency in production of health: a Stochastic frontier analysis for Indian states. In: Tavidze A (ed) Global economics: new research. Nova Science Publications, New York, pp 105–128

Chisholm D, Evans DB (2010) Improving health system efficiency as a means of moving towards universal coverage. World Health Report 2010, background paper, no. 28, World Health Organisation

Coelli TJ (1996) A guide to FRONTIER version 4.1: a computer program for Stochastic frontier production and cost function estimation. CEPA Working Paper 7/96, University of New England

Jain AK (1985) Determinants of regional variations in infant mortality in rural India. Population Studies 39(3):407–424

Kathuria V, Sankar D (2005) Inter-state disparities in health outcomes in rural India: an analysis using a Stochastic production frontier approach. Dev Policy Rev 23(2):145–163

MHFW (2012) Indian Public Health Standards (IPHS) Guidelines for Sub-Centres. Directorate General of Health Services, Ministry of Health & Family Welfare, Government of India

NHAC (2013) Health Sector Financing by Centre and States/UTs in India. Ministry of Health & Family Welfare Government of India

PC (2011) High Level Expert Group Report on Universal Health Coverage for India. page 43 Planning Commission

Prachitha J, Shanmugam KR (2012) Efficiency of raising health outcomes in the Indian states. Working Paper 70/2012, Madras School of Economics

RHS (2014) Rural Health Care System in India. National Health Mission, Ministry of Health and Family Welfare, pp 1–25

Shetty U, Pakkala T (2010) Technical efficiencies of healthcare system in major states of India: an application of NP-RDM of DEA formulation. J Health Manag 4(12):501–518

Tigga NS, Mishra US (2015) On measuring technical efficiency of the health system in India: an application of data envelopment analysis. J Health Manag 17(3):285–298

Chapter 12
Federalism: An Idea Behind the Success of Indian Democracy

Waseem Ahmad Sofi and Arshi Khan

Abstract India is the largest democracy with multireligious, multilingual, multiracial and multicultural country of the world. Its high complex and colourful social variety mosaic is clearly a discernible pattern, wherein sociocultural diversity draws its strength and sustenance from India's composite culture and civilizational plunge. The present study introduces a conceptual distinction between diversity claims and equality claims in order to reflect critically on the relation between federalism and democracy in India. Since, one of the most pressing issues facing by Indian democracy is the politicization of ethno-cultural diversity. Meanwhile, the paper engages with the issue of accommodation of diversity in the wake of federation building and the relation between federalism and democracy in India. A large attempt has been made in the paper to answer the sensitive question as, 'how far Indian federalism and decentralization contributed as well as succeeded in world's largest democratic State to foster its cultural diversity?' India's federal experiment has undergone, over the past sixty six years, an attempt has been made in the next part of paper therefore to capture the defining features of this experience, the hesitations, mistakes and failures as well as the success of Indian federal system. Viewed from this position, the paper finally concludes with an argument that federalism in India can be understood as a constitutional model, which would not only tolerate diversity but also foster it as an additional value for which the Indian multicultural state stands.

Keywords Federalism · Democracy · India · Diversity · Constitution
Conflict and autonomy

W.A. Sofi (✉) · A. Khan
Department of Political Science, Aligarh Muslim University, Aligarh, India
e-mail: sofiwaseemalig23@gmail.com

A. Khan
e-mail: arshikhan@gmail.com

N.A. Khan (ed.), *Challenges and Issues in Indian Fiscal Federalism*,
India Studies in Business and Economics, https://doi.org/10.1007/978-981-10-6217-9_12

12.1 Federalism and Democracy: Theoretical and Conceptual Framework

Federalism and democracy are much celebrated concepts, and sought after mechanisms for progress and development in the modern world. Although, these two concepts have remained essentially elusive and obscure ideals in most developing countries. However, these ideals have managed to provide relative stability for socio-economic development and have largely succeeded to guarantee durable peace in these countries. Democracy and democratic type of arrangement opened up political space and allowed long pent-up frustration and dissatisfaction to find expression in the resurgence of ethno-religious identities and agitations for minority rights. At the same time, federalism and federal type of governments have been increasingly explored to manage conflicts emanating from these emergent challenges. Challenges arising from arbitrary rule, exclusion and marginalization have persisted and assumed new dimensions through which democracy as a model of government has become both pervasive and controversial. However, it does not mean that democracy is a bad thing (Arshi Khan and Kushal Pal 2012, p. 20).

It is not the fault of democracy but the reflection of mounting desires for narrow gains of political leaders, petty interests, sectional objectives, impulsive aims, revisionism and irredentism. It is not the error of democratic institution but its wrongful operations. It is not the institution but the mankind who matters a lot in political schemes. What is more important today about democracy is to 'live with it'. Democracy treats both majority and minority as parts of a political community based on political parity. Moreover, it develops three layers of deep appreciations for diversity on the basis of institution, principle and value. Those who have endorsed democratic values have succeeded in achieving peace, harmony and development. Only as a political system, democracy is unstable, incredible and exploitative structure. It needs a social, economic and civic conditions corresponding with the political form. Democracy requires ideal democratic individual, thinking, behaviour and a way of life. A person who fights against repression, exploitation and injustice, it demands the existence of ideal democratic society where equality of opportunity and conditions for self-fulfilment are available. Democracy in order its broader meaning includes the condition of economic equality, unity in diversity and democratic morality, i.e. human values and welfare of human beings (Arshi Khan and Kushal Pal 2012, p. 20).

Let me now briefly turn to the concept of federalism which is basically not a descriptive but a normative term. Federalism refers to the advocacy of multi-tiered government combining elements of shared rule and regional self-rule. It is based on the presumed value and validity of combining unity and diversity and of accommodating, preserving and promoting distinct identities within a larger political union. It is a special mode of political association and organization that unites separate polities within a more comprehensive political system and to allow each to maintain its own fundamental political and respective integrity (Elazar 1995). Federalism is considered as a political concept, a situation whereby a group of members are bound together by covenant with a governing representative head. It is a form of government in which powers and responsibilities are divided between the national government and constitutional units and in which neither the national nor the constituent units of government are constitutionally subordinate to the other, i.e. each derived their sovereign powers from the constitution and each is empowered to deal directly with its citizens (Watts 2007).

Federalism can be understood as a constitutional model, which guarantees and implements a balance between the autonomy of the federal units (*self-rule*) and the participation of the federal units in the decision-making process of the federation (*share rule*). It is well-established form of government in which both the central government and provincial governments are *autonomous* within their own spheres and areas of competence. In this form of government, neither provinces are the mere delegates of the central power as in a decentralized state, nor is the central government a mere delegate of the provinces as in a confederation (Cyr 2014). Federalism can be understood as a constitutional model, which limits the governmental power and include different communities within the branches sharing governmental power and at the same time to enable them to govern and design themselves what is in their common interest. And let them share governmental power in a way that all inhabitants and all ethnicities can participate on the common endeavour to implement peace, justice and liberty. Viewed from this position, federalism is to be regarded as an instrument which implements the principle of diversity in unity. Federalism could so become a guarantor of the multicultural state, which does not only preserve diversity but also foster it as an additional value, for which the multicultural and democratic state stands. It aims at the prevention and the peaceful management of conflicts within multicultural and democratic states. Thus, federalism seems particularly suited to democracies with very large populations or territories or with highly diverse populations that are regionally concentrated (Fleiner and Lidija 2009).

12.2 Relationship Between Federalism and Democracy

In today's world, democracy and federalism are linked in various ways with different forms. The close and complex association between these two in real life requires a dialectical and sophisticated understanding of federalization and democratization. In the context of multinational or multicultural states, democratization can be understood as a process of federalization in which all parties or groups are to achieve dual domains on, or dual sovereignty over, the same land and same people, and to make dual identities (national and subnational) compatible and complementary. Two or more peoples are not mutually exclusive but inclusively cooperative. Democracy is beyond one narrow ethnic definition of people. People's rule must be understood as people's rule; that is, the coexistence of shared rule by all the peoples and self-rule by one group of people. Democracy means a set of rights for everyone, including minority nationalities. Civic and political liberties enjoyed by minorities' nationalities must be upheld. If democratization is narrowly designed for one people, such a process will lead to anti-federal measures (Baogang et al. 2007).

Conceptually, federalism can be defined in democratic terms and becomes fundamentally relevant as a principle of governance in terms of managing a bi-communal or multi-communal society. It manages in such a way that no community should dominate over another due to the risk of it becoming a permanent majority or permanent minority ruling community in a diverse society. Therefore, federalism should not only balance the interests of the federal and constituent governments but also the interests of diverse communities. It is now commonly recognized that federalism provides a safety value for minorities against the permanent domination of the majority. In other words, federal principles of governance in a diverse and multicultural society further boost democratic institutions and the democratization process by either creating a 'functional civic establishment' or by providing some viable measures for the protection of minorities (Arshi Khan and Kushal Pal 2012, p. 10). If democracy is about sharing political power, federalism is about sharing powers between the centre and local, or between the two levels of governments, or between mainstream nationality and minority nationalities. Thus, federalization can be seen as an effective way of deepening democratization in the sense of granting local autonomy and protecting minority rights, establishing new rules of the game with regard to the independence of the high court, and the democratizing of central and local relations.

Generally speaking, federalism contains the features of democracy in the following senses:

(a) The relationships between two governments are defined by the rule of laws and a set of procedures.
(b) Civic liberties and rights of minority nationalities are preserved and a set of constitutionally guaranteed scopes of action are enjoyed by minority nationalities.
(c) The idea of federalism relies on the idea of polycentricism, the practice of the division of power between federal and state governments, the balance of power and local autonomy (Baogang et al. 2007).

Quite often, how well or effectively federalism manages conflicts or brings about peace is, to a large extent, conditional on the extent of stresses of democracy. The ways, in which ethnic majorities relate with minorities, the ways in which larger or richer constituent units relate with smaller or poorer ones, all these have remarkable implications on the extent to which peaceful coexistence is nurtured and maintained and conflicts are managed in a federal democratic country. 'Unity in diversity' is a key objective of federalism, while pluralism and interest accommodation and primary concerns of democracy; but all these are easier said than done in most federal democracies. Often, minorities are excluded or suppressed; diversity is repressed in pursuit of unity, and so-called 'national integration', of course, with negative if not violent consequences. In fact, democracy and federalism have greatly helped to maximize commonalities and minimize differences, to maintain tolerance and reject violence, to echo peaceful coexistence and dislike separatism and to promote social justice and denounce regional imbalance. The perfect example is Continental Federal India which is not only the world's largest (i.e. populous) democracy but also probably the most complex (i.e. diverse) federal democracy. While its democratic structure protects its political unity, its federal form guarantees the harmonious coexistence of non-political diversities. The diversity of India's social realities and historical identities, as well as its centuries of experiences with social cohabitation, has brought about an evolving recognition of the federal polity. Indeed, none of the federal polities, old or new, bourgeois or socialist—Imperial Germany, the Austro-Hungarian Empire, Switzerland, the United States, Canada, Nigeria, Malaysia, Yugoslavia or the Soviet Union are known to encompass such a wide range of discrete subnational identities and that too with a distinct historical past, as is the case with India (Arshi Khan and Kushal Pal 2012, p. 11).

12.3 Federalism in the Context of Indian Democracy: A Historical Background

Democracy, equality, freedom, secularism, peace, non-violence, rule of law, attainment of rights and social justice usually set the Constitutional keynote of the Indian federal polity which negated all kinds of injustice, unlawful takeover and terrorism by any kinds of injustice, unlawful takeover and terrorism by any kind of actors—state or non-state. The diversity of India's social realities and historical identities, as well as its centuries of experiences with social cohabitation, has brought about an evolving recognition of the federal polity. The framers of the Indian constitution were fully aware of India's unique problems and peculiar needs that had not been tackled by other federations in history, like the United States, Canada, Switzerland and Australia and, therefore, they pursued '*the policy of pick and choose to see (what) would suit (them) best, (what) would suit the genius of the nation best....*' (Pal 1984). However, there were two options open before the Constituent Assembly: First, to adopt a unitary system of British type which India had been experiencing for a considerable period of history; second, to choose a federal polity in which there is a division of powers between the Centre and the States (Pal 1984). Initially, the first report of the Constituent Assembly imagined a weak centre as advocated by the Cripps and the Cabinet Mission Plans. However, the similarities were done to integrate and accommodate the Muslim League. The passing of the Indian Independence Act and the eventual Partition of India led the Constituent Assembly to adopt a more unitary version of federalism (Saez 2002).

Owing to the background of social federalism in Indian history, pre-modern rulers (until the takeover by the British colonialists in the eighteenth century) governed the vast proportion of people by employing schemes for autonomy and rendering protection for group rights. The British also recognized the need to respect different cultural identities, despite being in favour of centralizing the administration. They held some provinces directly under their full control while allowing hundreds of Princely States to remain functional in various provinces. Similarly, they also extended vast autonomy to the tribal populations and their territories in North-East India, in addition to other parts of the country. Despite their colonial approach, the British established several models of self-governance and provisions for the participation of Indians in the governance of the country. Since 1858, they have come up with various Acts and entered into the challenging era of reform of federal management through the Morley-Minto Reforms of 1909, the Montague-Chelmsford Report and Government of India Act 1919 and the Act of 1935 (Arshi Khan and Kushal Pal 2012, p. 09).

In the last phase of its colonial rule, the British drafted the Government of India Act, 1935, which became the bedrock of the present Indian Constitution of 1950. Despite borrowing from the Constitutions of Ireland, Canada and the United States of America, Indian Constitution is deeply rooted in the Government of India Act, 1935. The 1935 Act was based on a series of consultations and inquiries about the demands and choices of different communities in the country. This Act had introduced provisional autonomy and political safeguards for minorities in addition to granting cultural, religious, linguistic and educational rights embedded in the 1950 Constitution (Rudolph 2010, p. 10). On the other hand, India's territorial vastness and regional variations have been dealt with by federal political arrangements, both symmetrical and asymmetrical, for the states of the Indian Union on the basis of cultural, linguistic and ethnic factors. Besides accommodating various rights under federal arrangements for 28 states and the seven UTs within the Indian Union, the Indian Constitution and several later statutory developments envisaged compensatory measures for economically weak, historically discriminated people, as well as for alienated tribal populations of the country, in terms of reserving seats in elected bodies, employment, job promotions and, in many areas, community development schemes (Arshi Khan and Kushal Pal 2012, p. 09).

India is basically a federal society with the established attributes of cultural pluralism—autonomy, respect and identity. The diversities in the country are pre-political and have maintained their autonomous characters, traditions, family affairs, personal laws, lifestyles and many other cultural and social distinctions in which the government has only rarely intervened. Different sections and communities of Indian society have a history of fierce competition, cooperation and coordination. Despite the legacy of caste and communal conflicts in some parts of the country, communities have learnt to live in harmony based on mutual tolerance, mutual appreciation and accommodation. The two major communities (Hindus and Muslims) have remained the most active players in the inter-communal relationships mainly due to compatible values, ethics and experiences for mutual tolerance, respect and appreciations. Six other smaller religious communities (Christians, Sikhs, Buddhists, Jains, Zoroastrians and Jews) have all maintained their cultural distinctiveness with their respective contributions to build a viable federal India. One of the unique merits of Indian social federalism is that smaller religious communities have so far been prosperous, autonomous and represented in various sectors, more than their proportional share in some cases. Together they form a kind of human rainbow on this part of earth planet (Arshi Khan and Kushal Pal 2012, p. 09).

12.4 Emerging Challenges to Indian Federal Democracy

Federalism has been part of the public discussion in India for many decades, before and after independence in 1947, the period of six and half decades has brought both the Indian state and society in a new phase of development and crisis which is quite different from the turbulent and unstable situation in which India sought its independence. Those were the days when the young liberated Indian establishment was in need of its consolidation to begin its voyage for parliamentary democracy, national unity and development. In pursuit of these commitments, the constitution became instrumental in empowering the Indian Union towards rebuilding Indian state and society. However, socio-economic, political and international situations have changed much over during this period (Majeed 2001). Six decades of the working of India's federal system reveal flaws and weaknesses both at the structural and the functional levels. However, one realizes that certain flaws were inherent and innate in the pattern of federal India had adopted, namely the Union form, with its pronounced tilt towards centralization of authority. Certain other flaws and weaknesses became apparent, some in the very process of the unfolding of the federal system and its processes and some others when popular demands for greater rights for segments and autonomy of states and for redressed their grievances acquired momentum. Federalism in India after six decades of independence is witnessing significant changes in all walks of life and faces new set of challenges and therefore needs new and innovative responses (Khan 1992). In contemporary times, the India federal democracy is threatened by many factors, like:

- Centralization and concentration of powers
- The tyranny of majority and insensitivity to the rights of minorities
- Bad governance and poor intergovernmental relations
- Asymmetrical power relations
- Demand of state autonomy by the states and others (Malhotra 2012).

There are some challenges facing by our Indian federal system but it does not mean that India's federal design or constitutional provisions are outdated. At the same time, we should not ignore and avoid these challenges and issues which are apparent in our federal political system. I am quite confident that our 'cooperative federalism' requiring new approaches and methods so that we would find innovative solutions to these challenges and will create a new architecture for our Indian federal system. Therefore, the most vital change is necessary at this point to construct a new federal balance in India.

12.5 Success and Achievements of Indian Federalism

These are some challenges faced by our Indian federal system but it does not mean that India's federal design or constitutional provisions are outdated. India as a federal system is about 60 years old, compared to more than two centuries of the United States or Switzerland or Canada. The federal system has served extremely well for India to promote our democracy, to strengthen the national unity and to achieve economic progress. India is not only the world's largest populous (after China) but also probably the most complex, i.e. diverse, federal democracy. While its democratic structure protects its political unity, its federal form guarantees the harmonious coexistence of non-political diversities. Indeed, none of the federal polities, old or new, bourgeois or socialist—Imperial Germany, Austro-Hungarian Empire, Switzerland, the United States, Canada, Nigeria, Malaysia, Yugoslavia or the Soviet Union—are known to encompass such a wide range of discrete national identities and that too with a distinct historical past as is the case with India (Khan 1992). India did not start as a country with commitment to federalism as an organized principle and even did not have the term federalism incorporated in the preamble of the constitution. However, in about 60 years after independence, there has been a continuous development in constitutional theory and practices in regard to functioning of federalism in India. As federalism, India has shown remarkable capacity to adjust to the demands of the States for a larger show in governance (Hussain 2010).

India is a classic plural society and a massive federal polity which is apparent practically in every major aspect of its collective life, its social systems, economic formations, culture patterns; or language-dialect groupings, religious communities, castes, sub-castes and sects; or local variations of commonly prevalent mythologies and commonly revered deities; or ethnic identities, regional alignments and subregional attachments; or diversities of history marked by moments of triumphs and tragedies and differences in heroes and villains, and in the rich tapestry of folklore, folk dance, music, cuisine, crafts and artefacts of life (Khan 1992). The federal system has served extremely well for India to promote our democracy, to strengthen the national unity and to achieve economic progress. One of the reasons why India has been successful in this is perhaps the Indian federal system has one important attribute and that is the 'flexibility' of the system. Federalism respects diversity of our country, promotes pluralism, and balances national with state powers. It is best suited to our country which is a glaring example of Union of States with multi-social, multilingual and multicultural country of the world (Baogang et al. 2007).

While describing federalism, people have described it in many ways. For instance, some scholars have described federalism as 'administrative federalism;' some have argued for 'market preserving federalism' and some others have described it as 'coming together federalism' versus 'holding together federalism'. Countries like USA are unopposed to be examples of 'coming together' federalism while India is supposed to be an example of 'holding together' federalism. In my view, the important feature of Indian federalism is what in India we call the 'cooperative federalism' feature with formal and informal rules for maintaining the political system as well as for the peaceful change management. This is the feature that gives the 'flexibility' to our federation which greatly helped the country to maintain its unity while strengthening the democracy. The U.S. constitution, over its 200 years or more of existence, has been amended only 27 times while in India, we have amended the Constitution more than hundred times in the 65 years. In my view, this is the strength and not weakness of our system. There is perhaps no other country which is as heterogeneous and diverse as India in terms of religion, language, ethnicity, levels of income, etc. (Bhattacharyya 2015).

When India became independent, the States were formed which were more or less on the pattern that British had organized for administration in terms of various provinces. But there was a political demand that we need States organized on the basis of language as an organizing principle. This was a reflection of subnationalism and in 1956 the States Reorganization Commission divided the country into States on the basis of language. Now, fifty years later, there is a new demand coming up claiming for smaller units of administration as a language based big states are turning out to be too large to address the regional aspirations within a State. The country is responding to this demand and some large States like Uttar Pradesh and Bihar have already been bifurcated though language remains the same. Thus, Federalism has thus deepened democratization and promoted the democratic institutions of India. *James Manor* has rightly argued that democracy in India functions to a large extent because of its federalist arrangement. *Gurpreet Mahajan* highlights two ways in which federalism contributes to democracy: diversifying and pluralizing the national elites and accommodating the previously excluded people who have no national standing at regional level. Federalism has helped to minimize the domination of the majority that controls the centre and provided space for different kinds of groups and communities to share power (Baogang et al. 2007). Federalism in this sense is greatly a big asset as well as a great resource for the democratic country of India.

There are some measures are vital which I suggested for changing the present centralized federation into a cooperative and constructive federal polity in India. These measures are:

- Territorial reorganization of states on the criterion of providing to the States '*maximum homogeneity within and maximum identity without*'. Such a criterion can be determined on five principles, namely: (a) sociocultural affinity in terms of language, dialects, beliefs, religious communities and historical memories; (b) ethnic similarity in terms of *jatis*, tribes, etc. (c) administrative manageability in terms of territory and population; (d) distinct pattern of economy and (e) size of the state commensurate with the need for closer contact between the voters and their representatives, i.e. the rulers and ruled.
- Amendments to the Constitution for increasing the autonomy of the States by incorporating greater administrative and fiscal powers to the States, for effective socio-economic development and political stability.

- Activation of the Panchayati Raj and Nagarpalika System with necessary devolution of authority to build active grass roots democracy.
- Building a new federal-national consensus between parties, social activist groups and citizens, to fight vigorously communalism, casteism and separatism, and to defend the values of democracy secular polity, federal-national building and social justice.
- Nondependence of the states on Centre government for their financial resources. This concept will help the federal structure to act in harmony and will basically promote cooperation by minimizing tension among the various constituent governments of the federal union to pool their resources in order to achieve the desired results. In India, there are some constitutional mechanisms as also some extra constitutional mechanisms to foster the spirit of Cooperative federalism. The constitution makers might have deliberately provided for such features in the constitution in order to ensure the smooth working of the government.

12.6 Conclusion

The paper has sought to reflect critically on a thus-far neglected issue in federalism and also democracy scholarship, namely the relation between federalism and substantive democracy. Federalism is one of those good echo words that evokes a positive response toward many concepts as democracy, progress, constitution, etc. It is a system which is able to accommodate and foster the diversity and from all government systems, it is the one which is best suited to modern society to bring diversity together through sharing of power and resources, the responsibilities and benefits of democracy are made available to all. It is a system that respects diversity, promotes pluralism, and balances national with state powers. Beyond doubt, India has been a success story of federalism in accommodating many diversity claims in favour of upholding political order and stability and preventing secessionism. Thus, federalism is best suited to our country which is a glaring example of Union of States with multi-social, multilingual and multicultural country of the world. It has deepened democratization and promoted the democratic institutions of our country at the large extent. In this sense, federalism is surely a great asset as well as a big resource for Indian democracy.

References

Arshi Khan and Kushal Pal (2012) Federalism and nation-building in India. In: Arshi Khan & Kushal Pal (eds) Federalism, democracy and conflict resolution. Macmillan Publications Pvt. Ltd, New Delhi, pp 3–34

Baogang H, Brian G, Takashi I (2007) Federalism in India. Edward Elgar Publishing Limited, U.K. and U.S.A., pp 24–25

Bhattacharyya H (2015 June) Indian federalism and democracy: the growing salience of diversity-claims over equality-claims in comparative and Indian perspective. Reg Federal Stud, pp 211–227, 218–220
Cyr H (2014) Autonomy, subsidarity, solidarity: Foundations of cooperative federalism. Const Forum 23(4):20–40
Elazar DJ (1995) Federalism: an overview. HRSC Publishers, Pretoria, pp 1–2
Fleiner TF, Lidija B (2009) Constitutional democracy in a multicultural and globalised world. Springer Publishers, Berlin and London, pp 522–540
Hussain H (2010) Indian federalism: emerging trends. Manak Publications Pvt. Ltd, New Delhi, p 104
Khan R (1992a) Federal India: a design for new change. Vikas Publishing House Pvt. Ltd, New Delhi p 24
Khan R (1992b) Federal India: a design for new change. Vikas Publishing House Pvt. Ltd, New Delhi p 21
Khan R (1992c) Federal India: a design for new change. Vikas Publishing House Pvt. Ltd, New Delhi p 8
Majeed A (2001) Constitutional national building: half a century of India's success. Centre for Federal Studies (Jamia Hamdard) in association with Manak Publications, New Delhi, p 34
Malhotra VK (2012) Challenges before democracy in India. In: Pal AK (ed) Federalism, democracy and conflict resolution. Macmillan Publications Pvt. Ltd, New Delhi, 97–105
Pal Chandra (1984) State autonomy In Indian federation: emerging trends. Deep and Deep Publications, New Delhi, p 26
Rudolph LI (2010) Federalism as state formation in India: a theory of shared and negotiated sovereignty. Int Polit Sci Rev pp 1–20
Saez Lawrence (2002) Federalism without centre: the impact of political and economic reform on India's federal system. Sage Publications, New Delhi, pp 26–27
Watts RL (2007) Comparing federal systems. McGill-Queens University Press, Montreal and Kingston, pp 8–10

Chapter 13
Fiscal Reforms for High Economic Growth: An Indian Perspective

Naseer Ahmed Khan

Abstract Prior to the Liberalization of Indian economy, India's tax regime had many problems. In terms of Direct taxes, there was a high degree of progressiveness in 1960s and 1970s that led to adverse effect on tax collection efficiency; further there was a large number of exemptions eroded the narrow tax base in the country. Then enforcement of Direct taxes led to the tax evasion. The efforts reform India's tax system began in mid-1980s when government announced a Long-term Fiscal policy in 1985. This recognized that the fiscal position of the country is going down and there was a need to make changes in the tax system. Then the government of India appointed a tax reform committee headed by Prof Raja Chellaiah in 1991 to layout agenda for reforming India's tax system. The committee submitted its three reports in 1991, 1992 and 1993. The report reflected the tax cuts policy and Laffer curve hypothesis. Now much more of the Indian tax system depends on the implementation of second-generation fiscal reforms.

Keywords Laffer curve · Tax base · Direct taxes · Marginal tax rate · Tax cuts

JEL Codes H24 · H30 · H62

13.1 Introduction

Prior to the Liberalization of Indian economy, India's tax regime was marred with numerous problems. In terms of Direct taxes there was high degree of progressiveness in 1960s and 1970s that led to adverse effect on tax collection efficiency, further there were large number of exemptions that eroded the already narrow tax base in the country. Then the poor enforcement of Direct taxes led to high tax evasion.

N.A. Khan (✉)
School of Economics, University of Hyderabad, Hyderabad,
Telangana 500046, India
e-mail: drkhan58@gmail.com

N.A. Khan (ed.), *Challenges and Issues in Indian Fiscal Federalism*,
India Studies in Business and Economics, https://doi.org/10.1007/978-981-10-6217-9_13

13.2 Fifty Years of Trends in Indian Personal Taxes: Evolution of Income Tax Rates in India

The personal income tax rates were extraordinarily very high, during the decades of 1950s to 1980s. In 1970–1971, the personal Income Tax had 11 tax brackets with the tax rates progressively rising from 10 to 85%, when the surcharge of 10% was taken into account the maximum marginal rate for individuals was a mindboggling 93.50%. And in 1973–1974, the highest tax rate applicable to an individual could has gone up to an astronomical level of 97.50%. The then Direct taxes enquiry committee, 1971 attributed the large scale tax evasion, to the exorbitant tax rates and recommend reduction in the marginal tax rates up to 70%. This change was implemented in 1974–1975, when the marginal rate was brought down to 77%, including 10% surcharge and in 1976–1977, the rate was further reduced to 66%. A major simplification and rationalization initiative came when the number of tax brackets was reduced from 8 to 4 and highest marginal rate was brought down to 50%.

13.3 Liberalization of Personal Income Taxation in India: First Generation Fiscal Reforms-1991–2003

The last wave of reform in Indian personal income taxation was initiated on the basis of the recommendations of the TAX REFORM COMMITTEE (PROF RAJA CHALLIAH) in 1991. And this committee's recommendations were of TAX CUTSPOLICY MEASURES. The tax rates were considerably simplified to have 3(three) brackets of 20 and 30 and 40% in 1992–1993. Further, the three rates were brought down to 10, 20 and 30%. Finally now in India, thus Indian Direct Taxes highest slab is 30% only a very significantly very low as compare to in 1970s. Personal Income tax rates have remained very stable then with the same changes in the tax slabs.

13.4 Laffer Curve Hypothesis in India

The seventies of the twentieth century witnessed a phenomenon of stagflation. The terms stagflation means co-existence of inflation, consumption, saving and investment, as well as steady, rise in G.N.P. A new experiment of supply-side economics is made in the U.S.A to tackle all macroeconomic problems. Supply side economic is not a new phenomenon but can trace back to the ides of physiocracts and the classical economists like David Hume, Adam Smith, J.B. say and J.S. Mill. To quote David Hume, he said that 'Exorbitant taxes destroy industry by producing despair, and even before to reach this pitch they raise the wages of the labour and manufacturer and heighten the prices of all commodities' Physocracts argued with fundamental propositions that productivity and growth are related with decontrol and deregulation by the state.

The supply side economics follows say that aggregate supply creates production and growth for economy, while Keynes viewed that it is not supply side but demand that causes production, savings and investment. Jack Kemp, Laffer and Wimmisky are the main advocates, of supply side.

They hold the view those three decades of demand-side management has resulted in excess government expenditure along with high doses of taxation in economy. Excess money supply along with low rate of productions resulted in low rate G.N.P According to their version, tax reduction may help to generate more production and rise in G.N.P. Faster growth, higher employment, higher incomes and stable price are the main objectives of supply-side management. The main theme of supply-side economics is based on Laffer curve Analysis Laffer curve drawn below diagram shows negative relationship between tax rate revenue beyond and optimum level.

Looking to diagram, at zero level of tax rate, during primitive stage of economy, tax revenue is zero. Then with the increase in the rate of taxation, tax revenue tends to increase. At certain level- at 'M' point in the diagram shows highest rate of tax and tax revenue is also maximum. After crossing that stage, progressive reduction in revenue is seen with further increase in the rate of tax. It is a view of Laffer that tax rate and tax revenue are not positively related but also may change negatively after certain stage.

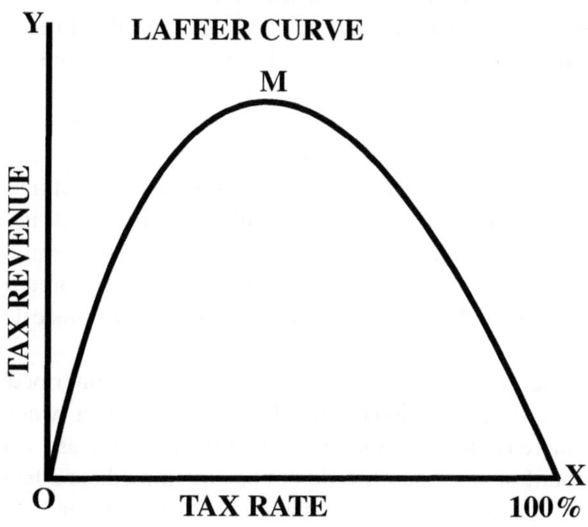

As a results at 100% rate of taxation, no one will be willing to work and tax base will shrink to zero untimely tax revenue will also zero. Thus, the main objective of supply-side economics is concerned with the changes in the structure of taxations to generate incentive effect in terms of more savings and investment and rise in productions. Here savings refer to corporate savings. It is that rise in corporate savings with internal savings and economics of scale will help a rise in productions, which untimely lead to rise in G.N.P Laffer has pleaded for neutral money policy and suggested to control a rate of growth of money supply and non-inflationary financing of the budget deficit.

Laffer curve analysis has led number of countries of including West Germany, Pureto Rico, U.K and Japan to adopt it as a tool of policy measure. Supply-side economists have adopted Laffer curve analysis for increased production and productivity through tax reduction. The Keynesian theory of employment could not solve the problem unemployment in developed as well as in developing nations. Keynes argues that unemployment is due to inadequate demand for labour. Firms do not hire more workers because aggregate demand low, rather than wages are too high. This implies that a minimum wage law would raise wage without reducing employment. But the actual effect of minimum wage law has been to raise the level unemployment among those with low skills and little experiences. Most of the countries misinterpreted the high rate of unemployment as indication of inadequate demand for labour and called for expansionary monetary and fiscal policies, in fact these policies did not come to our help but they exacerbated the unemployment and contributed to the raising rate of inflation.

It has been wieldy argued by many economists that our high rate of unemployment cannot be lowered by expansionary demand polices. An important aspect of supply-side economics has come to our rescue, that unemployment can only be reduced by policies that correct these labour market disincentives and distortions. The basic point of supply-side economics is that output the direct results of inputs and these input respond to incentives. In other words, if you make an activity more attentive people will in more of that activity and if we make an activity less attractive people do less of that activity. The change is the behaviour of people can be brought through the changes in incentives.

With the help of change in taxation regulation and government spending it is clear that taxes on production and accumulation of capital in the process of accelerated growth and hindrance and effect adversely output employment and our living standard. The tax policies of a government, not only force up to price level but wipes out market value of securities. The increase in piece level is not only restricted.

The final consumer goods but affects the prices of intermediate goods and increases the cost of productions. The demand for higher wage rate will also strengthen, but increase in wage rate will take time and increase will not always be by the same amount of tax. There would not be any immediate effect of tax on wage rate, clearly taxes contributed to the inflations and distort our living standards. In developing nations the level of employment can be increased through tax incentives in two ways. First, a reductions tax rate will stimulate the investment decision and the expansion in production. The rise in investment and production will provide more employment. Second, a tax cut will decrease the cost of production will increase the rate of profit. At a low cost and higher rate of profit more employment could be generated through more production, on the assumption that marginal propensity to consume (MPC) in the entrepreneurial class is negligible.

It is evident that entrepreneurs respond favourable to the tax incentives in developing countries. Even if these taxes are provided to any special sector or commodities, investment from sectors or commodities may enter into specific sectors, because of higher expectation, lead to generate more employment. Sometime, more investment is undesirable in housing, consumer durables and gold and silver and can be restricted through tax incentives for plant and equipment investment. In developing countries, there is regional imbalance of industrial development and labour is not perfectly mobile which causes the regional unemployment in these countries. The tax incentives in less developed areas would attract the entrepreneurs to establish new ventures in that area with more employment problem, these countries should provide more tax incentives to labour intensive industries, for generating more employment facilities. But with these positive points, may economists argue that tax incentives reduce tax revenue. This means increased investment decisions are financed from deficit financing or expansionary monetary policy which force up interest rate and lowers the investment decisions. In short run, tax incentives may cost exchequer but in long run with increases in the level of output and employment tax base also increase. Even if fiscal deficit exists it may be financed through extra generated savings by the higher incomes.

It is possible that at first instance, public investment may fall due to tax deduction. But eventually, private saving must rise because disposable income rises owing to the initial tax cut. The rise in private investment induced by the increase in the private saving must be able to offset the fall in public investment. Private investment can provide more output and higher employment than public investment. In developing countries, government projects are never completed in expected time, hence excalation of price cost exchequer more than the estimates. The scarce capital is destroyed in the process. Sometime wrong policy decisions by government also destroy the resource which could easily be spent on other productive purpose. For example, Indian government took a decision in 1978 to start district industrial centres at various district Head Quarters all over India. After 2 years of massive effort and expenditure to build infrastructure facilities, the project has been scraped in 1980.

It is widely argued that the monetary mismanagement has been the main cause of current high rate of inflation in developing countries. The expansionary effect of monetary policy was under estimated because of the failure to recognize the implications fiscal structure. Attempts of monetary authorities to encourage the investment by an easy money actually had an advise impact on investment in plant and equipment with monetary expansion nominal interest rates go up because of rise in general prices, but real interest rate goes up much less than nominal interest rate mismanagement of monetary policy can be term of mainly because of the ignorance of the impact of taxes. The effect of expansionary Monetary policy cannot be judged correctly unless the effects of taxations are included, tax rules not natural when there is inflation. It is evident that without indexing present tax rules in developing countries. The movements of the pre-tax real interest rate and of the post-tax interest rates are completely different. All of this shows that conventional macro-economic and in which ignores the fixed structure can be seriously misleading. It is now widely argued that fiscal incentivize for investment and saving or tax cut would increase the investment in plant and equipment.

The economists of the under-developed economics in recent years have sought to analyses their economic problems and develop policy measures essentially in terms of supply-side economics. They traced the application of the basic principles of the supply-side economics to their economic problems in the writing of the some of the leading economists have the post-World War II period. It has been pointed out that these there economists have primarily confined themselves to the analysis of the various factors, which have retarded productions in the counties. In others words while analysing the causes of the poverty of the nations these economists have highlighted the deficient infra-structural and productive capacities of these nations and suggested various policy measures to develop these facilities in order to provided necessary incentives to increases the supply.

Thus Sir W.A. Lewis a leading economist of this group in seminar paper analysed various factors, particularly excess labour force which are responsible for the retarded productive capacity of theses economics. According to him transfer of surplus labour in to more productive employment would increase the total output in the economy. In his subsequent works, he has discussed about various factors, which affect the transfer of labour and its effect on the supply. Similarly, the contributions of the doseschuttz, another leading developmental economist of the present age, is connected with the supply-side economics. Its important contributions is concerned with the investment in human resources, educations and technical change and their relationship with the productivity, are essentially concerned with the supply-side economics. The contributions of most of development through education and technical change and their relationship with the productivity are essentially concerned economists of the present age with regard to human resources development through educationist and health programmed, development of entrepreneurship and nurturance and development of infrastructure, etc. are essentially concerned with supply-side economics.

13.5 Relevance to Developing Countries

The development effort in countries like India, Bangladesh, Pakistan, Burma, Sri Lanka, and other have been based on wrong strategies of demand management under the influenced of Keynesians and western economic models of growth which resulted in the present formidable stagflation. These economies could as well follow the supply-side approach in their development efforts without being unduly scared of the negative redistributions effects of income. Moreover such a strategy is not against the basic philosophy and economic policy of mixed economy being followed in these countries with respectable rate for the private enterprise and free market. All that is required is to allow the free operations of these forces by removing unnecessary restrictions on economic activates by suitable amendments to rules and regulations affecting production and by encouraging incentives to produce by accelerated depreciation, investment tax credits, rationalisation, skill formation and reducing high rates results in parallel economy, black market, tax evasion, etc. assert the supply-side economists. Under development generally means non-utilization or under-utilisations of resource despite their availability. All developing countries are caught in the vicious circle of poverty. Poverty is acute in some fifteen countries including India where the G.N.P per capital is less than 200 dollars. The developing countries are striving to break the vicious circle of poverty and they have as bias for the manufacturing sector. Some of them have neglected agriculture. A proper approach would be to develop a favourable sector and create surplus and savings for the development of others sectors. Capital formation is their main need. Infrastructure including power and entrepreneurship are equally important. These counties lack a theoretical base of their own and ides like monetary expansions easy to create in a poor country are adopted by them. Capital formations, efficient use of capital scale of economics, return for earlier investments are aspect which supply-side economics should solve for these countries.

On the level of policy supply-side economics may have some interesting implications for underdevelopment. It pleads that factors governing the supply of goods must be given due weight in economic policy. It is not necessarily advocating a smaller role for government but it is insisting that influences of governmental actions and policies up on supply must explicitly taken into account. The policy makers have to consciously evolve economic policies in such a way that interventionist role of government does throttle individual initiative and effort. In our opinions this is the positive contributions which supply-side economics may make towards the analysis of under development. Until the supply of capital in developing countries is not increased they are not going to develop economically. The supply of capital comes from domestic source may be voluntarily or on voluntarily. Government savings may come-out of curtailment of unproductive civil expenditures. It may also arise out of the surplus of state enterprise, if of course the principal of no profit no loss is abandoned in favour of deliberate policy of obtaining surplus from public enterprises. Technological backwardness and lack of entrepreneurial ability are also two major obstacles the path of economic development of under developed countries. Technology and enterprise can be imported from abroad but it involves the foreign exchange problems. So the under developed countries have extended invitation to foreign collaborations.

13.6 Relevance to Indian Economy

Supply-side economics, although built in a capitalist economic setting, has got some relevance in present Indian context. Over the last decade budgetary deficit has increased three times in India. Excessive money creations, administered price rise, dogmatic pursuance of deficit financing coupled with oil shock have caused inflations. The situation was aggravated by irrational tax structure which was called for reform by Kaldor long ago. The system thus developed in India has not only generated any in built inflations process but also sapped individual initiative and growth. A parallel economics system has developed which is affecting the regular economic programme. Current effort of the government to regulate the unaccounted economy by bearer bonds and capital investment bonds are only playing a hide and seek game with block money along with administrative measures a policy of tax reforms for giving incentive to work effort and regulating parallel economy is worth considering. Thus to the extent encouragement of diversified economy and growth of productions and employment is possible through reductions of tax structures and regulations, supply side economics is relevant in India.

Indian economy suffers from resources constraints. The situation is not the same as the thirties in Europe where plenty of resources lay idle along recessions and deteriorating demand conditions. India can ill afford any wastage of resource and must work hard for their effective utilization, higher productivity and efficiency in resources use which are not quite comparable with the Keynesian model. Tax incentives along with improved tax collection and administrations and cutting down on essential items are some quasi supply-side features which could go a long way in improving by economic situations in India. Supply-side economics implies not merely to increase productive activity and supply of goods to reduce them but to alter the volume of productive activity and supply of goods in the market from time to time, so that there is neither an excess production not a deficit of it is in the market. It is this classical idea that has a relevance to the under-developed and developed counties like India with an abundant supply of labour and natural resources but relatively less of capital. Such economies should device a type of technology with a high labour adsorptive power but limited productive capacity. What are significant for such economies are the adoptions of labour-intensive techniques of production so that the twin objectives of supply management and demand management are achieved at the same time. Adoptions of such a technology will have two advantages for the labour-rich developing countries like India. First, on the supply-side it will increase supply at a rate commensurate with the rate of increase in demand and keep in check undesirable advances in productive capacity which results in a volume of output that cannot be matched by the prevailing volume of aggregate demand in the country. Second, on the demand side it will generate larger employment opportunities for the labours and will results in more income and purchasing power in the hands of the people. This creates the required demand in the economy in order give to moving equilibrium.

13.7 Way Forward

The Personal Income Tax rates have steadily declined in India after the implementation of first generation fiscal reforms started since 1991, with the maximum marginal rate of income tax coming down from a mind boggling 97.5% to much more manageable 30%, also the slabs at which the various tax rate are applicable have considerable widened over the years. It all happened due to the Tax Cuts policy measures and Of Laffer Curve philosophy in India (Table 13.1).

13.7.1 Second-Generation Fiscal Reforms (2003 onwards) in India

A major factor in introducing reforms was to control fiscal deficits and revenue deficits at the level of Federal and provincial governments, but unfortunately the Reform process after achieving some success in the initial years was not able to sustain it. Both the federal and provincial governments are facing the problem of Fiscal deficits as shown in (Table 13.2).

13.8 Causes

Two proximate causes have worked together to create Fiscal Imbalance—one related to the impact of the Federal pay commissions in pushing up sharply the expenditure of the government in salaries and pensions and secondly, the cyclical recession in economic activity retarding there growth of the tax revenues of the

Table 13.1 Total tax revenue and direct tax revenue (In Billion Rupees)

Year	Total tax revenue	Direct tax revenue
1991–92	500.69	101.03
1992–93	540.44	120.75
1993–94	534.49	125.22
1994–95	674.54	184.09
1995–96	819.39	222.87
1996–97	937.01	253.74
1997–98	956.72	271.72
1998–99	1046.52	321.2
1999–2000	1282.71	414.36
2000–01	1366.58	496.51
2001–02	1335.52	477.03

Source Federal government receipts, central bank of INDIA bulletin

Table 13.2 Federal and provincial's budgetary balance

Year	Fiscal deficit			Revenue deficit		
	Federal	Province	Combined	Federal	Province	Combined
1990–91	8.33	3.28	9.64	3.27	0.84	4.31
1991–92	5.89	2.93	7.17	2.64	0.81	3.45
1992–93	5.69	2.92	7.38	2.63	0.72	3.36
1993–94	7.43	2.49	8.68	4.04	0.47	4.51
1994–95	5.99	2.86	7.36	3.22	0.73	3.95
1995–96	5.38	2.75	6.81	2.66	0.77	3.43
1996–97	5.23	2.97	6.81	2.56	1.43	3.98
1997–98	6.21	3.1	7.74	3.24	1.29	4.53
1998–99	6.8	4.47	9.5	4.08	2.72	6.8
1999–2000	5.96	4.98	10.4	4.03	3.13	7.16

As % of GDP
Source Report of Thirteenth and Eleventh Finance Commission

Table 13.3 Tax buoyancies of federal and provinces

Decades	Combined	Federal	Provinces
1950–1960	1.38	1.38	1.39
1960–1970	1.16	1.15	1.17
1970–1980	1.3	1.27	1.35
1980–1990	1.14	1.15	1.12
1990–1999	0.96	0.91	1.04

Source Report of the eleventh finance commission 2000

Federal and Provincial governments. The next major item, which upset fiscal balance, was the interest on government borrowings. The composition of public debt has been more and more in favour of market rates of borrowings. The third major item contributing to higher revenue expenditure was the steady growth in subsidies. Subsidies accounted for 1.98% of GDP and 18.6% of the Federal's net revenue receipts in 1991–1992 (Table 13.3).

13.9 Fiscal Strategy in Second Federation Fiscal Reforms in India

The major thrust areas should be

(1) Reduction of fiscal deficit to a limit of 3% of GDP for federal and 2% for provincial governments.
(2) To achieve zero percent revenue deficit.
(3) To raise capital expenditure on rural infrastructure—to stimulate growth.

(4) To carry forward the programmes of dis-investment of loss-making enterprises in the public sector.
(5) To bringdown the subsidies on non-merit goods and also hidden subsidies.
(6) To create an environment for better cost-recovery in social as well as the economic services.

13.10 Fiscal Responsibility and Budget Management (FRBM) Act 2003

There was evidence of the fiscal correction during 1991–1992 to 1996–1997 in terms of a substantial increase in fiscal deficit indicators. Since then there has been a substantial reversal of trend mostly up to 2002–2003; in an endeavour to renew the process of fiscal consolidation and provide long-term macroeconomic stability. The Federal government enacted FRBM (fiscal responsibility and budget management) act in 2003. At the provincial levels, several legislations have also been enacted. The FRBM ACT widely seen as a landmark in Indian Economics Reform's history clearly recognizes that without an abiding dedication to Fiscal correction, no government can scale down the development mandate vested upon it by the masses.

13.11 Conclusion

Reduction in Fiscal Deficit to a sustainable level formed a significant component of the Stabilization and Reform process initiated in 1991 in India. It is a matter of concern for the long-term macroeconomic stability. First an effort has been made with the help of Tax-Cuts (Laffer curve hypothesis) to raise the tax revenues in Direct taxes and completion of the Tax reforms that have been introduced to Reduce tariffs, change to GST (Goods And Services Tax), Harmonize provincial taxes, abolish Octroi, impose pollution taxes, etc., widen the tax net and introducing the agriculture income tax at provinces. Now the second-generation reforms contemplated correctly for reducing the fiscal deficit and more reforms in public expenditure like to implement effectively Public Expenditure Management (PEM). Raising the government revenues by completing the tax reforms measures like bringing agricultural income under tax net at Provincial governments, removing non-merit subsidies and pricing economic services and ensuring high degree of productivity in government spending are some of the important policy measures for generating and realizing high growth through Fiscal policy Reforms.

TO SUM UP, the analysis about the working of Economic reforms in Fiscal policy area started INDIA in 1991, reveals that so far as spread of the reform process has been very narrow, limited to the corporate sector of the Indian Economy. Unless the second-generation reforms enlarge then and spread to

Agriculture and Small industry besides Reforms in fiscal policy, the much talked about expansion of employment opportunities and public investment cannot be created—in short, the objectives of second generation reforms in India should be GROWTH with social justice.

References

Blinder AS (1981) Tax cuts and investment incentives challenge

Cutt J (1969) Taxation and economic development in India. Vikas publications, New Delhi

Heller WW (1981) Kennedy's supply—side economics challenges, Publisher CHALLENGER

Jawed Akhtar SM, Naseem S (2013) Fiscal policy reforms in India since 1991. New Century publications, New Delhi

Joshi V, Little IMD (1998) India's economic reforms 1991–2001, Oxford Publications, Oxford

Mohan R (2010) India's economy: performances and challenges In: Acharya S, Mohan R. Oxford Publications, Oxford

Mukherjee R (2007) India's economic transition, Oxford publications economic surveys (2015–16). Government of India Publications

Musgrave RA (1981) What will the tax cut accomplish?, Publisher CHALLENGER

Hailstones TJ (1982) Some supply-side models–a guide to supply-side economics. Reston Publishers, Virginia

MIX
Papier aus verantwortungsvollen Quellen
Paper from responsible sources
FSC® C105338

If you have any concerns about our products,
you can contact us on
ProductSafety@springernature.com

In case Publisher is established outside the EU,
the EU authorized representative is:
Springer Nature Customer Service Center GmbH
Europaplatz 3, 69115 Heidelberg, Germany

Printed by Libri Plureos GmbH
in Hamburg, Germany